Ralph Waldo Emerson.

COMPLETE WORKS. *Centenary Edition.* 12 vols., crown 8vo. With Portraits, and copious notes by ED-WARD WALDO EMERSON. Price per volume, $1.75. 1. Nature, Addresses, and Lectures. 2. Essays: First Series. 3. Essays: Second Series. 4. Representative Men. 5. English Traits. 6. Conduct of Life. 7. Society and Solitude. 8. Letters and Social Aims. 9. Poems. 10. Lectures and Biographical Sketches. 11. Miscellanies. 12. Natural History of Intellect, and other Papers. With a General Index to Emerson's Collected Works.

Riverside Edition. With 2 Portraits. 12 vols., each, 12mo. gilt top, $1.75 ; the set, $21.00.

Little Classic Edition. 12 vols., in arrangement and contents identical with *Riverside Edition,* except that vol. 12 is without index. Each, 18mo, $1.25 ; the set, $15.00.

POEMS. *Household Edition.* With Portrait. 12mo, $1.50 ; full gilt, $2.00.

ESSAYS. First and Second Series. In Cambridge Classics. Crown 8vo, $1.00.

NATURE, LECTURES, AND ADDRESSES, together with REPRESENTATIVE MEN. In Cambridge Classics. Crown 8vo, $1.00.

PARNASSUS. A collection of Poetry edited by Mr. Emerson. Introductory Essay. *Household Edition.* 12mo, $1.50. *Holiday Edition.* 8vo, $3.00.

EMERSON BIRTHDAY BOOK. With Portrait and Illustrations. 18mo, $1.00.

EMERSON CALENDAR BOOK. 32mo, parchment-paper, 25 cents.

CORRESPONDENCE OF CARLYLE AND EMERSON, 834-1872. Edited by CHARLES ELIOT NORTON. 2 ols. crown 8vo, gilt top, $4.00.

Library Edition. 2 vols. 12mo, gilt top, $3.00.

CORRESPONDENCE OF JOHN STERLING AND EMERSON. Edited, with a sketch of Sterling's life, by ED-WARD WALDO EMERSON. 16mo, gilt top, $1.00.

LETTERS FROM RALPH WALDO EMERSON TO A FRIEND. 1838-1853. Edited by CHARLES ELIOT NORTON. 16mo, gilt top, $1.00.

THE CORRESPONDENCE BETWEEN EMERSON AND GRIMM. Edited by F. W. HOLLS. With Portraits. 16mo, $1.00, *net.* Postpaid, $1.05.

For various other editions of Emerson's works and Emerson Memoirs see catalogue.

HOUGHTON MIFFLIN COMPANY
BOSTON AND NEW YORK

Centenary Edition

THE COMPLETE WORKS OF
RALPH WALDO EMERSON

WITH

A BIOGRAPHICAL

INTRODUCTION AND NOTES

BY EDWARD WALDO EMERSON AND

A GENERAL INDEX

VOLUME

V

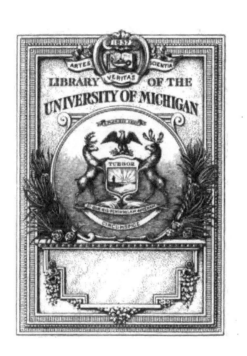

ENGLISH TRAITS

BY

RALPH WALDO EMERSON

BOSTON AND NEW YORK
HOUGHTON MIFFLIN COMPANY
The Riverside Press Cambridge

CONTENTS

ENGLISH TRAITS

CHAPTER I

FIRST VISIT TO ENGLAND

I HAVE been twice in England. In 1833, on my return from a short tour in Sicily, Italy and France, I crossed from Boulogne and landed in London at the Tower stairs. It was a dark Sunday morning; there were few people in the streets, and I remember the pleasure of that first walk on English ground, with my companion, an American artist,¹ from the Tower up through Cheapside and the Strand to a house in Russell Square, whither we had been recommended to good chambers. For the first time for many months we were forced to check the saucy habit of travellers' criticism, as we could no longer speak aloud in the streets without being understood. The shop-signs spoke our language; our country names were on the door-plates, and the public and private buildings wore a more native and wonted front.

Like most young men at that time, I was much indebted to the men of Edinburgh and of the Edinburgh Review, — to Jeffrey, Mackintosh,

Hallam, and to Scott, Playfair and De Quincey;[1] and my narrow and desultory reading had inspired the wish to see the faces of three or four writers, — Coleridge, Wordsworth, Landor, De Quincey, and the latest and strongest contributor to the critical journals, Carlyle; and I suppose if I had sifted the reasons that led me to Europe, when I was ill and was advised to travel, it was mainly the attraction of these persons. If Goethe had been still living I might have wandered into Germany also. Besides those I have named (for Scott was dead), there was not in Britain the man living whom I cared to behold, unless it were the Duke of Wellington, whom I afterwards saw at Westminster Abbey at the funeral of Wilberforce.[2] The young scholar fancies it happiness enough to live with people who can give an inside to the world; without reflecting that they are prisoners, too, of their own thought, and cannot apply themselves to yours. The conditions of literary success are almost destructive of the best social power, as they do not leave that frolic liberty which only can encounter a companion on the best terms. It is probable you left some obscure comrade at a tavern, or in the farms, with right mother-wit and equality to life, when you

crossed sea and land to play bo-peep with celebrated scribes. I have, however, found writers
superior to their books, and I cling to my first
belief that a strong head will dispose fast enough
of these impediments and give one the satisfaction of reality, the sense of having been met,
and a larger horizon.

On looking over the diary of my journey in
1833, I find nothing to publish in my memo-
randa of visits to places. But I have copied the
few notes I made of visits to persons, as they
respect parties quite too good and too transpar-
ent to the whole world to make it needful to
affect any prudery of suppression about a few
hints of those bright personalities.

At Florence, chief among artists I found
Horatio Greenough, the American sculptor.[1]
His face was so handsome and his person so
well formed that he might be pardoned, if, as
was alleged, the face of his Medora and the
figure of a colossal Achilles in clay, were ideal-
izations of his own. Greenough was a superior
man, ardent and eloquent, and all his opinions
had elevation and magnanimity. He believed
that the Greeks had wrought in schools or fra-
ternities, — the genius of the master imparting
his design to his friends and inflaming them

with it, and when his strength was spent, a new
hand with equal heat continued the work; and
so by relays, until it was finished in every part
with equal fire. This was necessary in so refrac-
tory a material as stone; and he thought art
would never prosper until we left our shy jealous ways and worked in society as they. All
his thoughts breathed the same generosity. He
was an accurate and a deep man. He was a
votary of the Greeks, and impatient of Gothic
art. His paper on Architecture, published
in 1843, announced in advance the leading
thoughts of Mr. Ruskin on the *morality* in
architecture, notwithstanding the antagonism
in their views of the history of art.   I have a
private letter from him, — later, but respecting
the same period, — in which he roughly sketches
his own theory. " Here is my theory of structure: A scientific arrangement of spaces and
forms to functions and to site; an emphasis of
features proportioned to their *gradated* importance in function; color and ornament to be
decided and arranged and varied by strictly
organic laws, having a distinct reason for each
decision; the entire and immediate banishment
of all make-shift and make-believe."

Greenough brought me, through a common

friend, an invitation from Mr. Landor, who lived at San Domenica di Fiesole. On the 15th May I dined with Mr. Landor. I found him noble and courteous, living in a cloud of pictures at his Villa Gherardesca, a fine house commanding a beautiful landscape. I had inferred from his books, or magnified from some anecdotes, an impression of Achillean wrath, — an untamable petulance. I do not know whether the imputation were just or not, but certainly on this May day his courtesy veiled that haughty mind and he was the most patient and gentle of hosts. He praised the beautiful cyclamen which grows all about Florence; he admired Washington; talked of Wordsworth, Byron, Massinger, Beaumont and Fletcher. To be sure, he is decided in his opinions, likes to surprise, and is well content to impress, if possible, his English whim upon the immutable past. No great man ever had a great son, if Philip and Alexander be not an exception; and Philip he calls the greater man. In art, he loves the Greeks, and in sculpture, them only. He prefers the Venus to everything else, and, after that, the head of Alexander, in the gallery here. He prefers John of Bologna to Michael Angelo; in painting, Raffaelle, and shares the growing

taste for Perugino and the early masters. The
Greek histories he thought the only good; and
after them, Voltaire's. I could not make him
praise Mackintosh, nor my more recent friends;
Montaigne very cordially, — and Charron also,
which seemed undiscriminating. He thought
Degerando indebted to " Lucas on Happiness "
and " Lucas on Holiness "!¹ He pestered me
with Southey; but who is Southey?

He invited me to breakfast on Friday. On
Friday I did not fail to go, and this time with
Greenough. He entertained us at once with
reciting half a dozen hexameter lines of Julius
Cæsar's ! — from Donatus, he said.² He glo-
rified Lord Chesterfield more than was necessary, and undervalued Burke, and undervalued
Socrates; designated as three of the greatest of
men, Washington, Phocion and Timoleon, —
much as our pomologists, in their lists, select
the three or the six best pears " for a small orchard ; " — and did not even omit to remark the
similar termination of their names. " A great
man," he said, " should make great sacrifices and
kill his hundred oxen without knowing whether
they would be consumed by gods and heroes, or
whether the flies would eat them." I had visited
Professor Amici, who had shown me his micro-

scopes, magnifying (it was said) two thousand diameters; and I spoke of the uses to which they were applied. Landor despised entomology, yet, in the same breath, said, " the sublime was in a grain of dust." I suppose I teased him about recent writers, but he professed never to have heard of Herschel, *not even by name*. One room was full of pictures, which he likes to show, especially one piece, standing before which he said " he would give fifty guineas to the man that would swear it was a Domenichino." I was more curious to see his library, but Mr. H——, one of the guests, told me that Mr. Landor gives away his books and has never more than a dozen at a time in his house.

Mr. Landor carries to its height the love of freak which the English delight to indulge, as if to signalize their commanding freedom. He has a wonderful brain, despotic, violent and inexhaustible, meant for a soldier, by what chance converted to letters; in which there is not a style nor a tint not known to him, yet with an English appetite for action and heroes. The thing done avails, and not what is said about it. An original sentence, a step forward, is worth more than all the censures. Landor is strangely undervalued in England; usually ignored and *s*ometimes savagely attacked in the Reviews. The criticism may be right or wrong, and is quickly forgotten ; but year after year the scholar must still go back to Landor for a multitude of elegant sentences ; for wisdom, wit, and indignation that are unforgetable.[1]

From London, on the 5th August, I went to Highgate, and wrote a note to Mr. Coleridge, requesting leave to pay my respects to him.[2] It was near noon. Mr. Coleridge sent a verbal message that he was in bed, but if I would call after one o'clock he would see me. I returned at one, and he appeared, a short, thick old man, with bright blue eyes and fine clear complexion, leaning on his cane. He took snuff freely, which presently soiled his cravat and neat black suit. He asked whether I knew Allston, and spoke warmly of his merits and doings when he knew him in Rome ; what a master of the Titianesque he was, etc., etc. He spoke of Dr. Channing. It was an unspeakable misfortune that he should have turned out a Unitarian after all. On this, he burst into a declamation on the folly and ignorance of Unitarianism, — its high unreasonableness ; and taking up Bishop Waterland's book,[3] which lay on the table, he read with ve-

hemence two or three pages written by himself
in the fly-leaves, — passages, too, which, I believe, are printed in the Aids to Reflection.
When he stopped to take breath, I interposed
that " whilst I highly valued all his explanations,
I was bound to tell him that I was born and bred
a Unitarian." "Yes," he said, " I supposed so ; "
and continued as before. It was a wonder that
after so many ages of unquestioning acquies-
cence in the doctrine of St. Paul, — the doctrine
of the Trinity, which was also according to Philo
Judæus the doctrine of the Jews before Christ,
— this handful of Priestleians should take on
themselves to deny it, etc., etc. He was very
sorry that Dr. Channing, a man to whom he
looked up, — no, to say that he looked *up* to
him would be to speak falsely, but a man whom
he looked *at* with so much interest, — should
embrace such views. When he saw Dr. Channing he had hinted to him that he was afraid he
loved Christianity for what was lovely and excellent, — he loved the good in it, and not the
true ; — " And I tell you, sir, that I have known
ten persons who loved the good, for one person
who loved the true ; but it is a far greater virtue
to love the true for itself alone, than to love
the good for itself alone." He (Coleridge) knew

all about Unitarianism perfectly well, because
he had once been a Unitarian and knew what
quackery it was. He had been called "the rising star of Unitarianism." He went on defining, or rather refining: "The Trinitarian doctrine was realism; the idea of God was not essential, but super-essential;" talked of *trinism*
and *tetrakism* and much more, of which I only
caught this, "that the will was that by which a
person is a person; because, if one should push
me in the street, and so I should force the man
next me into the kennel, I should at once exclaim, I did not do it, sir, meaning it was not
my will." And this also, that "if you should
insist on your faith here in England, and I on
mine, mine would be the hotter side of the
fagot."

I took advantage of a pause to say that he had
many readers of all religious opinions in America,
and I proceeded to inquire if the "extract" from
the Independent's pamphlet, in the third volume
of the Friend, were a veritable quotation. He
replied that it was really taken from a pamphlet
in his possession entitled "A Protest of one of
the Independents," or something to that effect.
I told him how excellent I thought it and how
much I wished to see the entire work. "Yes,"

he said, "the man was a chaos of truths, but lacked the knowledge that God was a God of order. Yet the passage would no doubt strike you more in the quotation than in the original, for I have filtered it."

When I rose to go, he said, " I do not know whether you care about poetry, but I will repeat some verses I lately made on my baptismal anniversary," and he recited with strong emphasis, standing, ten or twelve lines beginning, —

" Born unto God in Christ —— "

He inquired where I had been travelling; and on learning that I had been in Malta and Sicily, he compared one island with the other, repeating what he had said to the Bishop of London when he returned from that country, that Sicily was an excellent school of political economy; for, in any town there, it only needed to ask what the government enacted, and reverse that, to know what ought to be done; it was the most felicitously opposite legislation to anything good and wise. There were only three things which the government had brought into that garden of delights, namely, itch, pox and famine. Whereas in Malta, the force of law and mind was seen, in making that barren rock of semi-Saracen

inhabitants the seat of population and plenty.
Going out, he showed me in the next apartment
a picture of Allston's, and told me that Montague, a picture-dealer, once came to see him, and
glancing towards this, said, "Well, you have got
a picture!" thinking it the work of an old master;
afterwards, Montague, still talking with his back
to the canvas, put up his hand and touched it,
and exclaimed, "By Heaven! this picture is not
ten years old:"— so delicate and skilful was
that man's touch.

I was in his company for about an hour, but
find it impossible to recall the largest part of his
discourse, which was often like so many printed
paragraphs in his book, — perhaps the same, —
so readily did he fall into certain commonplaces.
As I might have foreseen, the visit was rather a
spectacle than a conversation, of no use beyond
the satisfaction of my curiosity. He was old and
preoccupied, and could not bend to a new companion and think with him.

From Edinburgh I went to the Highlands.
On my return I came from Glasgow to Dumfries, and being intent on delivering a letter which
I had brought from Rome, inquired for Craigen-
puttock. It was a farm in Nithsdale, in the

parish of Dunscore, sixteen miles distant. No public coach passed near it, so I took a private carriage from the inn. I found the house amid desolate heathery hills, where the lonely scholar nourished his mighty heart.[1] Carlyle was a man from his youth, an author who did not need to hide from his readers, and as absolute a man of the world, unknown and exiled on that hill-farm, as if holding on his own terms what is best in London. He was tall and gaunt, with a cliff-like brow,[2] self-possessed and holding his extraordinary powers of conversation in easy command; clinging to his northern accent with evident relish; full of lively anecdote and with a streaming humor which floated every thing he looked upon. His talk playfully exalting the familiar objects, put the companion at once into an acquaintance with his Lars and Lemurs, and it was very pleasant to learn what was predestined to be a pretty mythology. Few were the objects and lonely the man; "not a person to speak to within sixteen miles except the minister of Dunscore;" so that books inevitably made his topics.

He had names of his own for all the matters familiar to his discourse. Blackwood's was the " sand magazine;" Fraser's nearer approach to possibility of life was the "mud magazine;" a piece of road near by, that marked some failed enterprise, was the "grave of the last sixpence." When too much praise of any genius annoyed him he professed hugely to admire the talent shown by his pig. He had spent much time and contrivance in confining the poor beast to one enclosure in his pen, but pig, by great strokes of judgment, had found out how to let a board down, and had foiled him. For all that he still thought man the most plastic little fellow in the planet, and he liked Nero's death, "*Qualis artifex pereo!*" better than most history.[1] He worships a man that will manifest any truth to him. At one time he had inquired and read a good deal about America. Landor's principle was mere rebellion; and *that* he feared was the American principle. The best thing he knew of that country was that in it a man can have meat for his labor. He had read in Stewart's book that when he inquired in a New York hotel for the Boots, he had been shown across the street and had found Mungo in his own house dining on roast turkey.

We talked of books. Plato he does not read, and he disparaged Socrates; and, when pressed, persisted in making Mirabeau a hero. Gibbon

he called the " splendid bridge from the old
world to the new." His own reading had been
multifarious. Tristram Shandy was one of his
first books after Robinson Crusoe, and Robertson's America an early favorite. Rousseau's Con-
fessions had discovered to him that he was not
a dunce ; and it was now ten years since he had
learned German, by the advice of a man who
told him he would find in that language what he
wanted.

He took despairing or satirical views of literature at this moment ; recounted the incredible
sums paid in one year by the great booksellers
for puffing. Hence it comes that no newspaper
is trusted now, no books are bought, and the
booksellers are on the eve of bankruptcy.

He still returned to English pauperism, the
crowded country, the selfish abdication by public men of all that public persons should perform. Government should direct poor men
what to do. Poor Irish folk come wandering
over these moors. My dame makes it a rule to
give to every son of Adam bread to eat, and
supplies his wants to the next house. But here
are thousands of acres which might give them
all meat, and nobody to bid these poor Irish go
to the moor and till it. They burned the stacks

and so found a way to force the rich people to attend to them.

We went out to walk over long hills, and looked at Criffel, then without his cap, and down into Wordsworth's country. There we sat down and talked of the immortality of the soul. It was not Carlyle's fault that we talked on that topic, for he had the natural disinclination of every nimble spirit to bruise itself against walls, and did not like to place himself where no step can be taken. But he was honest and true, and cognizant of the subtile links that bind ages together, and saw how every event affects all the future. " Christ died on the tree ; that built Dunscore kirk yonder ; that brought you and me together. Time has only a relative existence." [1]

He was already turning his eyes towards London with a scholar's appreciation. London is the heart of the world, he said, wonderful only from the mass of human beings. He liked the huge machine. Each keeps its own round. The baker's boy brings muffins to the window at a fixed hour every day, and that is all the Londoner knows or wishes to know on the subject. But it turned out good men. He named certain individuals, especially one man of letters, his friend, the best mind he knew, whom London had well served.[1]

On the 28th August I went to Rydal Mount, to pay my respects to Mr. Wordsworth. His daughters called in their father, a plain, elderly, white-haired man, not prepossessing, and disfigured by green goggles. He sat down, and talked with great simplicity. He had just returned from a journey. His health was good, but he had broken a tooth by a fall, when walking with two lawyers, and had said that he was glad it did not happen forty years ago; whereupon they had praised his philosophy.

He had much to say of America, the more that it gave occasion for his favorite topic, — that society is being enlightened by a superficial tuition, out of all proportion to its being restrained by moral culture. Schools do no good. Tuition is not education. He thinks more of the education of circumstances than of tuition. 'T is not question whether there are offences of which the law takes cognizance, but whether there are offences of which the law does not take cognizance. Sin is what he fears, — and how society is to escape without gravest mischiefs from this source. He has even said, what seemed a paradox, that they needed a

civil war in America, to teach the necessity of
knitting the social ties stronger. " There may
be," he said, "in America some vulgarity in
manner, but that's not important. That comes
of the pioneer state of things. But I fear they
are too much given to the making of money;
and secondly, to politics; that they make political distinction the end and not the means. And
I fear they lack a class of men of leisure, — in
short, of gentlemen, — to give a tone of honor
to the community. I am told that things are
boasted of in the second class of society there,
which, in England, — God knows, are done in
England every day, but would never be spoken
of. In America I wish to know not how many
churches or schools, but what newspapers? My
friend Colonel Hamilton, at the foot of the hill,
who was a year in America, assures me that the
newspapers are atrocious, and accuse members of
Congress of stealing spoons!" He was against
taking off the tax on newspapers in England, —
which the reformers represent as a tax upon
knowledge, — for this reason, that they would be
inundated with base prints. He said he talked
on political aspects, for he wished to impress on
me and all good Americans to cultivate the
moral, the conservative, etc., etc., and never to
call into action the physical strength of the

people, as had just now been done in England in the Reform Bill, — a thing prophesied by Delolme. He alluded once or twice to his conversation with Dr. Channing, who had recently visited him (laying his hand on a particular chair in which the Doctor had sat).

The conversation turned on books. Lucretius he esteems a far higher poet than Virgil; not in his system, which is nothing, but in his power of illustration.' Faith is necessary to explain anything and to reconcile the foreknowledge of God with human evil. Of Cousin (whose lectures we had all been reading in Boston), he knew only the name.

I inquired if he had read Carlyle's critical articles and translations. He said he thought him sometimes insane. He proceeded to abuse Goethe's Wilhelm Meister heartily. It was full of all manner of fornication. It was like the crossing of flies in the air. He had never gone farther than the first part; so disgusted was he that he threw the book .across the room. I deprecated this wrath, and said what I could for the better parts of the book, and he courteously promised to look at it again. Carlyle he said wrote most obscurely. He was clever and deep, but he defied the sympathies of every body. Even Mr. Coleridge wrote more clearly, though he had always wished Coleridge would write more to be understood. He led me out into his garden, and showed me the gravel walk in which thousands of his lines were composed. His eyes are much inflamed. This is no loss except for reading, because he never writes prose, and of poetry he carries even hundreds of lines in his head before writing them. He had just returned from a visit to Staffa, and within three days had made three sonnets on Fingal's Cave, and was composing a fourth when he was called in to see me. He said, " If you are interested in my verses perhaps you will like to hear these lines." I gladly assented, and he recollected himself for a few moments and then stood forth and repeated, one after the other, the three entire sonnets with great animation. I fancied the second and third more beautiful than his poems are wont to be. The third is addressed to the flowers, which, he said, especially the ox-eye daisy, are very abundant on the top of the rock. The second alludes to the name of the cave, which is " Cave of Music;" the first to the circumstance of its being visited by the promiscuous company of the steamboat.

This recitation was so unlooked for and surprising, — he, the old Wordsworth, standing apart, and reciting to me in a garden-walk, like a school-boy declaiming, — that I at first was near to laugh; but recollecting myself, that I had come thus far to see a poet and he was chanting poems to me, I saw that he was right and I was wrong, and gladly gave myself up to hear. I told him how much the few printed extracts had quickened the desire to possess his unpublished poems. He replied he never was in haste to publish; partly because he corrected a good deal, and every alteration is ungraciously received after printing; but what he had written would be printed, whether he lived or died. I said Tintern Abbey appeared to be the favorite poem with the public, but more contemplative readers preferred the first books of the Excursion, and the Sonnèts. He said, " Yes, they are better." He preferred such of his poems as touched the affections, to any others; for whatever is didactic — what theories of society, and so on — might perish quickly; but whatever combined a truth with an affection was κτῆμα ἐς ἀεί,¹ good to-day and good forever. He cited the sonnet, On the feelings of a highminded Spaniard, which he preferred to any other (I so understood him), and the Two Voices; and quoted, with evident pleasure, the verses addressed To the Skylark. In this connection he said of the Newtonian theory that it might yet be superseded and forgotten; and Dalton's atomic theory.

When I prepared to depart he said he wished to show me what a common person in England could do, and he led me into the enclosure of his clerk, a young man to whom he had given this slip of ground, which was laid out, or its natural capabilities shown, with much taste. He then said he would show me a better way towards the inn; and he walked a good part of a mile, talking and ever and anon stopping short to impress the word or the verse, and finally parted from me with great kindness and returned across the fields.

Wordsworth honored himself by his simple adherence to truth, and was very willing not to shine; but he surprised by the hard limits of his thought. To judge from a single conversation, he made the impression of a narrow and very English mind; of one who paid for his rare elevation by general tameness and conformity. Off his own beat, his opinions were of no value. It is not very rare to find persons loving sympathy and ease, who expiate their departure from the common in one direction, by their conformity in every other.[1]

CHAPTER II

VOYAGE TO ENGLAND

THE occasion of my second visit to England was an invitation from some Mechanics' Institutes in Lancashire and Yorkshire, which separately are organized much in the same way as our New England Lyceums, but in 1847 had been linked into a "Union," which embraced twenty or thirty towns and cities and presently extended into the middle counties and northward into Scotland. I was invited, on liberal terms, to read a series of lectures in them all. The request was urged with every kind suggestion and every assurance of aid and comfort, by friendliest parties in Manchester, who, in the sequel, amply redeemed their word. The remuneration was equivalent to the fees at that time paid in this country for the like services. At all events it was sufficient to cover any travelling expenses, and the proposal offered an excellent opportunity of seeing the interior of England and Scotland, by means of a home and a committee of intelligent friends awaiting me in every town.

I did not go very willingly. I am not a good traveller, nor have I found that long journeys

yield a fair share of reasonable hours.' But the
invitation was repeated and pressed at a moment of more leisure and when I was a little
spent by some unusual studies. I wanted a
change and a tonic, and England was proposed
to me. Besides, there were at least the dread
attraction and salutary influences of the sea. So
I took my berth in the packet-ship Washington
Irving and sailed from Boston on Tuesday, 5th
October, 1847.

On Friday at noon we had only made one
hundred and thirty-four miles. A nimble Indian would have swum as far; but the captain
affirmed that the ship would show us in time
all her paces, and we crept along through the
floating drift of boards, logs and chips, which
the rivers of Maine and New Brunswick pour
into the sea after a freshet.

At last, on Sunday night, after doing one
day's work in four, the storm came, the winds
blew, and we flew before a northwester which
strained every rope and sail. The good ship
darts through the water all day, all night, like
a fish; quivering with speed, gliding through
liquid leagues, sliding from horizon to horizon.
She has passed Cape Sable; she has reached the
Banks; the land-birds are left; gulls, haglets,

ducks, petrels, swim, dive and hover around; no fishermen; she has passed the Banks, left five sail behind her far on the edge of the west at sundown, which were far east of us at morn, — though they say at sea a stern chase is a long race, — and still we fly for our lives. The shortest sea-line from Boston to Liverpool is 2850 miles. This a steamer keeps, and saves 150 miles. A sailing ship can never go in a shorter line than 3000, and usually it is much longer. Our good master keeps his kites up to the last moment, studding-sails alow and aloft, and by incessant straight steering, never loses a rod of way. Watchfulness is the law of the ship, — watch on watch, for advantage and for life. Since the ship was built, it seems, the master never slept but in his day-clothes whilst on board. "There are many advantages," says Saadi, "in sea-voyaging, but security is not one of them." Yet in hurrying over these abysses, whatever dangers we are running into, we are certainly running out of the risks of hundreds of miles every day, which have their own chances of squall, collision, sea-stroke, piracy, cold and thunder. Hour for hour, the risk on a steamboat is greater; but the speed is safety, or twelve days of danger instead of twenty-four.

Our ship was registered 750 tons, and weighed perhaps, with all her freight, 1500 tons. The mainmast, from the deck to the top-button, measured 115 feet; the length of the deck from stem to stern, 155. It is impossible not to personify a ship; every body does, in every thing they say:—she behaves well; she minds her rudder; she swims like a duck; she runs her nose into the water; she looks into a port. Then that wonderful *esprit du corps* by which we adopt into our self-love every thing we touch, makes us all champions of her sailing qualities.

The conscious ship hears all the praise. In one week she has made 1467 miles, and now, at night, seems to hear the steamer behind her, which left Boston to-day at two; has mended her speed and is flying before the gray south wind eleven and a half knots the hour. The sea-fire shines in her wake and far around wherever a wave breaks. I read the hour, 9h. 45', on my watch by this light. Near the equator you can read small print by it; and the mate describes the phosphoric insects, when taken up in a pail, as shaped like a Carolina potato.

I find the sea-life an acquired taste, like that for tomatoes and olives. The confinement, cold,

motion, noise and odor are not to be dispensed
with. The floor of your room is sloped at an
angle of twenty or thirty degrees, and I waked
every morning with the belief that some one was
tipping up my berth. Nobody likes to be treated
ignominiously, upset, shoved against the side
of the house, rolled over, suffocated with bilge,
mephitis and stewing oil. We get used to these
annoyances at last, but the dread of the sea remains longer. The sea is masculine, the type
of active strength. Look, what egg-shells are
drifting all over it, each one, like ours, filled
with men in ecstasies of terror, alternating with
cockney conceit, as the sea is rough or smooth.
Is this sad-colored circle an eternal cemetery?
In our graveyards we scoop a pit, but this aggressive water opens mile-wide pits and chasms
and makes a mouthful of a fleet. To the geolo-
gist the sea is the only firmament; the land is in
perpetual flux and change, now blown up like a
tumor, now sunk in a chasm, and the registered
observations of a few hundred years find it in a
perpetual tilt, rising and falling. The sea keeps
its old level; and 't is no wonder that the history of our race is so recent, if the roar of the
ocean is silencing our traditions. A rising of the
sea, such as has been observed, say an inch in

a century, from east to west on the land, will
bury all the towns, monuments, bones and
knowledge of mankind, steadily and insensibly.
If it is capable of these great and secular mischiefs, it is quite as ready at private and local
damage; and of this no landsman seems so
fearful as the seaman. Such discomfort and such
danger as the narratives of the captain and mate
disclose are bad enough as the costly fee we
pay for entrance to Europe; but the wonder is
always new that any sane man can be a sailor.
And here on the second day of our voyage,
stepped out a little boy in his shirt-sleeves, who
had hid himself whilst the ship was in port, in
the bread-closet, having no money and wishing
to go to England. The sailors have dressed
him in Guernsey frock, with a knife in his belt,
and he is climbing nimbly about after them; —
" likes the work first-rate, and if the captain will
take him, means now to come back again in the
ship." The mate avers that this is the history
of all sailors; nine out of ten are runaway boys;
and adds that all of them are sick of the sea, but
stay in it out of pride. Jack has a life of risks,
incessant abuse and the worst pay. It is a little
better with the mate and not very much better
with the captain. A hundred dollars a month is

reckoned high pay. If sailors were contented, if they had not resolved again and again not to go to sea any more, I should respect them.

Of course the inconveniences and terrors of the sea are not of any account to those whose minds are preoccupied. The water-laws, arctic frost, the mountain, the mine, only shatter cockneyism; every noble activity makes room for itself. A great mind is a good sailor, as a great heart is. And the sea is not slow in disclosing inestimable secrets to a good naturalist.

'T is a good rule in every journey to provide some piece of liberal study to rescue the hours which bad weather, bad company and taverns steal from the best economist. Classics which at home are drowsily read, have a strange charm in a country inn, or in the transom of a merchant brig. I remember that some of the happiest and most valuable hours I have owed to books, passed, many years ago, on shipboard.[1] The worst impediment I have found at sea is the want of light in the cabin.

We found on board the usual cabin library; Basil Hall, Dumas, Dickens, Bulwer, Balzac and Sand were our sea-gods. Among the passengers there was some variety of talent and profession; we exchanged our experiences and all

learned something. The busiest talk with leisure and convenience at sea, and sometimes a
memorable fact turns up, which you have long
had a vacant niche for, and seize with the joy of a
collector. But, under the best conditions, a voyage is one of the severest tests to try a man.
A college examination is nothing to it. Sea-days
are long— these lack-lustre, joyless days which
whistled over us; but they were few —only fifteen, as the captain counted, sixteen according
to me. Reckoned from the time when we left
soundings, our speed was such that the captain
drew the line of his course in red ink on his chart,
for the encouragement or envy of future navi-
gators.

It has been said that the King of England
would consult his dignity by giving audience to
foreign ambassadors in the cabin of a man-of-
war. And I think the white path of an Atlantic
ship the right avenue to the palace front of this
seafaring people, who for hundreds of years
claimed the strict sovereignty of the sea, and ex-
acted toll and the striking sail from the ships of
all other peoples. When their privilege was disputed by the Dutch and other junior marines,
on the plea that you could never anchor on the
same wave, or hold property in what was always

flowing, the English did not stick to claim the channel, or bottom of all the main: " As if," said they, " we contended for the drops of the sea, and not for its situation, or the bed of those waters. The sea is bounded by his majesty's empire."

As we neared the land, its genius was felt. This was inevitably the British side. In every man's thought arises now a new system, English sentiments, English loves and fears, English history and social modes. Yesterday every passenger had measured the speed of the ship by watching the bubbles over the ship's bulwarks. To-day, instead of bubbles, we measure by Kinsale, Cork, Waterford and Ardmore. There lay the green shore of Ireland, like some coast of plenty. We could see towns, towers, churches, harvests; but the curse of eight hundred years we could not discern.

CHAPTER III

LAND

ALFIERI thought Italy and England the only countries worth living in;[1] the former because there Nature vindicates her rights and triumphs over the evils inflicted by the governments; the latter because art conquers nature and transforms a rude, ungenial land into a paradise of comfort and plenty. England is a garden. Under an ash-colored sky, the fields have been combed and rolled till they appear to have been finished with a pencil instead of a plough. The solidity of the structures that compose the towns speaks the industry of ages. Nothing is left as it was made. Rivers, hills, valleys, the sea itself, feel the hand of a master. The long habitation of a powerful and ingenious race has turned every rood of land to its best use, has found all the capabilities, the arable soil, the quarriable rock, the highways, the byways, the fords, the navigable waters; and the new arts of intercourse meet you every where; so that England is a huge phalanstery, where all that man wants is provided within the precinct. Cushioned and comforted in every manner, the traveller rides

as on a cannon-ball, high and low, over rivers
and towns, through mountains in tunnels of
three or four miles, at near twice the speed of
our trains; and reads quietly the Times newspaper, which, by its immense correspondence
and reporting seems to have machinized the rest
of the world for his occasion.

The problem of the traveller landing at Liverpool is, Why England is England? What are
the elements of that power which the English
hold over other nations? If there be one test
of national genius universally accepted, it is success; and if there be one successful country in
the universe for the last millennium, that country
is England.

A wise traveller will naturally choose to visit
the best of actual nations; and an American has
more reasons than another to draw him to Britain.
In all that is done or begun by the Americans
towards right thinking or practice, we are met
by a civilization already settled and overpower-
ing. The culture of the day, the thoughts and
aims of men, are English thoughts and aims.'
A nation considerable for a thousand years since
Egbert, it has, in the last centuries, obtained the
ascendent, and stamped the knowledge, activity
and power of mankind with its impress. Those

who resist it do not feel it or obey it less. The Russian in his snows is aiming to be English. The Turk and Chinese also are making awkward efforts to be English. The practical common-sense of modern society, the utilitarian direction which labor, laws, opinion, religion take, is the natural genius of the British mind. The influence of France is a constituent of modern civility, but not enough opposed to the English for the most wholesome effect. The American is only the continuation of the English genius into new conditions, more or less propitious.

See what books fill our libraries. Every book we read, every biography, play, romance, in whatever form, is still English history and manners. So that a sensible Englishman once said to me, "As long as you do not grant us copyright, we shall have the teaching of you." [1]

But we have the same difficulty in making a social or moral estimate of England, that the sheriff finds in drawing a jury to try some cause which has agitated the whole community and on which every body finds himself an interested party. Officers, jurors, judges have all taken sides. England has inoculated all nations with her civilization, intelligence and tastes; and to resist the tyranny and prepossession of the Brit-

ish element, a serious man must aid himself by
comparing with it the civilizations of the farthest east and west, the old Greek, the Oriental,
and, much more, the ideal standard ; if only by
means of the very impatience which English
forms are sure to awaken in independent minds.

Besides, if we will visit London, the present
time is the best time, as some signs portend that
it has reached its highest point. It is observed
that the English interest us a little less within
a few years ; and hence the impression that the
British power has culminated, is in solstice, or
already declining.[1]

As soon as you enter England, which, with
Wales, is no larger than the State of Georgia,[2]
this little land stretches by an illusion to the
dimensions of an empire. Add South Carolina,
and you have more than an equivalent for the
area of Scotland. The innumerable details, the
crowded succession of towns, cities, cathedrals,
castles and great and decorated estates, the number and power of the trades and guilds, the military strength and splendor, the multitudes of
rich and of remarkable people, the servants and
equipages, — all these catching the eye and never
allowing it to pause, hide all boundaries by the
impression of magnificence and endless wealth.

I reply to all the urgencies that refer me to this and that object indispensably to be seen, — Yes, to see England well needs a hundred years; for what they told me was the merit of Sir John Soane's Museum, in London, — that it was well packed and well saved, — is the merit of England; — it is stuffed full, in all corners and crevices, with towns, towers, churches, villas, palaces, hospitals and charity-houses. In the history of art it is a long way from a cromlech to York minster; yet all the intermediate steps may still be traced in this all-preserving island.

The territory has a singular perfection. The climate is warmer by many degrees than it is entitled to by latitude. Neither hot nor cold, there is no hour in the whole year when one cannot work. Here is no winter, but such days as we have in Massachusetts in November, a temperature which makes no exhausting demand on human strength, but allows the attainment of the largest stature. Charles the Second said, " It invited men abroad more days in the year and more hours in the day than another country." Then England has all the materials of a working country except wood. The constant rain — a rain with every tide, in some parts of the island — keeps its multitude of rivers full

and brings agricultural production up to the
highest point. It has plenty of water, of stone,
of potter's clay, of coal, of salt and of iron. The
land naturally abounds with game; immense
heaths and downs are paved with quails, grouse
and woodcock, and the shores are animated by
water-birds. The rivers and the surrounding
sea spawn with fish; there are salmon for the
rich and sprats and herrings for the poor. In
the northern lochs, the herring are in innumerable shoals; at one season, the country people
say, the lakes contain one part water and two
parts fish.

The only drawback on this industrial conveniency is the darkness of its sky. The night and
day are too nearly of a color. It strains the
eyes to read and to write. Add the coal smoke.
In the manufacturing towns, the fine soot or
blacks darken the day, give white sheep the
color of black sheep, discolor the human saliva,
contaminate the air, poison many plants and
corrode the monuments and buildings.[1]

The London fog aggravates the distempers
of the sky, and sometimes justifies the epigram
on the climate by an English wit, " in a fine
day, looking up a chimney; in a foul day, looking down one." A gentleman in Liverpool told

me that he found he could do without a fire in
his parlor about one day in the year. It is however pretended that the enormous consumption
of coal in the island is also felt in modifying the
general climate.

Factitious climate, factitious position. England resembles a ship in its shape, and if it were
one, its best admiral could not have worked it
or anchored it in a more judicious or effective
position. Sir John Herschel said, " London is
the centre of the terrene globe." The shop-
keeping nation, to use a shop word, has a *good
stand*. The old Venetians pleased themselves
with the flattery that Venice was in 45°, midway
between the poles and the line ; as if that were
an imperial centrality. Long of old, the Greeks
fancied Delphi the navel of the earth, in their
favorite mode of fabling the earth to be an animal. The Jews believed Jerusalem to be the
centre. I have seen a kratometric chart designed
to show that the city of Philadelphia was in
the same thermic belt, and by inference in the
same belt of empire, as the cities of Athens,
Rome and London. It was drawn by a patriotic
Philadelphian, and was examined with pleasure, under his showing, by the inhabitants of
Chestnut Street. But when carried to Charles-

ton, to New Orleans and to Boston, it somehow failed to convince the ingenious scholars of all those capitals.

But England is anchored at the side of Europe, and right in the heart of the modern world. The sea, which, according to Virgil's famous line, divided the poor Britons utterly from the world,' proved to be the ring of marriage with all nations. It is not down in the books, — it is written only in the geologic strata, — that fortunate day when a wave of the German Ocean burst the old isthmus which joined Kent and Cornwall to France, and gave to this fragment of Europe its impregnable sea-wall, cutting off an island of eight hundred miles in length, with an irregular breadth reaching to three hundred miles ; a territory large enough for independence, enriched with every seed of national power, so near that it can see the harvests of the continent, and so far that who would cross the strait must be an expert mariner, ready for tempests. As America, Europe and Asia lie, these Britons have precisely the best commercial position in the whole planet, and are sure of a market for all the goods they can manufacture. And to make these advantages avail, the river Thames must dig its spacious outlet to the sea from the heart of the kingdom, giving road and landing to innumerable ships, and all the conveniency to trade that a people so skilful and sufficient in economizing water-front by docks, warehouses and lighters required. When James the First declared his purpose of punishing London by removing his Court, the Lord Mayor replied that "in removing his royal presence from his lieges, they hoped he would leave them the Thames."

In the variety of surface, Britain is a miniature of Europe, having plain, forest, marsh, river, seashore, mines in Cornwall; caves in Matlock and Derbyshire; delicious landscape in Dovedale, delicious sea-view at Tor Bay, Highlands in Scotland, Snowdon in Wales, and in Westmoreland and Cumberland a pocket Switzerland, in which the lakes and mountains are on a sufficient scale to fill the eye and touch the imagination. It is a nation conveniently small. Fontenelle thought that nature had sometimes a little affectation; and there is such an artificial completeness in this nation of artificers as if there were a design from the beginning to elaborate a bigger Birmingham. Nature held counsel with herself and said, ' My Romans are gone. To build my new empire, I will

choose a rude race, all masculine, with brutish
strength. I will not grudge a competition of
the roughest males. Let buffalo gore buffalo,
and the pasture to the strongest! For I have
work that requires the best will and sinew.
Sharp and temperate northern breezes shall
blow, to keep that will alive and alert. The sea
shall disjoin the people from others, and knit
them to a fierce nationality.' It shall give them
markets on every side. Long time I will keep
them on their feet, by poverty, border-wars,
seafaring, sea-risks and the stimulus of gain.
An island, — but not so large, the people not so
many as to glut the great markets and depress
one another, but proportioned to the size of
Europe and the continents.'

With its fruits, and wares, and money, must
its civil influence radiate. It is a singular coincidence to this geographic centrality, the spiritual
centrality which Emanuel Swedenborg ascribes to
the people. " For the English nation, the best
of them are in the centre of all Christians, because they have interior intellectual light. This
appears conspicuously in the spiritual world.
This light they derive from the liberty of speaking and writing, and thereby of thinking."

CHAPTER IV

RACE

A N ingenious anatomist has written a book[1]
to prove that races are imperishable, but
nations are pliant political constructions, easily
changed or destroyed. But this writer did not
found his assumed races on any necessary law,
disclosing their ideal or metaphysical necessity;
nor did he on the other hand count with precision the existing races and settle the true
bounds; a point of nicety, and the popular test
of the theory. The individuals at the extremes
of divergence in one race of men are as unlike as
the wolf to the lapdog. Yet each variety shades
down imperceptibly into the next, and you cannot draw the line where a race begins or ends.
Hence every writer makes a different count. Blu-
menbach reckons five races; Humboldt three;
and Mr. Pickering,[2] who lately in our Exploring
Expedition thinks he saw all the kinds of men
that can be on the planet, makes eleven.

The British Empire is reckoned to contain
(in 1848) 222,000,000 souls, — perhaps a fifth
of the population of the globe; and to comprise
a territory of 5,000,000 square miles. So far

have British people predominated. Perhaps forty of these millions are of British stock. Add the United States of America, which reckon (in the same year), exclusive of slaves, 20,000,000 of people, on a territory of 3,000,000 square miles, and in which the foreign element, however considerable, is rapidly assimilated, and you have a population of English descent and language of 60,000,000, and governing a population of 245,000,000 souls.

The British census proper reckons twenty-seven and a half millions in the home countries. What makes this census important is the quality of the units that compose it. They are free forcible men, in a country where life is safe and has reached the greatest value. They give the bias to the current age; and that, not by chance or by mass, but by their character and by the number of individuals among them of personal ability. It has been denied that the English have genius. Be it as it may, men of vast intellect have been born on their soil, and they have made or applied the principal inventions. They have sound bodies and supreme endurance in war and in labor. The spawning force of the race has sufficed to the colonization of great parts of the world; yet it remains to be seen whether they

ke good the exodus of millions from
ritain, amounting in 1852 to more than
ind a day. They have assimilating force,
ey are imitated by their foreign subjects;
y are still aggressive and propagandist,
g the dominion of their arts and liberty.
ws are hospitable, and slavery does not
ider them. What oppression exists is
al and temporary; their success is not
or fortunate, but they have maintained
:y and self-equality for many ages.

is power due to their race, or to some
use? Men hear gladly of the power of
r race. Every body likes to know that
intages cannot be attributed to air, soil,
to local wealth, as mines and quarries,
aws and traditions, nor to fortune; but
rior brain, as it makes the praise more
l to him.

inticipate in the doctrine of race some-
ce that law of physiology that whatever
uscle, or essential organ is found in one
individual, the same part or organ may
d in or near the same place in its con-
and we look to find in the son every
ind moral property that existed in the
:. In race, it is not the broad shoulders,

or litheness, or stature that give advantage, but
a symmetry that reaches as far as to the wit.
Then the miracle and renown begin. Then first
we care to examine the pedigree, and copy heed-
fully the training, — what food they ate, what
nursing, school, and exercises they had, which
resulted in this mother-wit, delicacy of thought
and robust wisdom. How came such men as
King Alfred, and Roger Bacon, William of
Wykeham, Walter Raleigh, Philip Sidney, Isaac
Newton, William Shakspeare, George Chapman,
Francis Bacon, George Herbert, Henry Vane,
to exist here? What made these delicate natures? was it the air? was it the sea? was it the
parentage? For it is certain that these men are
samples of their contemporaries. The hearing
ear is always found close to the speaking tongue,
and no genius can long or often utter any thing
which is not invited and gladly entertained by
men around him.

It is race, is it not, that puts the hundred
millions of India under the dominion of a remote island in the north of Europe? Race avails
much, if that be true which is alleged, that all
Celts are Catholics and all Saxons are Protest-
ants; that Celts love unity of power, and Saxons
the representative principle. Race is a controll-

ing influence in the Jew, who, for two millenniums, under every climate, has preserved the same character and employments. Race in the negro is of appalling importance. The French in Canada, cut off from all intercourse with the parent people, have held their national traits. I chanced to read Tacitus On the Manners of the Germans, not long since, in Missouri and the heart of Illinois, and I found abundant points of resemblance between the Germans of the Hercynian forest, and our *Hoosiers, Suckers* and *Badgers* of the American woods.

But whilst race works immortally to keep its own, it is resisted by other forces. Civilization is a re-agent, and eats away the old traits. The Arabs of to-day are the Arabs of Pharaoh; but the Briton of to-day is a very different person from Cassibelaunus or Ossian.[1] Each religious sect has its physiognomy. The Methodists have acquired a face; the Quakers, a face; the nuns, a face. An Englishman will pick out a dissenter by his manners. Trades and professions carve their own lines on face and form. Certain circumstances of English life are not less effective; as personal liberty; plenty of food; good ale and mutton; open market, or good wages for every kind of labor; high bribes to

talent and skill; the island life, or the million
opportunities and outlets for expanding and
misplaced talent; readiness of combination
among themselves for politics or for business;
strikes; [1] and sense of superiority founded on
habit of victory in labor and in war: and the
appetite for superiority grows by feeding.

It is easy to add to the counteracting forces to
race. Credence is a main element. 'T is said that
the views of nature held by any people deter-
mine all their institutions. Whatever influences
add to mental or moral faculty, take men out
of nationality as out of other conditions, and
make the national life a culpable compromise.

These limitations of the formidable doctrine
of race suggest others which threaten to under-
mine it, as not sufficiently based. The fixity or
inconvertibleness of races as we see them is a
weak argument for the eternity of these frail
boundaries, since all our historical period is a
point to the duration in which nature has
wrought. [2] Any the least and solitariest fact in
our natural history, such as the melioration of
fruits and of animal stocks, has the worth of a
power in the opportunity of geologic periods.
Moreover, though we flatter the self-love of
men and nations by the legend of pure races,

v

all our experience is of the gradation and resolution of races, and strange resemblances meet us everywhere. It need not puzzle us that Malay and Papuan, Celt and Roman, Saxon and Tartar should mix, when we see the rudiments of tiger and baboon in our human form, and know that the barriers of races are not so firm but that some spray sprinkles us from the antediluvian seas.

The low organizations are simplest; a mere mouth, a jelly, or a straight worm. As the scale mounts, the organizations become complex. We are piqued with pure descent, but nature loves inoculation. A child blends in his face the faces of both parents and some feature from every ancestor whose face hangs on the wall. The best nations are those most widely related; and navigation, as effecting a world-wide mixture, is the most potent advancer of nations.

The English composite character betrays a mixed origin. Everything English is a fusion of distant and antagonistic elements.' The language is mixed; the names of men are of different nations, — three languages, three or four nations; — the currents of thought are counter: contemplation and practical skill; active intellect and dead conservatism; world-wide enterprise and devoted use and wont; aggressive freedom and hospitable law with bitter class-legislation; a people scattered by their wars and affairs over the face of the whole earth, and homesick to a man; a country of extremes, — dukes and chartists, Bishops of Durham and naked heathen colliers; — nothing can be praised in it without damning exceptions, and nothing denounced without salvos of cordial praise.

Neither do this people appear to be of one stem, but collectively a better race than any from which they are derived. Nor is it easy to trace it home to its original seats. Who can call by right names what races are in Britain? Who can trace them historically? Who can discriminate them anatomically, or metaphysically?

In the impossibility of arriving at satisfaction on the historical question of race, and — come of whatever disputable ancestry — the indisputable Englishman before me, himself very well marked, and nowhere else to be found, — I fancied I could leave quite aside the choice of a tribe as his lineal progenitors. Defoe said in his wrath, " the Englishman was the mud of all races." I incline to the belief that, as water, lime and sand make mortar, so certain temperaments marry well, and, by well-managed contrarieties, develop as

drastic a character as the English. On the whole
it is not so much a history of one or of certain
tribes of Saxons, Jutes, or Frisians, coming
from one place and genetically identical, as it is
an anthology of temperaments out of them all.
Certain temperaments suit the sky and soil of
England, say eight or ten or twenty varieties,
as, out of a hundred pear-trees, eight or ten suit
the soil of an orchard and thrive, — whilst all
the unadapted temperaments die out.

The English derive their pedigree from such
a range of nationalities that there needs sea-
room and land-room to unfold the varieties of
talent and character. Perhaps the ocean serves
as a galvanic battery, to distribute acids at one
pole and alkalies at the other. So England tends
to accumulate her liberals in America, and her
conservatives at London. The Scandinavians
in her race still hear in every age the murmurs
of their mother, the ocean ; the Briton in the
blood hugs the homestead still.

Again, as if to intensate the influences that are
not of race, what we think of when we talk of
English traits really narrows itself to a small
district. It excludes Ireland and Scotland and
Wales, and reduces itself at last to London, that
is, to those who come and go thither. The por-

traits that hang on the walls in the Academy
Exhibition at London, the figures in Punch's
drawings of the public men or of the club-
houses, the prints in the shop-windows, are
distinctive English, and not American, no, nor
Scotch, nor Irish: but 't is a very restricted
nationality. As you go north into the manufacturing and agricultural districts, and to the
population that never travels; as you go into
Yorkshire, as you enter Scotland, the world's
Englishman is no longer found. In Scotland
there is a rapid loss of all grandeur of mien and
manners; a provincial eagerness and acuteness
appear; the poverty of the country makes itself
remarked, and a coarseness of manners; and,
among the intellectual, is the insanity of dia-
lectics.[1] In Ireland are the same climate and
soil as in England, but less food, no right relation to the land, political dependence, small
tenantry and an inferior or misplaced race.

These queries concerning ancestry and blood
may be well allowed, for there is no prosperity
that seems more to depend on the kind of man
than British prosperity. Only a hardy and wise
people could have made this small territory
great. We say, in a regatta or yacht-race, that
if the boats are anywhere nearly matched, it is

the man that wins. Put the best sailing-master
into either boat, and he will win.

Yet it is fine for us to speculate in face of unbroken traditions, though vague and losing themselves in fable. The traditions have got footing,
and refuse to be disturbed. The kitchen-clock
is more convenient than sidereal time. We must
use the popular category, as we do the Linnæan
classification, for convenience, and not as exact
and final. Otherwise we are presently confounded
when the best-settled traits of one race are claimed
by some new ethnologist as precisely characteristic of the rival tribe.

I found plenty of well-marked English types,
the ruddy complexion fair and plump, robust
men, with faces cut like a die, and a strong
island speech and accent; a Norman type, with
the complacency that belongs to that constitution. Others who might be Americans, for any
thing that appeared in their complexion or form;
and their speech was much less marked and their
thought much less bound. We will call them
Saxons. Then the Roman has implanted his
dark complexion in the trinity or quaternity of
bloods.

1. The sources from which tradition derives
their stock are mainly three. And first they are

of the oldest blood of the world, — the Celtic. Some peoples are deciduous or transitory.
Where are the Greeks? Where the Etrurians?
Where the Romans? But the Celts or Sidon-
ides are an old family, of whose beginning there
is no memory, and their end is likely to be still
more remote in the future; for they have endurance and productiveness. They planted
Britain, and gave to the seas and mountains
names which are poems and imitate the pure
voices of nature. They are favorably remembered in the oldest records of Europe. They
had no violent feudal tenure, but the husband-
man owned the land. They had an alphabet,
astronomy, priestly culture and a sublime creed.[1]
They have a hidden and precarious genius.
They made the best popular literature of the
Middle Ages in the songs of Merlin and the
tender and delicious mythology of Arthur.

2. The English come mainly from the Germans, whom the Romans found hard to conquer
in two hundred and ten years, — say impossible
to conquer, when one remembers the long sequel; — a people about whom in the old empire
the rumor ran there was never any that meddled
with them that repented it not.[2]

3. Charlemagne, halting one day in a town

of Narbonnese Gaul, looked out of a window and saw a fleet of Northmen cruising in the Mediterranean. They even entered the port of the town where he was, causing no small alarm and sudden manning and arming of his galleys. As they put out to sea again, the emperor gazed long after them, his eyes bathed in tears. "I am tormented with sorrow," he said, "when I foresee the evils they will bring on my posterity." There was reason for these Xerxes' tears. The men who have built a ship and invented the rig, cordage, sail, compass and pump; the working in and out of port, have acquired much more than a ship.' Now arm them and every shore is at their mercy. For if they have not numerical superiority where they anchor, they have only to sail a mile or two to find it. Bonaparte's art of war, namely of concentrating force on the point of attack, must always be theirs who have the choice of the battle-ground. Of course they come into the fight from a higher ground of power than the land-nations; and can engage them on shore with a victorious advantage in the retreat. As soon as the shores are sufficiently peopled to make piracy a losing business, the same skill and courage are ready for the service of trade.

The Heimskringla,¹ or Sagas of the Kings
of Norway, collected by Snorro Sturleson, is the
Iliad and Odyssey of English history. Its portraits, like Homer's, are strongly individualized.
The Sagas describe a monarchical republic like
Sparta. The government disappears before the
importance of citizens. In Norway, no Persian
masses fight and perish to aggrandize a king,
but the actors are bonders or landholders, every
one of whom is named and personally and pat-
ronymically described, as the king's friend and
companion. A sparse population gives this high
worth to every man. Individuals are often
noticed as very handsome persons, which trait
only brings the story nearer to the English race.
Then the solid material interest predominates,
so dear to English understanding, wherein the
association is logical, between merit and land.
The heroes of the Sagas are not the knights of
South Europe. No vaporing of France and
Spain has corrupted them. They are substantial
farmers whom the rough times have forced to
defend their properties. They have weapons
which they use in a determined manner, by no
means for chivalry, but for their acres. They
are people considerably advanced in rural arts,
living amphibiously on a rough coast, and draw-

ing half their food from the sea and half from the land. They have herds of cows, and malt, wheat, bacon, butter and cheese. They fish in the fiord and hunt the deer. A king among these farmers has a varying power, sometimes not exceeding the authority of a sheriff. A king was maintained, much as in some of our country districts a winter-schoolmaster is quartered, a week here, a week there, and a fortnight on the next farm, — on all the farms in rotation. This the king calls going into guest-quarters; and it was the only way in which, in a poor country, a poor king with many retainers could be kept alive when he leaves his own farm to collect his dues through the kingdom.

These Norsemen are excellent persons in the main, with good sense, steadiness, wise speech and prompt action. But they have a singular turn for homicide; their chief end of man is to murder or to be murdered; oars, scythes, harpoons, crowbars, peat-knives and hay-forks are tools valued by them all the more for their charming aptitude for assassinations. A pair of kings, after dinner, will divert themselves by thrusting each his sword through the other's body, as did Yngve and Alf. Another pair ride out on a morning for a frolic, and finding no weapon near, will take the bits out of their horses' mouths and crush each other's heads with them, as did Alric and Eric. The sight of a tent-cord or a cloak-string puts them on hanging somebody, a wife, or a husband, or, best of all, a king. If a farmer has so much as a hayfork, he sticks it into a King Dag. King Ingiald finds it vastly amusing to burn up half a dozen kings in a hall, after getting them drunk. Never was poor gentleman so surfeited with life, so furious to be rid of it, as the Northman. If he cannot pick any other quarrel, he will get himself comfortably gored by a bull's horns, like Egil, or slain by a land-slide, like the agricultural King Onund. Odin died in his bed, in Sweden; but it was a proverb of ill condition to die the death of old age. King Hake of Sweden cuts and slashes in battle, as long as he can stand, then orders his war-ship, loaded with his dead men and their weapons, to be taken out to sea, the tiller shipped and the sails spread; being left alone he sets fire to some tar-wood and lies down contented on deck. The wind blew off the land, the ship flew, burning in clear flame, out between the islets into the ocean, and there was the right end of King Hake.

The early Sagas are sanguinary and piratical;

the later are of a noble strain. History rarely yields us better passages than the conversation between King Sigurd the Crusader and King Eystein his brother, on their respective merits, — one the soldier, and the other a lover of the arts of peace.[1]

But the reader of the Norman history must steel himself by holding fast the remote compensations which result from animal vigor. As the old fossil world shows that the first steps of reducing the chaos were confided to saurians and other huge and horrible animals, so the foundations of the new civility were to be laid by the most savage men.

The Normans came out of France into England worse men than they went into it one hundred and sixty years before. They had lost their own language and learned the Romance or barbarous Latin of the Gauls, and had acquired, with the language, all the vices it had names for. The conquest has obtained in the chronicles the name of the " memory of sorrow." Twenty thousand thieves landed at Hastings. These founders of the House of Lords were greedy and ferocious dragoons, sons of greedy and ferocious pirates. They were all alike, they took everything they could carry, they burned, harried, violated, tortured and killed, until everything English was brought to the verge of ruin. Such however is the illusion of antiquity and wealth, that decent and dignified men now existing boast their descent from these filthy thieves, who showed a far juster conviction of their own merits, by assuming for their types the swine, goat, jackal, leopard, wolf and snake, which they severally resembled.[1]

England yielded to the Danes and Northmen in the tenth and eleventh centuries, and was the receptacle into which all the mettle of that strenuous population was poured. The continued draught of the best men in Norway, Sweden and Denmark to these piratical expeditions exhausted those countries, like a tree which bears much fruit when young, and these have been second-rate powers ever since. The power of the race migrated and left Norway void. King Olaf said, "When King Harold, my father, went westward to England, the chosen men in Norway followed him; but Norway was so emptied then, that such men have not since been to find in the country, nor especially such a leader as King Harold was for wisdom and bravery."

It was a tardy recoil of these invasions, when,

in 1801, the British government sent Nelson to bombard the Danish forts in the Sound, and, in 1807, Lord Cathcart, at Copenhagen, took the entire Danish fleet, as it lay in the basins, and all the equipments from the Arsenal, and carried them to England. Konghelle, the town where the kings of Norway, Sweden and Denmark were wont to meet, is now rented to a private English gentleman for a hunting ground.

It took many generations to trim and comb and perfume the first boat-load of Norse pirates into royal highnesses and most noble Knights of the Garter; but every sparkle of ornament dates back to the Norse boat. There will be time enough to mellow this strength into civility and religion. It is a medical fact that the children of the blind see; the children of felons have a healthy conscience. Many a mean, dastardly boy is, at the age of puberty, transformed into a serious and generous youth.[1]

The mildness of the following ages has not quite effaced these traits of Odin; as the rudiment of a structure matured in the tiger is said to be still found unabsorbed in the Caucasian man. The nation has a tough, acrid, animal nature, which centuries of churching and civilizing have not been able to sweeten. Alfieri said "the crimes of Italy were the proof of the superiority of the stock;" and one may say of England that this watch moves on a splinter of adamant. The English uncultured are a brutal nation. The crimes recorded in their calendars leave nothing to be desired in the way of cold malignity. Dear to the English heart is a fair stand-up fight. The brutality of the manners in the lower class appears in the boxing, bear-baiting, cock-fighting, love of executions, and in the readiness for a set-to in the streets, delightful to the English of all classes. The coster-mongers of London streets hold cowardice in loathing : — "we must work our fists well; we are all handy with our fists." The public schools are charged with being bear-gardens of brutal strength, and are liked by the people for that cause. The fagging is a trait of the same quality. Medwin, in the Life of Shelley, relates that at a military school they rolled up a young man in a snowball, and left him so in his room while the other cadets went to church; — and crippled him for life. They have retained impressment, deck-flogging, army-flogging and school-flogging. Such is the ferocity of the army discipline that a soldier, sentenced to flogging, sometimes prays that his sentence may be commuted to death. Flogging, banished from the armies of Western Europe, remains here by the sanction of the Duke of Wellington. The right of the husband to sell the wife has been retained down to our times. The Jews have been the favorite victims of royal and popular persecution. Henry III. mortgaged all the Jews in the kingdom to his brother the Earl of Cornwall, as security for money which he borrowed. The torture of criminals, and the rack for extorting evidence, were slowly disused. Of the criminal statutes, Sir Samuel Romilly said, " I have examined the codes of all nations, and ours is the worst, and worthy of the Anthropophagi." ¹ In the last session (1848), the House of Commons was listening to the details of flogging and torture practised in the jails.²

As soon as this land, thus geographically posted, got a hardy people into it, they could not help becoming the sailors and factors of the globe. From childhood, they dabbled in water, they swam like fishes, their playthings were boats. In the case of the ship-money, the judges delivered it for law, that " England being an island, the very midland shires therein are all to be accounted maritime ;" and Fuller adds, "the genius even of landlocked counties driving the

natives with a maritime dexterity." As early as
the conquest it is remarked, in explanation of
the wealth of England, that its merchants trade
to all countries.

The English at the present day have great
vigor of body and endurance. Other countrymen look slight and undersized beside them,
and invalids. They are bigger men than the
Americans. I suppose a hundred English taken
at random out of the street would weigh a fourth
more than so many Americans. Yet, I am told,
the skeleton is not larger. They are round,
ruddy and handsome; at least the whole bust
is well formed, and there is a tendency to stout
and powerful frames. I remarked the stoutness
on my first landing at Liverpool; porter, dray-
man, coachman, guard, — what substantial, respectable, grandfatherly figures, with costume
and manners to suit. The American has arrived
at the old mansion-house and finds himself
among uncles, aunts and grandsires. The pictures on the chimney-tiles of his nursery were
pictures of these people. Here they are in the
identical costumes and air which so took him.

It is the fault of their forms that they grow
stocky, and the women have that disadvantage,
— few tall, slender figures of flowing shape, but

v

stunted and thickset persons. The French say that the Englishwomen have two left hands. But in all ages they are a handsome race. The bronze monuments of crusaders lying cross-legged in the Temple Church at London, and those in Worcester and in Salisbury cathedrals, which are seven hundred years old, are of the same type as the best youthful heads of men now in England;—please by beauty of the same character, an expression blending good-nature, valor and refinement, and mainly by that un-corrupt youth in the face of manhood, which is daily seen in the streets of London.

Both branches of the Scandinavian race are distinguished for beauty. The anecdote of the handsome captives which Saint Gregory found at Rome, A. D. 600, is matched by the testimony of the Norman chroniclers, five centuries later, who wondered at the beauty and long flowing hair of the young English captives. Mean-time the Heimskringla has frequent occasion to speak of the personal beauty of its heroes. When it is considered what humanity, what resources of mental and moral power the traits of the blonde race betoken, its accession to empire marks a new and finer epoch, wherein the old mineral force shall be subjugated at last by humanity and shall plough in its furrow henceforward. It is not a final race, once a crab always crab,—but a race with a future.

On the English face are combined decision and nerve with the fair complexion, blue eyes and open and florid aspect. Hence the love of truth, hence the sensibility, the fine perception and poetic construction. The fair Saxon man, with open front and honest meaning, domestic, affectionate, is not the wood out of which cannibal, or inquisitor, or assassin is made, but he is moulded for law, lawful trade, civility, marriage, the nurture of children, for colleges, churches, charities and colonies.

They are rather manly than warlike. When the war is over, the mask falls from the affectionate and domestic tastes, which make them women in kindness. This union of qualities is fabled in their national legend of "Beauty and the Beast," or, long before, in the Greek legend of Hermaphrodite. The two sexes are co-present in the English mind. I apply to Britannia, queen of seas and colonies, the words in which her latest novelist portrays his heroine; "She is as mild as she is game, and as game as she is mild." The English delight in the antagonism which combines in one person the extremes of

courage and tenderness. Nelson, dying at Trafalgar, sends his love to Lord Collingwood, and
like an innocent schoolboy that goes to bed,
says "Kiss me, Hardy," and turns to sleep.
Lord Collingwood, his comrade, was of a nature
the most affectionate and domestic. Admiral
Rodney's figure approached to delicacy and effeminacy, and he declared himself very sensible
to fear, which he surmounted only by considerations of honor and public duty. Clarendon
says the Duke of Buckingham was so modest
and gentle, that some courtiers attempted to
put affronts on him, until they found that this
modesty and effeminacy was only a mask for
the most terrible determination. And Sir Edward Parry said of Sir John Franklin, that "if
he found Wellington Sound open, he explored
it; for he was a man who never turned his back
on a danger, yet of that tenderness that he would
not brush away a mosquito." Even for their
highwaymen the same virtue is claimed, and
Robin Hood comes described to us as *mitissi-
mus prædonum;* the gentlest thief. But they
know where their war-dogs lie. Cromwell,
Blake, Marlborough, Chatham, Nelson and
Wellington are not to be trifled with, and the
brutal strength which lies at the bottom of

society, the animal ferocity of the quays and
cockpits, the bullies of the costermongers of
Shoreditch, Seven Dials and Spitalfields, they
know how to wake up.

They have a vigorous health and last well
into middle and old age. The old men are as
red as roses, and still handsome. A clear skin,
a peach-bloom complexion and good teeth are
found all over the island. They use a plentiful
and nutritious diet. The operative cannot sub-
sist on water-cresses. Beef, mutton, wheat-bread
and malt-liquors are universal among the first-
class laborers. Good feeding is a chief point of
national pride among the vulgar, and in their caricatures they represent the Frenchman as a poor,
starved body. It is curious that Tacitus found
the English beer already in use among the Germans: "They make from barley or wheat a
drink corrupted into some resemblance to wine."
Lord Chief Justice Fortescue, in Henry VI.'s
time, says, "The inhabitants of England drink
no water, unless at certain times on a religious
score and by way of penance." The extremes
of poverty and ascetic penance, it would seem,
never reach cold water in England. Wood the
antiquary, in describing the poverty and macer-
ation of Father Lacey, an English Jesuit, does

not deny him beer. He says, "His bed was under a thatching, and the way to it up a ladder; his fare was coarse; his drink, of a penny a gawn, or gallon."

They have more constitutional energy than any other people. They think, with Henri Quatre, that manly exercises are the foundation of that elevation of mind which gives one nature ascendant over another; or with the Arabs, that the days spent in the chase are not counted in the length of life. They box, run, shoot, ride, row, and sail from pole to pole. They eat and drink, and live jolly in the open air, putting a bar of solid sleep between day and day.[1] They walk and ride as fast as they can, their head bent forward, as if urged on some pressing affair. The French say that Englishmen in the street always walk straight before them like mad dogs. Men and women walk with infatuation. As soon as he can handle a gun, hunting is the fine art of every Englishman of condition. They are the most voracious people of prey that ever existed. Every season turns out the aristocracy into the country to shoot and fish. The more vigorous run out of the island to America, to Asia, to Africa and Australia, to hunt with fury by gun, by trap, by harpoon, by lasso, with dog, with horse, with elephant or with dromedary, all the game that is in nature. These men have written the game-books of all countries, as Hawker, Scrope, Murray, Herbert, Maxwell, Cumming and a host of travellers. The people at home are addicted to boxing, running, leaping and rowing matches.

I suppose the dogs and horses must be thanked for the fact that the men have muscles almost as tough and supple as their own. If in every efficient man there is first a fine animal, in the English race it is of the best breed, a wealthy, juicy, broad-chested creature, steeped in ale and good cheer and a little overloaded by his flesh. Men of animal nature rely, like animals, on their instincts. The Englishman associates well with dogs and horses. His attachment to the horse arises from the courage and address required to manage it. The horse finds out who is afraid of it, and does not disguise its opinion. Their young boiling clerks and lusty collegians like the company of horses better than the company of professors. I suppose the horses are better company for them. The horse has more uses than Buffon noted. If you go into the streets, every driver in 'bus or dray is a bully, and if I wanted a good troop of soldiers,

I should recruit among the stables. Add a certain degree of refinement to the vivacity of these
riders, and you obtain the precise quality which
makes the men and women of polite society
formidable.

They come honestly by their horsemanship,
with *Hengst* and *Horsa* for their Saxon founders.
The other branch of their race had been Tartar
nomads. The horse was all their wealth. The
children were fed on mares' milk. The pastures
of Tartary were still remembered by the tenacious practice of the Norsemen to eat horseflesh
at religious feasts. In the Danish invasions the
marauders seized upon horses where they landed,
and were at once converted into a body of expert
cavalry.

At one time this skill seems to have declined.
Two centuries ago the English horse never performed any eminent service beyond the seas;
and the reason assigned was that the genius of
the English hath always more inclined them to
foot-service, as pure and proper manhood, without any mixture; whilst in a victory on horseback, the credit ought to be divided betwixt the
man and his horse. But in two hundred years
a change has taken place.[1] Now, they boast that
they understand horses better than any other

people in the world, and that their horses are become their second selves.

"William the Conqueror being," says Camden, "better affected to beasts than to men, imposed heavy fines and punishments on those that should meddle with his game." The Saxon Chronicle says "he loved the tall deer as if he were their father." And rich Englishmen have followed his example, according to their ability, ever since, in encroaching on the tillage and commons with their game-preserves. It is a proverb in England that it is safer to shoot a man than a hare. The severity of the game-laws certainly indicates an extravagant sympathy of the nation with horses and hunters. The gentlemen are always on horseback, and have brought horses to an ideal perfection; the English racer is a factitious breed. A score or two of mounted gentlemen may frequently be seen running like centaurs down a hill nearly as steep as the roof of a house. Every inn-room is lined with pictures of races; telegraphs communicate, every hour, tidings of the heats from Newmarket and Ascot; and the House of Commons adjourns over the "Derby Day."

CHAPTER V

ABILITY

THE Saxon and the Northman are both Scandinavians. History does not allow us to fix the limits of the application of these names with any accuracy, but from the residence of a portion of these people in France, and from some effect of that powerful soil on their blood and manners, the Norman has come popularly to represent in England the aristocratic, and the Saxon the democratic principle. And though, I doubt not, the nobles are of both tribes, and the workers of both, yet we are forced to use the names a little mythically, one to represent the worker and the other the enjoyer.

The island was a prize for the best race. Each of the dominant races tried its fortune in turn. The Phœnician, the Celt and the Goth had already got in. The Roman came, but in the very day when his fortune culminated. He looked in the eyes of a new people that was to supplant his own. He disembarked his legions, erected his camps and towers, — presently he heard bad news from Italy, and worse and worse, every year; at last, he made a handsome com-

pliment of roads and walls, and departed. But
the Saxon seriously settled in the land, builded,
tilled, fished and traded, with German truth and
adhesiveness. The Dane came and divided with
him. Last of all the Norman or French-Dane .
arrived, and formally conquered, harried and
ruled the kingdom. A century later it came out
that the Saxon had the most bottom and lon-
gevity, had managed to make the victor speak
the language and accept the law and usage of
the victim; forced the baron to dictate Saxon
terms to Norman kings; and, step by step, got
all the essential securities of civil liberty invented
and confirmed. The genius of the race and the
genius of the place conspired to this effect. The
island is lucrative to free labor, but not worth
possession on other terms. The race was so intellectual that a feudal or military tenure could
not last longer than the war. The power of the
Saxon-Danes, so thoroughly beaten in the war
that the name of English and villein were syn-
onymous, yet so vivacious as to extort charters
from the kings, stood on the strong personality
of these people. Sense and economy must rule
in a world which is made of sense and economy,
and the banker, with his seven per cent., drives
the earl out of his castle. A nobility of sol-

diers cannot keep down a commonalty of shrewd scientific persons. What signifies a pedigree of a hundred links, against a cotton-spinner with steam in his mill; or against a company of broad-shouldered Liverpool merchants, for whom Stephenson and Brunel are contriving locomotives and a tubular bridge? [1]

These Saxons are the hands of mankind. They have the taste for toil, a distaste for pleasure or repose, and the telescopic appreciation of distant gain. They are the wealth-makers, — and by dint of mental faculty which has its own conditions. The Saxon works after liking, or only for himself; and to set him at work and to begin to draw his monstrous values out of barren Britain, all dishonor, fret and barrier must be removed, and then his energies begin to play.

The Scandinavian fancied himself surrounded by Trolls, — a kind of goblin men with vast power of work and skilful production, — divine stevedores, carpenters, reapers, smiths and masons, swift to reward every kindness done them, with gifts of gold and silver. In all English history this dream comes to pass. Certain Trolls or working brains, under the names of Alfred, Bede, Caxton, Bracton, Camden, Drake, Selden, Dugdale, Newton, Gibbon, Brindley, Watt, Wedgwood, dwell in the troll-mounts of Britain and turn the sweat of their face to power and renown.[1]

If the race is good, so is the place. Nobody landed on this spellbound island with impunity. The enchantments of barren shingle and rough weather transformed every adventurer into a laborer. Each vagabond that arrived bent his neck to the yoke of gain, or found the air too tense for him. The strong survived, the weaker went to the ground. Even the pleasure-hunters and sots of England are of a tougher texture. A hard temperament had been formed by Saxon and Saxon-Dane, and such of these French or Normans as could reach it were naturalized in every sense.

All the admirable expedients or means hit upon in England must be looked at as growths or irresistible offshoots of the expanding mind of the race. A man of that brain thinks and acts thus; and his neighbor, being afflicted with the same kind of brain, though he is rich and called a baron or a duke, thinks the same thing, and is ready to allow the justice of the thought and act in his retainer or tenant, though sorely against his baronial or ducal will.

The island was renowned in antiquity for its breed of mastiffs, so fierce that when their teeth were set you must cut their heads off to part them. The man was like his dog. The people have that nervous bilious temperament which is known by medical men to resist every means employed to make its possessor subservient to the will of others. The English game is main force to main force, the planting of foot to foot, fair play and open field, — a rough tug without trick or dodging, till one or both come to pieces. King Ethelwald spoke the language of his race when he planted himself at Wimborne and said he " would do one of two things, or there live, or there lie." They hate craft and subtlety. They neither poison, nor waylay, nor assassinate ; and when they have pounded each other to a poultice, they will shake hands and be friends for the remainder of their lives.

You shall trace these Gothic touches at school, at country fairs, at the hustings and in parliament. No artifice, no breach of truth and plain dealing, — not so much as secret ballot, is suffered in the island. In parliament, the tactics of the opposition is to resist every step of the government by a pitiless attack : and in a bargain, no prospect of advantage is so dear to the

merchant as the thought of being tricked is
mortifying.

Sir Kenelm Digby, a courtier of Charles and
James, who won the sea-fight of Scanderoon,
was a model Englishman in his day. "His
person was handsome and gigantic, he had so
graceful elocution and noble address, that, had
he been dropt out of the clouds in any part
of the world, he would have made himself respected : he was skilled in six tongues, and
master of arts and arms." [1] Sir Kenelm wrote a
book, Of Bodies and of Souls, in which he
propounds, that "syllogisms do breed, or rather
are all the variety of man's life. They are the
steps by which we walk in all our businesses.
Man, as he is man, doth nothing else but weave
such chains. Whatsoever he doth, swarving
from this work, he doth as deficient from the
nature of man : and, if he do aught beyond this,
by breaking out into divers sorts of exterior
actions, he findeth, nevertheless, in this linked
sequel of simple discourses, the art, the cause,
the rule, the bounds and the model of it." [2]

There spoke the genius of the English people. There is a necessity on them to be logical.
They would hardly greet the good that did not
logically fall, — as if it excluded their own merit,

or shook their understandings. They are jealous of minds that have much facility of association, from an instinctive fear that the seeing many relations to their thought might impair this serial continuity and lucrative concentration. They are impatient of genius, or of minds addicted to contemplation, and cannot conceal their contempt for sallies of thought, however lawful, whose steps they cannot count by their wonted rule. Neither do they reckon better a syllogism that ends in syllogism. For they have a supreme eye to facts, and theirs is a logic that brings salt to soup, hammer to nail, oar to boat; the logic of cooks, carpenters and chemists, following the sequence of nature, and one on which words make no impression. Their mind is not dazzled by its own means, but locked and bolted to results. They love men who, like Samuel Johnson, a doctor in the schools, would jump out of his syllogism the instant his major proposition was in danger, to save that at all hazards. Their practical vision is spacious, and they can hold many threads without entangling them. All the steps they orderly take; but with the high logic of never confounding the minor and major proposition; keeping their eye on their aim, in all the com-

plicity and delay incident to the several series
of means they employ. There is room in their
minds for this and that, — a science of degrees.
In the courts the independence of the judges
and the loyalty of the suitors are equally excellent. In parliament they have hit on that
capital invention of freedom, a constitutional
opposition. And when courts and parliament
are both deaf, the plaintiff is not silenced. Calm,
patient, his weapon of defence from year to year
is the obstinate reproduction of the grievance,
with calculations and estimates. But, meantime,
he is drawing numbers and money to his opinion,
resolved that if all remedy fails, right of revolution is at the bottom of his charter-box. They
are bound to see their measure carried, and
stick to it through ages of defeat.

Into this English logic, however, an infusion
of justice enters, not so apparent in other races;
— a belief in the existence of two sides, and the
resolution to see fair play. There is on every
question an appeal from the assertion of the
parties to the proof of what is asserted. They
kiss the dust before a fact. Is it a machine, is
it a charter, is it a boxer in the ring, is it a
candidate on the hustings, — the universe of
Englishmen will suspend their judgment until

the trial can be had. They are not to be led by
a phrase, they want a working plan, a working
machine, a working constitution, and will sit
out the trial and abide by the issue and reject
all preconceived theories. In politics they put
blunt questions, which must be answered; Who
is to pay the taxes? What will you do for trade?
What for corn? What for the spinner?

This singular fairness and its results strike
the French with surprise. Philip de Commines
says, " Now, in my opinion, among all the sov-
ereignties I know in the world, that in which
the public good is best attended to, and the
least violence exercised on the people, is that of
England." Life is safe, and personal rights;
and what is freedom without security? whilst,
in France, "fraternity," "equality," and "in-
divisible unity" are names for assassination.
Montesquieu said, " England is the freest country in the world. If a man in England had as
many enemies as hairs on his head, no harm
would happen to him."

Their self-respect, their faith in causation, and
their realistic logic or coupling of means to ends,
have given them the leadership of the modern
world. Montesquieu said, "No people have
true common-sense but those who are born in

England." This common-sense is a perception
of all the conditions of our earthly existence; of
laws that can be stated, and of laws that cannot be stated, or that are learned only by practice, in which allowance for friction is made.
They are impious in their skepticism of theory,
and in high departments they are cramped and
sterile. But the unconditional surrender to facts,
and the choice of means to reach their ends, are
as admirable as with ants and bees.

The bias of the nation is a passion for utility.
They love the lever, the screw and pulley, the
Flanders draught-horse, the waterfall, wind-
mills, tide-mills; the sea and the wind to bear
their freight ships. More than the diamond
Koh-i-noor, which glitters among their crown
jewels, they prize that dull pebble which is wiser
than a man, whose poles turn themselves to the
poles of the world, and whose axis is parallel to
the axis of the world.[1] Now, their toys are steam
and galvanism. They are heavy at the fine arts,
but adroit at the coarse; not good in jewelry or
mosaics, but the best iron-masters, colliers, wool-
combers and tanners in Europe. They apply
themselves to agriculture, to draining, to resisting encroachments of sea, wind, travelling sands,
cold and wet sub-soil; to fishery, to manufac-

ture of indispensable staples, — salt, plumbago, leather, wool, glass, pottery and brick, — to bees and silkworms; — and by their steady combinations they succeed. A manufacturer sits down to dinner in a suit of clothes which was wool on a sheep's back at sunrise. You dine with a gentleman on venison, pheasant, quail, pigeons, poultry, mushrooms and pine-apples, all the growth of his estate. They are neat husbands for ordering all their tools pertaining to house and field. All are well kept. There is no want and no waste. They study use and fitness in their building, in the order of their dwellings and in their dress. The Frenchman invented the ruffle; the Englishman added the shirt. The Englishman wears a sensible coat buttoned to the chin, of rough but solid and lasting texture. If he is a lord, he dresses a little worse than a commoner. They have diffused the taste for plain substantial hats, shoes and coats through Europe. They think him the best dressed man whose dress is so fit for his use that you cannot notice or remember to describe it.

They secure the essentials in their diet, in their arts and manufactures. Every article of cutlery shows, in its shape, thought and long experience of workmen. They put the expense

in the right place, as, in their sea-steamers, in
the solidity of the machinery and the strength
of the boat.[1] The admirable equipment of their
arctic ships carries London to the pole. They
build roads, aqueducts; warm and ventilate
houses. And they have impressed their directness and practical habit on modern civilization.

In trade, the Englishman believes that nobody
breaks who ought not to break; and that if he
do not make trade everything, it will make him
nothing; and acts on this belief. The spirit of
system, attention to details, and the subordi-
nation of details, or the not driving things too
finely (which is charged on the Germans), constitute that dispatch of business which makes
the mercantile power of England.

In war, the Englishman looks to his means.
He is of the opinion of Civilis, his German ancestor, whom Tacitus reports as holding that
"the gods are on the side of the strongest;" —
a sentence which Bonaparte unconsciously translated, when he said that " he had noticed that
Providence always favored the heaviest battal-
ion." Their military science propounds that if
the weight of the advancing column is greater
than that of the resisting, the latter is destroyed.
Therefore Wellington, when he came to the

army in Spain, had every man weighed, first
with accoutrements, and then without; believing that the force of an army depended on the
weight and power of the individual soldiers, in
spite of cannon. Lord Palmerston told the
House of Commons that more care is taken of
the health and comfort of English troops than
of any other troops in the world; and that hence
the English can put more men into the rank, on
the day of action, on the field of battle, than
any other army. Before the bombardment of
the Danish forts in the Baltic, Nelson spent day
after day, himself, in the boats, on the exhausting service of sounding the channel. Clerk of
Eldin's ' celebrated manœuvre of breaking the
line of sea-battle, and Nelson's feat of *doubling*,
or stationing his ships one on the outer bow,
and another on the outer quarter of each of the
enemy's, were only translations into naval tactics of Bonaparte's rule of concentration. Lord
Collingwood was accustomed to tell his men
that if they could fire three well-directed broad-
sides in five minutes, no vessel could resist them;
and from constant practice they came to do it in
three minutes and a half.

But conscious that no race of better men exists, they rely most on the simplest means, and

do not like ponderous and difficult tactics, but
delight to bring the affair hand to hand ;[1] where
the victory lies with the strength, courage and
endurance of the individual combatants. They
adopt every improvement in rig, in motor, in
weapons, but they fundamentally believe that
the best stratagem in naval war is to lay your
ship close alongside of the enemy's ship and
bring all your guns to bear on him, until you
or he go to the bottom. This is the old fashion,
which never goes out of fashion, neither in nor
out of England.

It is not usually a point of honor, nor a religious sentiment, and never any whim, that
they will shed their blood for ; but usually property, and right measured by property, that
breeds revolution.[2] They have no Indian taste
for a tomahawk-dance, no French taste for a
badge or a proclamation. The Englishman is
peaceably minding his business and earning his
day's wages. But if you offer to lay hand on
his day's wages, on his cow, or his right in common, or his shop, he will fight to the Judgment.
Magna-charta, jury-trial, *habeas-corpus*, star-
chamber, ship-money, Popery, Plymouth col-
ony, American Revolution, are all questions
involving a yeoman's right to his dinner, and

except as touching that, would not have lashed the British nation to rage and revolt.

Whilst they are thus instinct with a spirit of order and of calculation, it must be owned they are capable of larger views; but the indulgence is expensive to them, costs great crises, or accumulations of mental power. In common, the horse works best with blinders. Nothing is more in the line of English thought than our unvarnished Connecticut question, "Pray, sir, how do you get your living when you are at home?" The questions of freedom, of taxation, of privilege, are money questions. Heavy fellows, steeped in beer and fleshpots, they are hard of hearing and dim of sight. Their drowsy minds need to be flagellated by war and trade and politics and persecution. They cannot well read a principle, except by the light of fagots and of burning towns.

Tacitus says of the Germans, "Powerful only in sudden efforts, they are impatient of toil and labor." This highly destined race, if it had not somewhere added the chamber of patience to its brain, would not have built London. I know not from which of the tribes and temperaments that went to the composition of the people this tenacity was supplied, but they clinch every nail

they drive. They have no running for luck, and
no immoderate speed. They spend largely on
their fabric, and await the slow return. Their
leather lies tanning seven years in the vat. At
Rogers's mills, in Sheffield, where I was shown
the process of making a razor and a penknife,
I was told there is no luck in making good
steel; that they make no mistakes, every blade
in the hundred and in the thousand is good.
And that is characteristic of all their work, —
no more is attempted than is done.

When Thor and his companions arrive at
Utgard, he is told that "nobody is permitted
to remain here, unless he understand some art,
and excel in it all other men." [1] The same question is still put to the posterity of Thor. A
nation of laborers, every man is trained to some
one art or detail and aims at perfection in that;
not content unless he has something in which he
thinks he surpasses all other men. He would
rather not do anything at all than not do it well.
I suppose no people have such thoroughness;
— from the highest to the lowest, every man
meaning to be master of his art.

"To show capacity," a Frenchman described
as the end of a speech in debate: "No," said an
Englishman, "but to set your shoulder at the

wheel, — to advance the business." Sir Samuel
Romilly refused to speak in popular assemblies,
confining himself to the House of Commons,
where a measure can be carried by a speech.
The business of the House of Commons is
conducted by a few persons, but these are hard-
worked. Sir Robert Peel "knew the Blue Books
by heart." His colleagues and rivals carry Han-
sard¹ in their heads. The high civil and legal
offices are not beds of ease, but posts which exact frightful amounts of mental labor. Many
of the great leaders, like Pitt, Canning, Castlereagh, Romilly, are soon worked to death.
They are excellent judges in England of a good
worker, and when they find one, like Clarendon, Sir Philip Warwick, Sir William Coventry,
Ashley, Burke, Thurlow, Mansfield, Pitt, Eldon, Peel, or Russell, there is nothing too good
or too high for him.

They have a wonderful heat in the pursuit
of a public aim. Private persons exhibit, in scientific and antiquarian researches, the same per-
tinacity as the nation showed in the coalitions
in which it yoked Europe against the empire
of Bonaparte, one after the other defeated, and
still renewed, until the sixth hurled him from
his seat.

Sir John Herschel, in completion of the work of his father, who had made the catalogue of the stars of the northern hemisphere, expatriated himself for years at the Cape of Good Hope, finished his inventory of the southern heaven, came home, and redacted it in eight years more; — a work whose value does not begin until thirty years have elapsed, and thenceforward a record to all ages of the highest import. The Admiralty sent out the Arctic expeditions year after year, in search of Sir John Franklin, until at last they have threaded their way through polar pack and Behring's Straits and solved the geographical problem. Lord Elgin, at Athens, saw the imminent ruin of the Greek remains, set up his scaffoldings, in spite of epigrams, and, after five years' labor to collect them, got his marbles on ship-board. The ship struck a rock and went to the bottom. He had them all fished up by divers, at a vast expense, and brought to London; not knowing that Haydon, Fuseli and Canova, and all good heads in all the world, were to be his applauders. In the same spirit, were the excavation and research by Sir Charles Fellowes for the Xanthian monument, and of Layard for his Nineveh sculptures.[1]

The nation sits in the immense city they have
builded, a London extended into every man's
mind, though he live in Van Dieman's Land
or Capetown. Faithful performance of what is
undertaken to be performed, they honor in
themselves, and exact in others, as certificate
of equality with themselves. The modern world
is theirs. They have made and make it day by
day. The commercial relations of the world are
so intimately drawn to London, that every dollar on earth contributes to the strength of the
English government. And if all the wealth in
the planet should perish by war or deluge, they
know themselves competent to replace it.

They have approved their Saxon blood, by
their sea-going qualities; their descent from
Odin's smiths, by their hereditary skill in working in iron; their British birth, by husbandry
and immense wheat harvests; and justified their
occupancy of the centre of habitable land, by
their supreme ability and cosmopolitan spirit.[1]
They have tilled, builded, forged, spun and
woven. They have made the island a thorough-
fare, and London a shop, a law-court, a record-
office and scientific bureau, inviting to strangers;
a sanctuary to refugees of every political and
religious opinion; and such a city that almost

every active man, in any nation, finds himself
at one time or other forced to visit it.

In every path of practical activity they have
gone even with the best. There is no secret
of war in which they have not shown mastery.
The steam-chamber of Watt, the locomotive of
Stephenson, the cotton-mule of Roberts, perform the labor of the world. There is no de-
partment of literature, of science, or of useful
art, in which they have not produced a first-rate
book. It is England whose opinion is waited
for on the merit of a new invention, an improved
science. And in the complications of the trade
and politics of their vast empire, they have been
equal to every exigency, with counsel and with
conduct. Is it their luck, or is it in the chambers of their brain, — it is their commercial
advantage that whatever light appears in better
method or happy invention, breaks out *in their
race*. They are a family to which a destiny
attaches, and the Banshee[1] has sworn that a
male heir shall never be wanting. They have
a wealth of men to fill important posts, and the
vigilance of party criticism insures the selection
of a competent person.

A proof of the energy of the British people

is the highly artificial construction of the whole fabric. The climate and geography, I said, were factitious, as if the hands of man had arranged the conditions. The same character pervades the whole kingdom. Bacon said, "Rome was a state not subject to paradoxes;" but England subsists by antagonisms and contradictions. The foundations of its greatness are the rolling waves; and from first to last it is a museum of anomalies. This foggy and rainy country furnishes the world with astronomical observations. Its short rivers do not afford water-power, but the land shakes under the thunder of the mills. There is no gold-mine of any importance, but there is more gold in England than in all other countries. It is too far north for the culture of the vine, but the wines of all countries are in its docks. The French Comte de Lauraguais said, "No fruit ripens in England but a baked apple;" but oranges and pine-apples are as cheap in London as in the Mediterranean. The Mark-Lane Express, or the Custom House Returns, bear out to the letter the vaunt of Pope, —

> "Let India boast her palms, nor envy we
> The weeping amber, nor the spicy tree,
> While, by our oaks, those precious loads are borne,
> And realms commanded which those trees adorn." [1]

The native cattle are extinct, but the island is full of artificial breeds. The agriculturist Bakewell created sheep and cows and horses to order, and breeds in which every thing was omitted but what is economical. The cow is sacrificed to her bag, the ox to his sirloin. Stall-feeding makes sperm-mills of the cattle, and converts the stable to a chemical factory. The rivers, lakes and ponds, too much fished, or obstructed by factories, are artificially filled with the eggs of salmon, turbot and herring.

Chat Moss and the fens of Lincolnshire and Cambridgeshire are unhealthy and too barren to pay rent. By cylindrical tiles and gutta-percha tubes, five millions of acres of bad land have been drained and put on equality with the best, for rape-culture and grass. The climate too, which was already believed to have become milder and drier by the enormous consumption of coal, is so far reached by this new action, that fogs and storms are said to disappear. In due course, all England will be drained and rise a second time out of the waters. The latest step was to call in the aid of steam to agriculture. Steam is almost an Englishman. I do not know but they will send him to Parliament next, to make laws. He weaves, forges, saws, pounds,

fans, and now he must pump, grind, dig and
plough for the farmer. The markets created by
the manufacturing population have erected agriculture into a great thriving and spending industry. The value of the houses in Britain is
equal to the value of the soil. Artificial aids of
all kinds are cheaper than the natural resources.
No man can afford to walk, when the parlia-
mentary-train carries him for a penny a mile.
Gas-burners are cheaper than daylight in num-
berless floors in the cities. All the houses in
London buy their water. The English trade
does not exist for the exportation of native products, but on its manufactures, or the making
well every thing which is ill-made elsewhere.
They make ponchos for the Mexican, ban-
dannas for the Hindoo, ginseng for the Chinese, beads for the Indian, laces for the Flem-
ings, telescopes for astronomers, cannons for
kings.

The Board of Trade caused the best models
of Greece and Italy to be placed within the reach
of every manufacturing population. They caused
to be translated from foreign languages and illustrated by elaborate drawings, the most approved works of Munich, Berlin and Paris.
They have ransacked Italy to find new forms,

to add a grace to the products of their looms,
their potteries and their foundries.[1]

The nearer we look, the more artificial is their
social system. Their law is a network of fictions.
Their property, a scrip or certificate of right to
interest on money that no man ever saw. Their
social classes are made by statute. Their ratios
of power and representation are historical and
legal. The last Reform-bill took away political
power from a mound, a ruin and a stone wall,
whilst Birmingham and Manchester, whose mills
paid for the wars of Europe, had no representative.[2] Purity in the elective Parliament is secured by the purchase of seats.[3] Foreign power
is kept by armed colonies; power at home, by
a standing army of police. The pauper lives
better than the free laborer, the thief better than
the pauper, and the transported felon better than
the one under imprisonment. The crimes are
factitious; as smuggling, poaching, noncon-
formity, heresy and treason. The sovereignty
of the seas is maintained by the impressment
of seamen. " The impressment of seamen,"
said Lord Eldon,[4] "is the life of our navy."
Solvency is maintained by means of a national
debt, on the principle, "If you will not lend
me the money, how can I pay you?" For the

v

administration of justice, Sir Samuel Romilly's expedient for clearing the arrears of business in Chancery was, the Chancellor's staying away entirely from his court. Their system of education is factitious. The Universities galvanize dead languages into a semblance of life. Their church is artificial. The manners and customs of society are artificial;—made-up men with made-up manners;—and thus the whole is Birmingham-ized, and we have a nation whose existence is a work of art;—a cold, barren, almost arctic isle being made the most fruitful, luxurious and imperial land in the whole earth.

Man in England submits to be a product of political economy. On a bleak moor a mill is built, a banking-house is opened, and men come in as water in a sluice-way, and towns and cities rise. Man is made as a Birmingham button. The rapid doubling of the population dates from Watt's steam-engine. A landlord who owns a province says, "The tenantry are unprofitable; let me have sheep." He unroofs the houses and ships the population to America.' The nation is accustomed to the instantaneous creation of wealth. It is the maxim of their economists, "that the greater part in value of the wealth now existing in England has been produced by

human hands within the last twelve months."
Meantime, three or four days' rain will reduce
hundreds to starving in London.

One secret of their power is their mutual good
understanding. Not only good minds are born
among them, but all the people have good
minds. Every nation has yielded some good
wit, if, as has chanced to many tribes, only one.
But the intellectual organization of the English
admits a communicableness of knowledge and
ideas among them all. An electric touch by any
of their national ideas, melts them into one family and brings the hoards of power which their
individuality is always hiving, into use and play
for all. Is it the smallness of the country, or is
it the pride and affection of race, — they have
solidarity, or responsibleness, and trust in each
other.

Their minds, like wool, admit of a dye which
is more lasting than the cloth. They embrace
their cause with more tenacity than their life.
Though not military, yet every common subject
by the poll is fit to make a soldier of. These
private, reserved, mute family-men can adopt a
public end with all their heat, and this strength
of affection makes the romance of their heroes.
The difference of rank does not divide the na-

tional heart. The Danish poet Oehlenschläger complains that who writes in Danish writes to two hundred readers.[1] In Germany there is one speech for the learned, and another for the masses, to that extent that, it is said, no sentiment or phrase from the works of any great German writer is ever heard among the lower classes. But in England, the language of the noble is the language of the poor. In Parliament, in pulpits, in theatres, when the speakers rise to thought and passion, the language becomes idiomatic; the people in the street best understand the best words. And their language seems drawn from the Bible, the Common Law and the works of Shakspeare, Bacon, Milton, Pope, Young, Cowper, Burns and Scott. The island has produced two or three of the greatest men that ever existed, but they were not solitary in their own time. Men quickly embodied what Newton found out, in Greenwich observatories and practical navigation. The boys know all that Hutton[2] knew of strata, or Dalton of atoms, or Harvey of blood-vessels; and these studies, once dangerous, are in fashion. So what is invented or known in agriculture, or in trade, or in war, or in art, or in literature and antiquities. A great ability, not amassed on a few giants, but poured into the general mind, so that each of them could at a pinch stand in the shoes of the other; and they are more bound in character than differenced in ability or in rank. The laborer is a possible lord. The lord is a possible basket-maker. Every man carries the English system in his brain, knows what is confided to him and does therein the best he can. The chancellor carries England on his mace, the midshipman at the point of his dirk, the smith on his hammer, the cook in the bowl of his spoon; the postilion cracks his whip for England, and the sailor times his oars to "God save the King!" The very felons have their pride in each other's English stanchness. In politics and in war they hold together as by hooks of steel. The charm in Nelson's history is the unselfish greatness, the assurance of being supported to the uttermost by those whom he supports to the uttermost. Whilst they are some ages ahead of the rest of the world in the art of living; whilst in some directions they do not represent the modern spirit but constitute it; — this vanguard of civility and power they coldly hold, marching in phalanx, lockstep, foot after foot, file after file of heroes, ten thousand deep.

CHAPTER VI

MANNERS

I FIND the Englishman to be him of all men who stands firmest in his shoes. They have in themselves what they value in their horses, — mettle and bottom. On the day of my arrival at Liverpool, a gentleman, in describing to me the Lord Lieutenant of Ireland, happened to say, " Lord Clarendon has pluck like a cock and will fight till he dies ; " and what I heard first I heard last, and the one thing the English value is *pluck*. The word is not beautiful, but on the quality they signify by it the nation is unanimous. The cabmen have it ; the merchants have it ; the bishops have it ; the women have it ; the journals have it ; — the Times newspaper they say is the pluckiest thing in England, and Sydney Smith had made it a proverb that little Lord John Russell, the minister, would take the command of the Channel fleet to-morrow.

They require you to dare to be of your own opinion, and they hate the practical cowards who cannot in affairs answer directly yes or no. They dare to displease, nay, they will let you break all the commandments, if you do it natively and with spirit. You must be somebody; then you may do this or that, as you will.

Machinery has been applied to all work, and carried to such perfection that little is left for the men but to mind the engines and feed the furnaces. But the machines require punctual service, and as they never tire, they prove too much for their tenders. Mines, forges, mills, breweries, railroads, steam-pump, steam-plough, drill of regiments, drill of police, rule of court and shop-rule have operated to give a mechanical regularity to all the habit and action of men. A terrible machine has possessed itself of the ground, the air, the men and women, and hardly even thought is free.

The mechanical might and organization requires in the people constitution and answering spirits; and he who goes among them must have some weight of metal. At last, you take your hint from the fury of life you find, and say, one thing is plain, this is no country for fainthearted people: don't creep about diffidently; make up your mind; take your own course, and you shall find respect and furtherance.

It requires, men say, a good constitution to travel in Spain. I say as much of England, for other cause, simply on account of the vigor and brawn of the people. Nothing but the most serious business could give one any counterweight to these Baresarks, though they were only to order eggs and muffins for their breakfast. The Englishman speaks with all his body. His elocution is stomachic,—as the American's is labial. The Englishman is very petulant and precise about his accommodation at inns and on the roads; a quiddle about his toast and his chop and every species of convenience, and loud and pungent in his expressions of impatience at any neglect. His vivacity betrays itself at all points, in his manners, in his respiration, and the inarticulate noises he makes in clearing the throat; —all significant of burly strength. He has stamina; he can take the initiative in emergencies. He has that *aplomb* which results from a good adjustment of the moral and physical nature and the obedience of all the powers to the will; as if the axes of his eyes were united to his backbone, and only moved with the trunk.

This vigor appears in the incuriosity and stony neglect, each of every other. Each man walks, eats, drinks, shaves, dresses, gesticulates, and, in every manner acts and suffers without reference to the bystanders, in his own fashion, only careful not to interfere with them or annoy them; not that he is trained to neglect the eyes of his neighbors,—he is really occupied with his own affair and does not think of them. Every man in this polished country consults only his convenience, as much as a solitary pioneer in Wisconsin. I know not where any personal eccentricity is so freely allowed, and no man gives himself any concern with it. An Englishman walks in a pouring rain, swinging his closed umbrella like a walking-stick; wears a wig, or a shawl, or a saddle, or stands on his head, and no remark is made. And as he has been doing this for several generations, it is now in the blood.

In short, every one of these islanders is an island himself, safe, tranquil, incommunicable. In a company of strangers you would think him deaf; his eyes never wander from his table and newspaper. He is never betrayed into any curiosity or unbecoming emotion. They have all been trained in one severe school of manners, and never put off the harness. He does not give his hand. He does not let you meet his eye. It is almost an affront to look a man in the face without being introduced. In mixed or in select companies they do not introduce persons; so that a presentation is a circumstance as valid as

a contract. Introductions are sacraments. He
withholds his name. At the hotel, he is hardly
willing to whisper it to the clerk at the book-
office. If he give you his private address on a
card, it is like an avowal of friendship; and
his bearing, on being introduced, is cold, even
though he is seeking your acquaintance and is
studying how he shall serve you.

It was an odd proof of this impressive energy,
that in my lectures I hesitated to read and threw
out for its impertinence many a disparaging
phrase which I had been accustomed to spin,
about poor, thin, unable mortals;—so much
had the fine physique and the personal vigor of
this robust race worked on my imagination.

I happened to arrive in England at the moment of a commercial crisis. But it was evident
that let who will fail, England will not. These
people have sat here a thousand years, and here
will continue to sit. They will not break up, or
arrive at any desperate revolution, like their
neighbors; for they have as much energy, as
much continence of character as they ever had.
The power and possession which surround them
are their own creation, and they exert the same
commanding industry at this moment.

They are positive, methodical, cleanly and

formal, loving routine and conventional ways;
loving truth and religion, to be sure, but inexorable on points of form. All the world praises
the comfort and private appointments of an
English inn, and of English households. You
are sure of neatness and of personal decorum.
A Frenchman may possibly be clean; an Englishman is conscientiously clean. A certain order
and complete propriety is found in his dress and
in his belongings.

Born in a harsh and wet climate, which keeps
him in doors whenever he is at rest, and being
of an affectionate and loyal temper, he dearly
loves his house. If he is rich, he buys a demesne
and builds a hall; if he is in middle condition,
he spares no expense on his house. Without,
it is all planted; within, it is wainscoted, carved,
curtained, hung with pictures and filled with
good furniture. 'Tis a passion which survives
all others, to deck and improve it. Hither he
brings all that is rare and costly, and with the
national tendency to sit fast in the same spot for
many generations, it comes to be, in the course of
time, a museum of heirlooms, gifts and trophies
of the adventures and exploits of the family.
He is very fond of silver plate, and though he
have no gallery of portraits of his ancestors,

he has of their punch-bowls and porringers.
Incredible amounts of plate are found in good
houses, and the poorest have some spoon or
saucepan, gift of a godmother, saved out of
better times.

An English family consists of a few persons,
who, from youth to age, are found revolving
within a few feet of each other, as if tied by some
invisible ligature, tense as that cartilage which we
have seen attaching the two Siamese. England
produces under favorable conditions of ease and
culture the finest women in the world. And as
the men are affectionate and true-hearted, the
women inspire and refine them. Nothing can be
more delicate without being fantastical, nothing
more firm and based in nature and sentiment,
than the courtship and mutual carriage of the
sexes. The song of 1596 says, "The wife of
every Englishman is counted blest." The sentiment of Imogen in Cymbeline is copied from
English nature; and not less the Portia of Brutus,
the Kate Percy and the Desdemona. The romance does not exceed the height of noble passion
in Mrs. Lucy Hutchinson,¹ or in Lady Russell,
or even as one discerns through the plain prose
of Pepys's Diary, the sacred habit of an English
wife. Sir Samuel Romilly could not bear the

death of his wife. Every class has its noble and tender examples.

Domesticity is the taproot which enables the nation to branch wide and high. The motive and end of their trade and empire is to guard the independence and privacy of their homes. Nothing so much marks their manners as the concentration on their household ties. This domesticity is carried into court and camp. Wellington governed India and Spain and his own troops, and fought battles, like a good family-man, paid his debts, and though general of an army in Spain, could not stir abroad for fear of public creditors. This taste for house and parish merits has of course its doting and foolish side. Mr. Cobbett attributes the huge popularity of Perceval, prime minister in 1810, to the fact that he was wont to go to church every Sunday, with a large quarto gilt prayer-book under one arm, his wife hanging on the other, and followed by a long brood of children.

They keep their old customs, costumes, and pomps, their wig and mace, sceptre and crown. The Middle Ages still lurk in the streets of London. The Knights of the Bath take oath to defend injured ladies; the gold-stick-in-waiting survives. They repeated the ceremonies of the

eleventh century in the coronation of the present
Queen. A hereditary tenure is natural to them.
Offices, farms, trades and traditions descend so.
Their leases run for a hundred and a thousand
years. Terms of service and partnership are lifelong, or are inherited. "Holdship has been with
me," said Lord Eldon, "eight-and-twenty years,
knows all my business and books." Antiquity of
usage is sanction enough. Wordsworth says of
the small freeholders of Westmoreland, " Many
of these humble sons of the hills had a con-
sciousness that the land which they tilled had
for more than five hundred years been possessed
by men of the same name and blood." The ship-
carpenter in the public yards, my lord's gardener
and porter, have been there for more than a
hundred years, grandfather, father, and son.

The English power resides also in their dislike of change. They have difficulty in bringing
their reason to act, and on all occasions use their
memory first. As soon as they have rid themselves of some grievance and settled the better
practice, they make haste to fix it as a finality,
and never wish to hear of alteration more.

Every Englishman is an embryonic chancellor: his instinct is to search for a precedent.
The favorite phrase of their law is, "a custom

whereof the memory of man runneth not back to the contrary." The barons say, "*Nolumus mutari;*" and the cockneys stifle the curiosity of the foreigner on the reason of any practice with " Lord, sir, it was always so." They hate innovation. Bacon told them, Time was the right reformer; Chatham, that " confidence was a plant of slow growth ; " Canning, to " advance with the times ; " and Wellington, that " habit was ten times nature." All their statesmen learn the irresistibility of the tide of custom, and have invented many fine phrases to cover this slowness of perception and prehensility of tail.

A sea-shell should be the crest of England, not only because it represents a power built on the waves, but also the hard finish of the men. The Englishman is finished like a cowry or a murex. After the spire and the spines are formed, or with the formation, a juice exudes and a hard enamel varnishes every part.[1] The keeping of the proprieties is as indispensable as clean linen. No merit quite countervails the want of this whilst this sometimes stands in lieu of all. "'T is in bad taste," is the most formidable word an Englishman can pronounce. But this japan costs them dear. There is a prose in certain Englishmen which exceeds in wooden deadness all rivalry with other countrymen. There is a knell in the conceit and externality of their voice, which seems to say, *Leave all hope behind.* In this Gibraltar of propriety, mediocrity gets intrenched and consolidated and founded in adamant. An Englishman of fashion is like one of those souvenirs, bound in gold vellum, enriched with delicate engravings on thick hot-pressed paper, fit for the hands of ladies and princes, but with nothing in it worth reading or remembering.

A severe decorum rules the court and the cottage. When Thalberg the pianist was one evening performing before the Queen at Windsor, in a private party, the Queen accompanied him with her voice. The circumstance took air, and all England shuddered from sea to sea. The indecorum was never repeated. Cold, repressive manners prevail. No enthusiasm is permitted except at the opera. They avoid every thing marked. They require a tone of voice that excites no attention in the room. Sir Philip Sidney is one of the patron saints of England, of whom Wotton said, "His wit was the measure of congruity."

Pretension and vaporing are once for all distasteful. They keep to the other extreme of low tone in dress and manners. They avoid preten-

sion and go right to the heart of the thing.
They hate nonsense, sentimentalism and high-
flown expression; they use a studied plainness.
Even Brummel, their fop, was marked by the
severest simplicity in dress. They value themselves on the absence of every thing theatrical in
the public business, and on conciseness and going to the point, in private affairs.

In an aristocratical country like England, not
the Trial by Jury, but the dinner, is the capital
institution. It is the mode of doing honor to a
stranger, to invite him to eat, — and has been for
many hundred years. " And they think," says
the Venetian traveller of 1500, " no greater honor
can be conferred or received, than to invite others
to eat with them, or to be invited themselves, and
they would sooner give five or six ducats to provide an entertainment for a person, than a groat
to assist him in any distress." [1] It is reserved to
the end of the day, the family-hour being generally six, in London, and if any company is expected, one or two hours later. Every one dresses
for dinner, in his own house, or in another man's.
The guests are expected to arrive within half an
hour of the time fixed by card of invitation, and
nothing but death or mutilation is permitted to
detain them.[2] The English dinner is precisely

v

the model on which our own are constructed in the Atlantic cities. The company sit one or two hours before the ladies leave the table. The gentlemen remain over their wine an hour longer, and rejoin the ladies in the drawing-room and take coffee. The dress-dinner generates a talent of table-talk which reaches great perfection: the stories are so good that one is sure they must have been often told before, to have got such happy turns. Hither come all manner of clever projects, bits of popular science, of practical intervention, of miscellaneous humor; political, literary and personal news; railroads, horses, diamonds, agriculture, horticulture, pisciculture and wine.

English stories, *bon-mots* and the recorded table-talk of their wits, are as good as the best of the French. In America, we are apt scholars, but have not yet attained the same perfection : for the range of nations from which London draws, and the steep contrasts of condition, create the picturesque in society, as broken country makes picturesque landscape; whilst our prevailing equality makes a prairie tameness : and secondly, because the usage of a dress-dinner every day at dark has a tendency to hive and produce to advantage every thing good. Much

attrition has worn every sentence into a bullet.
Also one meets now and then with polished men
who know every thing, have tried every thing,
and can do every thing, and are quite superior
to letters and science. What could they not, if
only they would?

CHAPTER VII

TRUTH

THE Teutonic tribes have a national single-ness of heart, which contrasts with the Latin races. The German name has a proverbial significance of sincerity and honest meaning. The arts bear testimony to it. The faces of clergy and laity in old sculptures and illuminated missals are charged with earnest belief. Add to this hereditary rectitude the punctuality and precise dealing which commerce creates, and you have the English truth and credit.[1] The government strictly performs its engagements. The subjects do not understand trifling on its part. When any breach of promise occurred, in the old days of prerogative, it was resented by the people as an intolerable grievance. And in modern times, any slipperiness in the government of political faith, or any repudiation or crookedness in matters of finance, would bring the whole nation to a committee of inquiry and reform. Private men keep their promises, never so trivial. Down goes the flying word on the tablets, and is indelible as Domesday Book.

Their practical power rests on their national

sincerity. Veracity derives from instinct, and marks superiority in organization. Nature has endowed some animals with cunning, as a compensation for strength withheld; but it has provoked the malice of all others, as if avengers of public wrong. In the nobler kinds, where strength could be afforded, her races are loyal to truth, as truth is the foundation of the social state. Beasts that make no truce with man, do not break faith with each other. 'T is said that the wolf, who makes a *cache* of his prey and brings his fellows with him to the spot, if, on digging, it is not found, is instantly and unresistingly torn in pieces. English veracity seems to result on a sounder animal structure, as if they could afford it.[1] They are blunt in saying what they think, sparing of promises, and they require plain dealing of others. We will not have to do with a man in a mask. Let us know the truth. Draw a straight line, hit whom and where it will. Alfred, whom the affection of the nation makes the type of their race, is called by a writer at the Norman Conquest, the *truth-speaker; Alueredus veridicus*. Geoffrey of Monmouth says of King Aurelius, uncle of Arthur, that "above all things he hated a lie." The Northman Guttorm said to King Olaf, "It is royal work to

fulfil royal words." The mottoes of their families are monitory proverbs, as, *Fare fac*, — Say,
do, — of the Fairfaxes ; *Say and seal*, of the
house of Fiennes ; *Vero nil verius*, of the De
Veres. To be king of their word is their pride.
When they unmask cant, they say, " The English of this is," etc. ; and to give the lie is the
extreme insult. The phrase of the lowest of the
people is " honor-bright," and their vulgar praise,
" His word is as good as his bond." They hate
shuffling and equivocation, and the cause is dam-
aged in the public opinion, on which any palter-
ing can be fixed. Even Lord Chesterfield, with
his French breeding, when he came to define a
gentleman, declared that truth made his distinction ; and nothing ever spoken by him would
find so hearty a suffrage from his nation. The
Duke of Wellington, who had the best right to
say so, advises the French General Kellermann
that he may rely on the parole of an English
officer. The English, of all classes, value themselves on this trait, as distinguishing them from
the French, who, in the popular belief, are more
polite than true. An Englishman understates,
avoids the superlative, checks himself in compliments,' alleging that in the French language one
cannot speak without lying.

They love reality in wealth, power, hospitality, and do not easily learn to make a show, and
take the world as it goes. They are not fond of
ornaments, and if they wear them, they must be
gems. They read gladly in old Fuller¹ that a
lady in the reign of Elizabeth " would have as
patiently digested a lie, as the wearing of false
stones or pendants of counterfeit pearl." They
have the earth-hunger, or preference for property in land, which is said to mark the Teutonic nations. They build of stone: public and
private buildings are massive and durable. In
comparing their ships' houses and public offices
with the American, it is commonly said that
they spend a pound where we spend a dollar.
Plain rich clothes, plain rich equipage, plain
rich finish throughout their house and belongings mark the English truth.

They confide in each other,—English believes
in English. The French feel the superiority of
this probity. The Englishman is not springing
a trap for his admiration, but is honestly minding
his business. The Frenchman is vain. Madame de Staël says that the English irritated Napoleon, mainly because they have found out how
to unite success with honesty. She was not aware
how wide an application her foreign readers

would give to the remark. Wellington discovered the ruin of Bonaparte's affairs, by his own
probity. He augured ill of the empire as soon
as he saw that it was mendacious and lived by
war.[1] If war do not bring in its sequel new
trade, better agriculture and manufactures, but
only games, fireworks and spectacles, — no prosperity could support it; much less a nation
decimated for conscripts and out of pocket, like
France. So he drudged for years on his military
works at Lisbon, and from this base at last extended his gigantic lines to Waterloo, believing
in his countrymen and their syllogisms above
all the rhodomontade of Europe.[2]

At a St. George's festival, in Montreal, where
I happened to be a guest since my return home,
I observed that the chairman complimented his
compatriots, by saying, " they confided that
wherever they met an Englishman, they found
a man who would speak the truth." And one
cannot think this festival fruitless, if, all over
the world, on the 23d of April, wherever two
or three English are found, they meet to en-
courage each other in the nationality of veracity.

In the power of saying rude truth, sometimes
in the lion's mouth, no men surpass them. On
the king's birthday, when each bishop was ex-

pected to offer the king a purse of gold, Latimer gave Henry VIII. a copy of the Vulgate, with a mark at the passage, "Whoremongers and adulterers God will judge;" and they so honor stoutness in each other that the king passed it over. They are tenacious of their belief and cannot easily change their opinions to suit the hour. They are like ships with too much head on to come quickly about, nor will prosperity or even adversity be allowed to shake their habitual view of conduct. Whilst I was in London, M. Guizot arrived there on his escape from Paris, in February, 1848. Many private friends called on him. His name was immediately proposed as an honorary member of the Athenæum. M. Guizot was blackballed. Certainly they knew the distinction of his name. But the Englishman is not fickle. He had really made up his mind now for years as he read his newspaper, to hate and despise M. Guizot; and the altered position of the man as an illustrious exile and a guest in the country, makes no difference to him, as it would instantly to an American.

They require the same adherence, thorough conviction and reality, in public men. It is the want of character which makes the low reputation of the Irish members. "See them," they said, "one hundred and twenty-seven all voting like sheep, never proposing any thing, and all but four voting the income tax," — which was an ill-judged concession of the government, relieving Irish property from the burdens charged on English.

They have a horror of adventurers in or out of Parliament. The ruling passion of Englishmen in these days is a terror of humbug. In the same proportion they value honesty, stoutness, and adherence to your own. They like a man committed to his objects. They hate the French, as frivolous; they hate the Irish, as aimless; they hate the Germans, as professors. In February, 1848, they said, Look, the French king and his party fell for want of a shot; they had not conscience to shoot, so entirely was the pith and heart of monarchy eaten out.

They attack their own politicians every day, on the same grounds, as adventurers. They love stoutness in standing for your right, in declining money or promotion that costs any concession.[1] The barrister refuses the silk gown of Queen's Counsel, if his junior have it one day earlier. Lord Collingwood would not accept his medal for victory on 14 February, 1797, if he did not receive one for victory on 1st June, 1794; and the long withholden medal was accorded. When Castlereagh dissuaded Lord Wellington from going to the king's levee until the unpopular Cintra business had been explained, he replied, "You furnish me a reason for going. I will go to this, or I will never go to a king's levee."[1] The radical mob at Oxford cried after the tory Lord Eldon, "There's old Eldon; cheer him; he never ratted."[2] They have given the parliamentary nickname of *Trimmers* to the timeservers, whom English character does not love.[3]

They are very liable in their politics to extraordinary delusions; thus to believe what stands recorded in the gravest books, that the movement of 10 April, 1848, was urged or assisted by foreigners: which, to be sure, is paralleled by the democratic whimsy in this country which I have noticed to be shared by men sane on other points, that the English are at the bottom of the agitation of slavery, in American politics: and then again by the French popular legends on the subject of *perfidious Albion*. But suspicion will make fools of nations as of citizens.

A slow temperament makes them less rapid and ready than other countrymen, and has given

occasion to the observation that English wit
comes afterwards, — which the French denote
as *esprit d'escalier*. This dulness makes their
attachment to home and their adherence in all
foreign countries to home habits. The Englishman who visits Mount Etna will carry his tea-
kettle to the top. The old Italian author of the
" Relation of England " (in 1500), says, "I have
it on the best information, that, when the war is
actually raging most furiously, they will seek for
good eating and all their other comforts, without
thinking what harm might befall them." Then
their eyes seem to be set at the bottom of a
tunnel, and they affirm the one small fact they
know, with the best faith in the world that
nothing else exists. And as their own belief in
guineas is perfect, they readily, on all occasions,
apply the pecuniary argument as final. Thus
when the Rochester rappings [1] began to be heard
of in England, a man deposited £100 in a sealed
box in the Dublin Bank, and then advertised in
the newspapers to all somnambulists, mesmer-
izers and others, that whoever could tell him
the number of his note should have the money.
He let it lie there six months, the newspapers
now and then, at his instance, stimulating the
attention of the adepts; but none could ever

tell him; and he said, "Now let me never be
bothered more with this proven lie." It is told
of a good Sir John that he heard a case stated
by counsel, and made up his mind; then the
counsel for the other side taking their turn to
speak, he found himself so unsettled and per-
plexed that he exclaimed, "So help me God!
I will never listen to evidence again." Any
number of delightful examples of this English
stolidity are the anecdotes of Europe. I knew
a very worthy man,—a magistrate, I believe he
was, in the town of Derby,—who went to the
opera to see Malibran. In one scene, the heroine
was to rush across a ruined bridge. Mr. B. arose
and mildly yet firmly called the attention of the
audience and the performers to the fact that,
in his judgment, the bridge was unsafe! This
English stolidity contrasts with French wit and
tact. The French, it is commonly said, have
greatly more influence in Europe than the English. What influence the English have is by
brute force of wealth and power; that of the
French by affinity and talent. The Italian is
subtle, the Spaniard treacherous: tortures, it is
said, could never wrest from an Egyptian the con-
fession of a secret. None of these traits belong
to the Englishman. His choler and conceit force

every thing out.   Defoe, who knew his countrymen well, says of them, —

> " In close intrigue, their faculty 's but weak,
>   For generally whate'er they know, they speak,
>   And often their own counsels undermine
>   By mere infirmity without design ;
>   From whence, the learned say, it doth proceed,
>   That English treasons never can succeed ;
>   For they 're so open-hearted, you may know
>   Their own most secret thoughts, and others' too." '

CHAPTER VIII

CHARACTER

THE English race are reputed morose. I do not know that they have sadder brows than their neighbors of northern climates. They are sad by comparison with the singing and dancing nations: not sadder, but slow and staid, as finding their joys at home. They, too, believe that where there is no enjoyment of life there can be no vigor and art in speech or thought; that your merry heart goes all the way, your sad one tires in a mile. This trait of gloom has been fixed on them by French travellers, who, from Froissart, Voltaire, Le Sage, Mirabeau, down to the lively journalists of the *feuilletons*, have spent their wit on the solemnity of their neighbors. The French say, gay conversation is unknown in their island. The Englishman finds no relief from reflection, except in reflection. When he wishes for amusement, he goes to work. His hilarity is like an attack of fever. Religion, the theatre and the reading the books of his country all feed and increase his natural melancholy. The police does not interfere with public diversions. It thinks itself bound in duty to respect the pleasures and rare gayety of this inconsolable nation; and their well-known courage is entirely attributable to their disgust of life.

I suppose their gravity of demeanor and their few words have obtained this reputation. As compared with the Americans, I think them cheerful and contented. Young people in this country are much more prone to melancholy. The English have a mild aspect and a ringing cheerful voice. They are large-natured and not so easily amused as the southerners, and are among them as grown people among children, requiring war, or trade, or engineering, or science, instead of frivolous games. They are proud and private, and even if disposed to recreation, will avoid an open garden. They sported sadly ; *ils s'amusaient tristement, selon la coutume de leur pays,* said Froissart ;[1] and I suppose never nation built their party-walls so thick, or their garden-fences so high. Meat and wine produce no effect on them. They are just as cold, quiet and composed, at the end, as at the beginning of dinner.

The reputation of taciturnity they have enjoyed for six or seven hundred years ; and a kind of pride in bad public speaking is noted in the House of Commons, as if they were willing to show that they did not live by their tongues, or thought they spoke well enough if they had the tone of gentlemen. In mixed company they shut their mouths. A Yorkshire mill-owner told me he had ridden more than once all the way from London to Leeds, in the first-class carriage, with the same persons, and no word exchanged. The club-houses were established to cultivate social habits, and it is rare that more than two eat together, and oftenest one eats alone. Was it then a stroke of humor in the serious Swedenborg, or was it only his pitiless logic, that made him shut up the English souls in a heaven by themselves?

They are contradictorily described as sour, splenetic and stubborn,—and as mild, sweet and sensible. The truth is they have great range and variety of character. Commerce sends abroad multitudes of different classes. The choleric Welshman, the fervid Scot, the bilious resident in the East or West Indies, are wide of the perfect behavior of the educated and dignified man of family. So is the burly farmer; so is the country squire, with his narrow and violent life. In every inn is the Commercial-Room, in which 'travellers,' or bagmen who carry patterns and solicit orders for the manufacturers, are wont to be entertained. It easily happens that this class should characterize England to the foreigner, who meets them on the road and at every public house, whilst the gentry avoid the taverns, or seclude themselves whilst in them.

But these classes are the right English stock, and may fairly show the national qualities, before yet art and education have dealt with them. They are good lovers, good haters, slow but obstinate admirers, and in all things very much steeped in their temperament, like men hardly awaked from deep sleep, which they enjoy. Their habits and instincts cleave to nature. They are of the earth, earthy; and of the sea, as the sea-kinds, attached to it for what it yields them, and not from any sentiment. They are full of coarse strength, rude exercise, butcher's meat and sound sleep; and suspect any poetic insinuation or any hint for the conduct of life which reflects on this animal existence, as if somebody were fumbling at the umbilical cord and might stop their supplies. They doubt a man's sound judgment if he does not eat with appetite, and shake their heads if he is particularly chaste. Take them as they come, you shall find in the common people a surly indifference, sometimes gruffness and ill temper; and in minds of more power, magazines of inexhaustible war, challenging

"The ruggedest hour that time and spite dare bring
To frown upon the enraged Northumberland."[1]

They are headstrong believers and defenders of
their opinion, and not less resolute in maintaining
their whim and perversity. Hezekiah Wood-
ward wrote a book against the Lord's Prayer.
And one can believe that Burton, the Anatomist of Melancholy, having predicted from the
stars the hour of his death, slipped the knot
himself round his own neck, not to falsify his
horoscope.

Their looks bespeak an invincible stoutness:
they have extreme difficulty to run away, and will
die game. Wellington said of the young cox-
combs of the Life-Guards, delicately brought up,
"But the puppies fight well;" and Nelson said
of his sailors, "They really mind shot no more
than peas." Of absolute stoutness no nation has
more or better examples. They are good at
storming redoubts, at boarding frigates, at dying
in the last ditch, or any desperate service which
has daylight and honor in it; but not, I think,
at enduring the rack, or any passive obedience,
like jumping off a castle-roof at the word of a
czar. Being both vascular and highly organized,
so as to be very sensible of pain; and intellectual, so as to see reason and glory in a matter.

Of that constitutional force which yields the supplies of the day, they have the more than enough; the excess which creates courage on fortitude, genius in poetry, invention in mechanics, enterprise in trade, magnificence in wealth, splendor in ceremonies, petulance and projects in youth. The young men have a rude health which runs into peccant humors. They drink brandy like water, cannot expend their quantities of waste strength on riding, hunting, swimming and fencing, and run into absurd frolics with the gravity of the Eumenides. They stoutly carry into every nook and corner of the earth their turbulent sense; leaving no lie uncontradicted; no pretension unexamined. They chew hasheesh; cut themselves with poisoned creases; swing their hammock in the boughs of the Bohon Upas; taste every poison; buy every secret; at Naples they put St. Januarius's blood in an alembic; they saw a hole into the head of the "winking Virgin," to know why she winks; measure with an English footrule every cell of the Inquisition, every Turkish caaba, every Holy of holies; translate and send to Bentley the arcanum bribed and bullied away from shuddering Bramins; and measure their own strength by the terror they cause. These travellers are of every class, the

best and the worst ; and it may easily happen
that those of rudest behavior are taken notice of
and remembered. The Saxon melancholy in the
vulgar rich and poor appears as gushes of ill-
humor, which every check exasperates into sar-
casm and vituperation. There are multitudes of
rude young English who have the self-sufficiency
and bluntness of their nation, and who, with their
disdain of the rest of mankind· and with this
indigestion and choler, have made the English
traveller a proverb for uncomfortable and offensive manners. It was no bad description of the
Briton generically, what was said two hundred
years ago of one particular Oxford scholar : " He
was a very bold man, uttered any thing that came
into his mind, not only among his companions,
but in public coffee-houses, and would often
speak his mind of particular persons then acci-
dentally present, without examining the company
he was in ; for which he was often reprimanded
and several times threatened to be kicked and
beaten."

The common Englishman is prone to forget
a cardinal article in the bill of social rights, that
every man has a right to his own ears. No man
can claim to usurp more than a few cubic feet of
the audibilities of a public room, or to put upon

the company with the loud statement of his
crotchets or personalities.

But it is in the deep traits of race that the fortunes of nations are written, and however derived,
— whether a happier tribe or mixture of tribes,
the air, or what circumstance that mixed for them
the golden mean of temperament, — here exists
the best stock in the world, broad-fronted, broad-
bottomed, best for depth, range and equability ;
men of aplomb and reserves, great range and
many moods, strong instincts, yet apt for culture;
war-class as well as clerks ; earls and tradesmen ;
wise minority, as well as foolish majority; abys-
mal temperament, hiding wells of wrath, and
glooms on which no sunshine settles, alternated
with a common sense and humanity which hold
them fast to every piece of cheerful duty ; making
this temperament a sea to which all storms are
superficial ; a race to which their fortunes flow,
as if they alone had the elastic organization at
once fine and robust enough for dominion ; as if
the burly inexpressive, now mute and contumacious, now fierce and sharp-tongued dragon,
which once made the island light with his fiery
breath, had bequeathed his ferocity to his conqueror. They hide virtues under vices, or the
semblance of them. It is the misshapen hairy

Scandinavian troll again, who lifts the cart out of
the mire, or threshes

" The corn

That ten day-laborers could not end," [1]

but it is done in the dark and with muttered mal-
edictions. He is a churl with a soft place in his
heart, whose speech is a brash of bitter waters,
but who loves to help you at a pinch. He says
no, and serves you, and your thanks disgust him.
Here was lately a cross-grained miser, odd and
ugly, resembling in countenance the portrait of
Punch with the laugh left out ; rich by his own
industry ; sulking in a lonely house ; who never
gave a dinner to any man and disdained all cour-
tesies : yet as true a worshipper of beauty in form
and color as ever existed, and profusely pouring
over the cold mind of his countrymen creations
of grace and truth, removing the reproach of sterility from English art, catching from their savage
climate every fine hint, and importing into their
galleries every tint and trait of sunnier cities and
skies ; making an era in painting ; and when he
saw that the splendor of one of his pictures in
the Exhibition dimmed his rival's that hung next
it, secretly took a brush and blackened his own.[a]

They do not wear their heart in their sleeve for
daws to peck at.[1] They have that phlegm or

staidness which it is a compliment to disturb. " Great men," said Aristotle, " are always of a nature originally melancholy." 'T is the habit of a mind which attaches to abstractions with a passion which gives vast results. They dare to displease, they do not speak to expectation. They like the sayers of No, better than the sayers of Yes. Each of them has an opinion which he feels it becomes him to express all the more that it differs from yours. They are meditating opposition. This gravity is inseparable from minds of great resources.

There is an English hero superior to the French, the German, the Italian, or the Greek. When he is brought to the strife with fate, he sacrifices a richer material possession, and on more purely metaphysical grounds. He is there with his own consent, face to face with fortune, which he defies. On deliberate choice and from grounds of character, he has elected his part to live and die for, and dies with grandeur. This race has added new elements to humanity and has a deeper root in the world.

They have great range of scale, from ferocity to exquisite refinement. With larger scale, they have great retrieving power. After running each tendency to an extreme, they try another tack with equal heat. More intellectual than other races, when they live with other races they do not take their language, but bestow their own. They subsidize other nations, and are not subsidized. They proselyte, and are not proselyted. They assimilate other races to themselves, and are not assimilated. The English did not calculate the conquest of the Indies. It fell to their character. So they administer, in different parts of the world, the codes of every empire and race; in Canada, old French law; in the Mauritius, the Code Napoléon; in the West Indies, the edicts of the Spanish Cortes; in the East Indies, the Laws of Menu; in the Isle of Man, of the Scandinavian Thing; at the Cape of Good Hope, of the old Netherlands; and in the Ionian Islands, the Pandects of Justinian.

They are very conscious of their advantageous position in history. England is the lawgiver, the patron, the instructor, the ally. Compare the tone of the French and of the English press: the first querulous, captious, sensitive about English opinion; the English press never timorous about French opinion, but arrogant and contemptuous.

They are testy and headstrong through an excess of will and bias; churlish as men sometimes please to be who do not forget a debt, who ask no favors and who will do what they like with their own. With education and intercourse, these asperities wear off and leave the good-will pure. If anatomy is reformed according to national tendencies, I suppose the spleen will hereafter be found in the Englishman, not found in the American, and differencing the one from the other. I anticipate another anatomical discovery, that this organ will be found to be cortical and caducous; that they are superficially morose, but at last tender-hearted, herein differing from Rome and the Latin nations. Nothing savage, nothing mean resides in the English heart. They are subject to panics of credulity and of rage, but the temper of the nation, however disturbed, settles itself soon and easily, as, in this temperate zone, the sky after whatever storms clears again, and serenity is its normal condition.

A saving stupidity masks and protects their perception, as the curtain of the eagle's eye. Our swifter Americans, when they first deal with English, pronounce them stupid; but, later, do them justice as people who wear well, or hide their strength. To understand the power of performance that is in their finest wits, in the patient Newton, or in the versatile transcendent poets, or in the Dugdales, Gibbons, Hallams, Eldons and Peels, one should see how English day-laborers hold out. High and low, they are of an unctuous texture. There is an adipocere in their constitution, as if they had oil also for their mental wheels and could perform vast amounts of work without damaging themselves.

Even the scale of expense on which people live, and to which scholars and professional men conform, proves the tension of their muscle, when vast numbers are found who can each lift this enormous load. I might even add, their daily feasts argue a savage vigor of body.

No nation was ever so rich in able men; "Gentlemen," as Charles I. said of Strafford, " whose abilities might make a prince rather afraid than ashamed in the greatest affairs of state ; " men of such temper, that, like Baron Vere, " had one seen him returning from a victory, he would by his silence have suspected that he had lost the day ; and, had he beheld him in a retreat, he would have collected him a conqueror by the cheerfulness of his spirit." [1]

The following passage from the " Heims-kringla " might almost stand as a portrait of the modern Englishman : — " Haldor was very stout and strong and remarkably handsome in appearances. King Harold gave him this testimony, that he, among all his men, cared least about doubtful circumstances, whether they betokened danger or pleasure ; for whatever turned up, he was never in higher nor in lower spirits, never slept less nor more on account of them, nor ate nor drank but according to his custom. Haldor was not a man of many words, but short in conversation, told his opinion bluntly and was obstinate and hard : and this could not please the king, who had many clever people about him, zealous in his service. Haldor remained a short time with the king, and then came to Iceland, where he took up his abode in Hiardaholt and dwelt in that farm to a very advanced age." [1]

The national temper, in the civil history, is not flashy or whiffling. The slow, deep English mass smoulders with fire, which at last sets all its borders in flame. The wrath of London is not French wrath, but has a long memory, and, in its hottest heat, a register and rule.

Half their strength they put not forth. They are capable of a sublime resolution, and if hereafter the war of races, often predicted, and making itself a war of opinions also (a question of despotism and liberty coming from Eastern Europe), should menace the English civilization,

these sea-kings may take once again to their floating castles and find a new home and a second
millennium of power in their colonies.

The stability of England is the security of
the modern world. If the English race were as
mutable as the French, what reliance? But the
English stand for liberty. The conservative,
money-loving, lord-loving English are yet lib-
erty-loving; and so freedom is safe: for they
have more personal force than any other people.
The nation always resist the immoral action of
their government. They think humanely on
the affairs of France, of Turkey, of Poland, of
Hungary, of Schleswig Holstein, though over-
borne by the statecraft of the rulers at last.

Does the early history of each tribe show the
permanent bias, which, though not less potent, is
masked as the tribe spreads its activity into colonies, commerce, codes, arts, letters? The early
history shows it, as the musician plays the air
which he proceeds to conceal in a tempest of variations. In Alfred, in the Northmen, one may
read the genius of the English society, namely
that private life is the place of honor. Glory, a
career, and ambition, words familiar to the longi-
tude of Paris, are seldom heard in English speech.
Nelson wrote from their hearts his homely tele-

graph, " England expects every man to do his
duty."

For actual service, for the dignity of a profession, or to appease diseased or inflamed talent,
the army and navy may be entered (the worst
boys doing well in the navy) ; and the civil service in departments where serious official work
is done; and they hold in esteem the barrister
engaged in the severer studies of the law. But
the calm, sound and most British Briton shrinks
from public life as charlatanism, and respects an
economy founded on agriculture, coal-mines,
manufactures or trade, which secures an independence through the creation of real values.

They wish neither to command nor obey, but
to be kings in their own houses. They are intellectual and deeply enjoy literature; they like
well to have the world served up to them in
books, maps, models, and every mode of exact
information, and, though not creators in art, they
value its refinement. They are ready for leisure,
can direct and fill their own day, nor need so
much as others the constraint of a necessity.
But the history of the nation discloses, at every
turn, this original predilection for private independence, and however this inclination may have
been disturbed by the bribes with which their

vast colonial power has warped men out of orbit,
the inclination endures, and forms and reforms
the laws, letters, manners and occupations. They
choose that welfare which is compatible with
the commonwealth, knowing that such alone is
stable ; as wise merchants prefer investments in
the three per cents.

CHAPTER IX

COCKAYNE

THE English are a nation of humorists.[1] Individual right is pushed to the uttermost bound compatible with public order. Property is so perfect that it seems the craft of that race, and not to exist elsewhere. The king cannot step on an acre which the peasant refuses to sell.[2] A testator endows a dog or a rookery, and Europe cannot interfere with his absurdity. Every individual has his particular way of living, which he pushes to folly, and the decided sympathy of his compatriots is engaged to back up Mr. Crump's whim by statutes and chancellors and horse-guards. There is no freak so ridiculous but some Englishman has attempted to immortalize by money and law. British citizenship is as omnipotent as Roman was. Mr. Cockayne is very sensible of this. The pursy man means by freedom the right to do as he pleases, and does wrong in order to feel his freedom, and makes a conscience of persisting in it.

He is intensely patriotic, for his country is so small. His confidence in the power and performance of his nation makes him provokingly

incurious about other nations. He dislikes foreigners. Swedenborg, who lived much in England, notes "the similitude of minds among the
English, in consequence of which they contract
familiarity with friends who are of that nation,
and seldom with others; and they regard foreigners as one looking through a telescope from
the top of a palace regards those who dwell or
wander about out of the city." A much older
traveller, the Venetian who wrote the "Relation
of England," in 1500, says : — "The English
are great lovers of themselves and of every thing
belonging to them. They think that there are
no other men than themselves and no other world
but England; and whenever they see a handsome foreigner, they say that he looks like an
Englishman and it is a great pity he should not
be an Englishman; and whenever they partake
of any delicacy with a foreigner, they ask him
whether such a thing is made in his country."
When he adds epithets of praise, his climax is,
"So English;" and when he wishes to pay you
the highest compliment, he says, "I should not
know you from an Englishman." France is, by
its natural contrast, a kind of blackboard on
which English character draws its own traits in
chalk.[1] This arrogance habitually exhibits itself

in allusions to the French. I suppose that all men of English blood in America, Europe or Asia, have a secret feeling of joy that they are not French natives. Mr. Coleridge is said to have given public thanks to God, at the close of a lecture, that he had defended him from being able to utter a single sentence in the French language. I have found that Englishmen have such a good opinion of England, that the ordinary phrases in all good society, of postponing or disparaging one's own things in talking with a stranger, are seriously mistaken by them for an insuppressible homage to the merits of their nation ; and the New Yorker or Pennsylvanian who modestly laments the disadvantage of a new country, log-huts and savages, is surprised by the instant and unfeigned commiseration of the whole company, who plainly account all the world out of England a heap of rubbish.

The same insular limitation pinches his foreign politics. He sticks to his traditions and usages, and, so help him God! he will force his island by-laws down the throat of great countries, like India, China, Canada, Australia,¹ and not only so, but impose Wapping on the Congress of Vienna and trample down all nationalities with his taxed boots. Lord Chatham goes for liberty and no taxation without representation; — for that is British law; but not a hobnail shall they dare make in America, but buy their nails in England; — for that also is British law; and the fact that British commerce was to be re-created by the independence of America, took them all by surprise.

In short, I am afraid that English nature is so rank and aggressive as to be a little incompatible with every other. The world is not wide enough for two.

But beyond this nationality, it must be admitted, the island offers a daily worship to the old Norse god Brage, celebrated among our Scandinavian forefathers for his eloquence and majestic air. The English have a steady courage that fits them for great attempts and endurance: they have also a petty courage, through which every man delights in showing himself for what he is and in doing what he can; so that in all companies, each of them has too good an opinion of himself to imitate anybody. He hides no defect of his form, features, dress, connection, or birthplace, for he thinks every circumstance belonging to him comes recommended to you. If one of them have a bald, or a red, or a green head, or bow legs, or a scar, or mark, or a paunch, or a squeaking or a raven voice, he has persuaded himself that there is something modish and becoming in it, and that it sits well on him.

But nature makes nothing in vain, and this little superfluity of self-regard in the English brain is one of the secrets of their power and history. It sets every man on being and doing what he really is and can. It takes away a dodging, skulking, secondary air, and encourages a frank and manly bearing, so that each man makes the most of himself and loses no opportunity for want of pushing. A man's personal defects will commonly have, with the rest of the world, precisely that importance which they have to himself. If he makes light of them, so will other men. We all find in these a convenient metre of character, since a little man would be ruined by the vexation. I remember a shrewd politician, in one of our western cities, told me that " he had known several successful statesmen made by their foible." And another, an ex-governor of Illinois, said to me, "If the man knew anything, he would sit in a corner and be modest ; but he is such an ignorant peacock that he goes bustling up and down and hits on extraordinary discoveries."

There is also this benefit in brag, that the speaker is unconsciously expressing his own ideal.

Humor him by all means, draw it all out and hold him to it.[1] Their culture generally enables the travelled English to avoid any ridiculous extremes of this self-pleasing, and to give it an agreeable air. Then the natural disposition is fostered by the respect which they find entertained in the world for English ability. It was said of Louis XIV., that his gait and air were becoming enough in so great a monarch, yet would have been ridiculous in another man; so the prestige of the English name warrants a certain confident bearing, which a Frenchman or Belgian could not carry. At all events, they feel themselves at liberty to assume the most extraordinary tone on the subject of English merits.

An English lady on the Rhine hearing a German speaking of her party as foreigners, exclaimed, " No, we are not foreigners; we are English ; it is you that are foreigners." They tell you daily in London the story of the Frenchman and Englishman who quarrelled. Both were unwilling to fight, but their companions put them up to it ; at last it was agreed that they should fight alone, in the dark, and with pistols : the candles were put out, and the Englishman, to make sure not to hit any body, fired up the chimney, — and brought down the Frenchman.

They have no curiosity about foreigners, and answer any information you may volunteer with " Oh, Oh ! " until the informant makes up his mind that they shall die in their ignorance, for any help he will offer. There are really no limits to this conceit, though brighter men among them make painful efforts to be candid.

The habit of brag runs through all classes, from the " Times " newspaper through politicians and poets, through Wordsworth, Carlyle, Mill and Sydney Smith, down to the boys of Eton. In the gravest treatise on political economy, in a philosophical essay, in books of science, one is surprised by the most innocent exhibition of unflinching nationality. In a tract on Corn, a most amiable and accomplished gentleman writes thus : — " Though Britain, according to Bishop Berkeley's idea, were surrounded by a wall of brass ten thousand cubits in height, still she would as far excel the rest of the globe in riches, as she now does both in this secondary quality and in the more important ones of freedom, virtue and science." [1]

The English dislike the American structure of society, whilst yet trade, mills, public education and Chartism are doing what they can to create in England the same social condition. [2]

America is the paradise of the economists ; is the favorable exception invariably quoted to the rules of ruin ; but when he speaks directly of the Americans the islander forgets his philosophy and remembers his disparaging anecdotes.

But this childish patriotism costs something, like all narrowness. The English sway of their colonies has no root of kindness. They govern by their arts and ability ; they are more just than kind ; and whenever an abatement of their power is felt, they have not conciliated the affection on which to rely.

Coarse local distinctions, as those of nation, province or town, are useful in the absence of real ones ; but we must not insist on these accidental lines. Individual traits are always triumphing over national ones. There is no fence in metaphysics discriminating Greek, or English, or Spanish science. Æsop and Montaigne, Cervantes and Saadi are men of the world ; and to wave our own flag at the dinner table or in the University is to carry the boisterous dulness of a fire-club into a polite circle. Nature and destiny are always on the watch for our follies. Nature trips us up when we strut ; and there are curious examples in history on this very point of national pride.

George of Cappadocia, born at Epiphania in
Cilicia, was a low parasite who got a lucrative
contract to supply the army with bacon. A rogue
and informer, he got rich and was forced to run
from justice. He saved his money, embraced
Arianism, collected a library, and got promoted
by a faction to the episcopal throne of Alexan-
dria. When Julian came, A. D. 361, George was
dragged to prison; the prison was burst open
by the mob and George was lynched, as he de-
served. And this precious knave became, in
good time, Saint George of England, patron of
chivalry, emblem of victory and civility and the
pride of the best blood of the modern world.

Strange, that the solid truth-speaking Briton
should derive from an impostor. Strange, that
the New World should have no better luck, —
that broad America must wear the name of a
thief. Amerigo Vespucci, the pickle-dealer at
Seville, who went out, in 1499, a subaltern with
Hojeda, and whose highest naval rank was boat-
swain's mate in an expedition that never sailed,
managed in this lying world to supplant Columbus and baptize half the earth with his own dishonest name. Thus nobody can throw stones.
We are equally badly off in our founders; and
the false pickle-dealer is an offset to the false
bacon-seller.[1]

CHAPTER X

WEALTH

THERE is no country in which so absolute a homage is paid to wealth. In America there is a touch of shame when a man exhibits the evidences of large property, as if after all it needed apology. But the Englishman has pure pride in his wealth, and esteems it a final certificate. A coarse logic rules throughout all English souls; — if you have merit, can you not show it by your good clothes and coach and horses? How can a man be a gentleman without a pipe of wine? Haydon says, "There is a fierce resolution to make every man live according to the means he possesses."[1] There is a mixture of religion in it. They are under the Jewish law, and read with sonorous emphasis that their days shall be long in the land, they shall have sons and daughters, flocks and herds, wine and oil. In exact proportion is the reproach of poverty. They do not wish to be represented except by opulent men. An Englishman who has lost his fortune is said to have died of a broken heart. The last term of insult is, "a beggar." Nelson said, "The want of fortune is a crime which I can never get over." Sydney

Smith said, " Poverty is infamous in England."
And one of their recent writers speaks, in reference to a private and scholastic life, of " the grave
moral deterioration which follows an empty exchequer." You shall find this sentiment, if not
so frankly put, yet deeply implied in the novels
and romances of the present century, and not
only in these, but in biography and in the votes
of public assemblies, in the tone of the preaching and in the table-talk.

I was lately turning over Wood's *Athenæ Oxonienses*, and looking naturally for another standard in a chronicle of the scholars of Oxford for
two hundred years. But I found the two disgraces
in that, as in most English books, are, first, dis-
loyalty to Church and State, and second, to be
born poor, or to come to poverty. A natural fruit
of England is the brutal political economy. Mal-
thus finds no cover laid at Nature's table for the
laborer's son. In 1809, the majority in Parliament expressed itself by the language of Mr.
Fuller in the House of Commons, " If you do
not like the country, damn you, you can leave
it." When Sir S. Romilly proposed his bill for-
bidding parish officers to bind children appren-
tices at a greater distance than forty miles from
their home, Peel opposed, and Mr. Wortley

said, " though, in the higher ranks, to cultivate family affections was a good thing, it was not so among the lower orders. Better take them away from those who might deprave them. And it was highly injurious to trade to stop binding to manufacturers, as it must raise the price of labor and of manufactured goods." [1]

The respect for truth of facts in England is equalled only by the respect for wealth. It is at once the pride of art of the Saxon, as he is a wealth-maker, and his passion for independence. The Englishman believes that every man must take care of himself, and has himself to thank if he do not mend his condition. To pay their debts is their national point of honor. From the Exchequer and the East India House to the huckster's shop, every thing prospers because it is solvent. The British armies are solvent and pay for what they take. The British empire is solvent; for in spite of the huge national debt, the valuation mounts. During the war from 1789 to 1815, whilst they complained that they were taxed within an inch of their lives, and by dint of enormous taxes were subsidizing all the continent against France, the English were growing rich every year faster than any people ever grew before. It is their maxim that the weight of taxes must be calculated, not by what is taken, but by what is left. Solvency is in the ideas and mechanism of an Englishman. The Crystal Palace is not considered honest until it pays; no matter how much convenience, beauty, or *éclat*, it must be self-supporting. They are contented with slower steamers, as long as they know that swifter boats lose money. They proceed logically by the double method of labor and thrift. Every household exhibits an exact economy, and nothing of that uncalculated headlong expenditure which families use in America. If they cannot pay, they do not buy; for they have no presumption of better fortunes next year, as our people have; and they say without shame, I cannot afford it. Gentlemen do not hesitate to ride in the second-class cars, or in the second cabin. An economist, or a man who can proportion his means and his ambition, or bring the year round with expenditure which expresses his character without embarrassing one day of his future, is already a master of life, and a freeman. Lord Burleigh writes to his son that " one ought never to devote more than two thirds of his income to the ordinary expenses of life, since the extraordinary will be certain to absorb the other third." [1]

The ambition to create value evokes every kind of ability; government becomes a manufacturing corporation, and every house a mill. The headlong bias to utility will let no talent lie in a napkin, — if possible will teach spiders to weave silk stockings. An Englishman, while he eats and drinks no more or not much more than another man, labors three times as many hours in the course of a year as another European; or, his life as a workman is three lives. He works fast. Everything in England is at a quick pace. They have reinforced their own productivity by the creation of that marvellous machinery which differences this age from any other age.

It is a curious chapter in modern history, the growth of the machine-shop. Six hundred years ago, Roger Bacon explained the precession of the equinoxes, the consequent necessity of the reform of the calendar; measured the length of the year; invented gunpowder; and announced (as if looking from his lofty cell, over five centuries, into ours) that "machines can be constructed to drive ships more rapidly than a whole galley of rowers could do; nor would they need anything but a pilot to steer them. Carriages also might be constructed to move with an incredible speed, without the aid of any animal.

Finally, it would not be impossible to make machines which by means of a suit of wings should fly in the air in the manner of birds." But the secret slept with Bacon. The six hundred years have not yet fulfilled his words. Two centuries ago the sawing of timber was done by hand; the carriage wheels ran on wooden axles; the land was tilled by wooden ploughs. And it was to little purpose that they had pit-coal, or that looms were improved, unless Watt and Stephenson had taught them to work force-pumps and power-looms by steam. The great strides were all taken within the last hundred years. The Life of Sir Robert Peel, in his day the model Englishman, very properly has, for a frontispiece, a drawing of the spinning-jenny, which wove the web of his fortunes. Hargreaves invented the spinning-jenny, and died in a work-house. Arkwright improved the invention, and the machine dispensed with the work of ninety-nine men; that is, one spinner could do as much work as one hundred had done before. The loom was improved further. But the men would sometimes strike for wages and combine against the masters, and, about 1829–30, much fear was felt lest the trade would be drawn away by these interruptions and the emigration of the spinners

to Belgium and the United States. Iron and
steel are very obedient. Whether it were not
possible to make a spinner that would not rebel,
nor mutter, nor scowl, nor strike for wages, nor
emigrate? At the solicitation of the masters,
after a mob and riot at Staley Bridge, Mr. Roberts of Manchester undertook to create this
peaceful fellow, instead of the quarrelsome fellow God had made. After a few trials, he succeeded, and in 1830 procured a patent for his
self-acting mule; a creation, the delight of mill-
owners, and "destined," they said, "to restore
order among the industrious classes;" a machine
requiring only a child's hand to piece the broken
yarns. As Arkwright had destroyed domestic
spinning, so Roberts destroyed the factory spinner. The power of machinery in Great Britain,
in mills, has been computed to be equal to
600,000,000 men, one man being able by the
aid of steam to do the work which required two
hundred and fifty men to accomplish fifty years
ago. The production has been commensurate.
England already had this laborious race, rich
soil, water, wood, coal, iron and favorable climate. Eight hundred years ago commerce had
made it rich, and it was recorded, "England is
the richest of all the northern nations." The

Norman historians recite that " in 1067, William carried with him into Normandy, from England, more gold and silver than had ever before been seen in Gaul." But when, to this labor and trade and these native resources was added this goblin of steam, with his myriad arms, never tired, working night and day everlastingly, the amassing of property has run out of all figures. It makes the motor of the last ninety years. The steam-pipe has added to her population and wealth the equivalent of four or five Englands. Forty thousand ships are entered in Lloyd's lists. The yield of wheat has gone on from 2,000,000 quarters in the time of the Stuarts, to 13,000,000 in 1854. A thousand million of pounds sterling are said to compose the floating money of commerce. In 1848, Lord John Russell stated that the people of this country had laid out £300,000,000 of capital in railways, in the last four years. But a better measure than these sounding figures is the estimate that there is wealth enough in England to support the entire population in idleness for one year.

The wise, versatile, all-giving machinery makes chisels, roads, locomotives, telegraphs. Whitworth divides a bar to a millionth of an inch. Steam twines huge cannon into wreaths, as easily as it braids straw, and vies with the volcanic forces which twisted the strata. It can clothe shingle mountains with ship-oaks, make sword-blades that will cut gun-barrels in two. In Egypt, it can plant forests, and bring rain after three thousand years. Already it is rudder-ing the balloon, and the next war will be fought in the air. But another machine more potent in England than steam is the Bank. It votes an issue of bills, population is stimulated and cities rise; it refuses loans, and emigration emp-ties the country; trade sinks; revolutions break out; kings are dethroned. By these new agents our social system is moulded. By dint of steam and of money, war and commerce are changed. Nations have lost their old omnipotence; the patriotic tie does not hold. Nations are getting obsolete, we go and live where we will. Steam has enabled men to choose what law they will live under. Money makes place for them. The telegraph is a limp band that will hold the Fen-ris-wolf of war.[1] For now that a telegraph line runs through France and Europe from London, every message it transmits makes stronger by one thread the band which war will have to cut.

v

The introduction of these elements gives new resources to existing proprietors. A sporting duke may fancy that the state depends on the House of Lords, but the engineer sees that every stroke of the steam-piston gives value to the duke's land, fills it with tenants ; doubles, quadruples, centuples the duke's capital, and creates new measures and new necessities for the culture of his children. Of course it draws the nobility into the competition, as stockholders in the mine, the canal, the railway, in the application of steam to agriculture, and sometimes into trade. But it also introduces large classes into the same competition ; the old energy of the Norse race arms itself with these magnificent powers ; new men prove an overmatch for the land-owner, and the mill buys out the castle. Scandinavian Thor, who once forged his bolts in icy Hecla and built galleys by lonely fiords, in England has advanced with the times, has shorn his beard, enters Parliament, sits down at a desk in the India House and lends Miöllnir to Birmingham for a steam-hammer.[1]

The creation of wealth in England in the last ninety years is a main fact in modern history. The wealth of London determines prices all over the globe. All things precious, or useful,

or amusing, or intoxicating, are sucked into this
commerce and floated to London. Some English private fortunes reach, and some exceed a
million of dollars a year. A hundred thousand
palaces adorn the island. All that can feed the
senses and passions, all that can succor the talent
or arm the hands of the intelligent middle class,
who never spare in what they buy for their own
consumption; all that can aid science, gratify
taste, or soothe comfort, is in open market. Whatever is excellent and beautiful in civil, rural, or
ecclesiastic architecture, in fountain, garden, or
grounds, — the English noble crosses sea and
land to see and to copy at home. The taste and
science of thirty peaceful generations; the gardens which Evelyn planted; the temples and
pleasure-houses which Inigo Jones and Christo-
pher Wren built; the wood that Gibbons carved;
the taste of foreign and domestic artists, Shen-
stone, Pope, Brown, Loudon, Paxton,[1] — are in
the vast auction, and the hereditary principle
heaps on the owner of to-day the benefit of ages
of owners. The present possessors are to the
full as absolute as any of their fathers in choosing and procuring what they like. This comfort
and splendor, the breadth of lake and mountain,
tillage, pasture and park, sumptuous castle and

modern villa, — all consist with perfect order. They have no revolutions ; no horse-guards dictating to the crown ; no Parisian *poissardes* and barricades; no mob : but drowsy habitude, daily dress-dinners, wine and ale and beer and gin and sleep.

With this power of creation and this passion for independence, property has reached an ideal perfection. It is felt and treated as the national life-blood. The laws are framed to give property the securest possible basis, and the provisions to lock and transmit it have exercised the cunningest heads in a profession which never admits a fool. The rights of property nothing but felony and treason can override. The house is a castle which the king cannot enter. The Bank is a strong box to which the king has no key. Whatever surly sweetness possession can give, is tasted in England to the dregs. Vested rights are awful things, and absolute possession gives the smallest freeholder identity of interest with the duke. High stone fences and padlocked garden-gates announce the absolute will of the owner to be alone. Every whim of exaggerated egotism is put into stone and iron, into silver and gold, with costly deliberation and detail.

An Englishman hears that the Queen Dowager wishes to establish some claim to put her park paling a rod forward into his grounds, so as to get a coachway and save her a mile to the avenue. Instantly he transforms his paling into stone-masonry, solid as the walls of Cuma, and all Europe cannot prevail on him to sell or compound for an inch of the land. They delight in a freak as the proof of their sovereign freedom. Sir Edward Boynton, at Spic Park at Cadenham, on a precipice of incomparable prospect, built a house like a long barn, which had not a window on the prospect side. Strawberry Hill of Horace Walpole, Fonthill Abbey of Mr. Beckford, were freaks; and Newstead Abbey became one in the hands of Lord Byron.

But the proudest result of this creation has been the great and refined forces it has put at the disposal of the private citizen. In the social world an Englishman to-day has the best lot. He is a king in a plain coat. He goes with the most powerful protection, keeps the best company, is armed by the best education, is seconded by wealth; and his English name and accidents are like a flourish of trumpets announcing him. This, with his quiet style of manners, gives him the power of a sovereign without the inconveniences which belong to that rank. I much prefer the condition of an English gentleman of the better class to that of any potentate in Europe, — whether for travel, or for opportunity of society, or for access to means of science or study, or for mere comfort and easy healthy relation to people at home.

Such as we have seen is the wealth of England ; a mighty mass, and made good in whatever details we care to explore. The cause and spring of it is the wealth of temperament in the people. The wonder of Britain is this plenteous nature. Her worthies are ever surrounded by as good men as themselves ; [1] each is a captain a hundred strong, and that wealth of men is represented again in the faculty of each individual, — that he has waste strength, power to spare. The English are so rich and seem to have established a tap-root in the bowels of the planet, because they are constitutionally fertile and creative.

But a man must keep an eye on his servants, if he would not have them rule him. Man is a shrewd inventor and is ever taking the hint of a new machine from his own structure, adapting some secret of his own anatomy in iron, wood and leather to some required function in the work of the world. But it is found that the

machine unmans the user. What he gains in
making cloth, he loses in general power. There
should be temperance in making cloth, as well
as in eating. A man should not be a silk-worm,
nor a nation a tent of caterpillars.[1] The robust
rural Saxon degenerates in the mills to the Leicester stockinger, to the imbecile Manchester spinner, — far on the way to be spiders and needles.
The incessant repetition of the same hand-work
dwarfs the man, robs him of his strength, wit
and versatility, to make a pin-polisher, a buckle-
maker, or any other specialty ; and presently, in
a change of industry, whole towns are sacrificed
like ant-hills, when the fashion of shoe-strings
supersedes buckles, when cotton takes the place
of linen, or railways of turnpikes, or when commons are enclosed by landlords. Then society is
admonished of the mischief of the division of
labor, and that the best political economy is care
and culture of men ; for in these crises all are
ruined except such as are proper individuals,
capable of thought and of new choice and the
application of their talent to new labor. Then
again come in new calamities. England is aghast
at the disclosure of her fraud in the adulteration
of food, of drugs and of almost every fabric in
her mills and shops; finding that milk will not

nourish, nor sugar sweeten, nor bread satisfy, nor pepper bite the tongue, nor glue stick. In true England all is false and forged. This too is the reaction of machinery, but of the larger machinery of commerce. 'T is not, I suppose, want of probity, so much as the tyranny of trade, which necessitates a perpetual competition of underselling, and that again a perpetual deterioration of the fabric.

The machinery has proved, like the balloon, unmanageable, and flies away with the aeronaut. Steam from the first hissed and screamed to warn him; it was dreadful with its explosion, and crushed the engineer. The machinist has wrought and watched, engineers and firemen without number have been sacrificed in learning to tame and guide the monster. But harder still it has proved to resist and rule the dragon Money, with his paper wings. Chancellors and Boards of Trade, Pitt, Peel and Robinson and their Parliaments and their whole generation adopted false principles, and went to their graves in the belief that they were enriching the country which they were impoverishing. They congratulated each other on ruinous expedients. It is rare to find a merchant who knows why a crisis occurs in trade, why prices rise or fall, or who knows the mischief of paper-money. In the culmination of national prosperity, in the annexation of countries; building of ships, depots, towns; in the influx of tons of gold and silver; amid the chuckle of chancellors and financiers, it was found that bread rose to famine prices, that the yeoman was forced to sell his cow and pig, his tools and his acre of land; and the dreadful barometer of the poor-rates was touching the point of ruin. The poor-rate was sucking in the solvent classes and forcing an exodus of farmers and mechanics. What befalls from the violence of financial crises, befalls daily in the violence of artificial legislation.[1]

Such a wealth has England earned, ever new, bounteous and augmenting. But the question recurs, does she take the step beyond, namely to the wise use, in view of the supreme wealth of nations? We estimate the wisdom of nations by seeing what they did with their surplus capital. And, in view of these injuries, some compensation has been attempted in England. A part of the money earned returns to the brain to buy schools, libraries, bishops, astronomers, chemists and artists with; and a part to repair the wrongs of this intemperate weaving, by hospitals, savings-banks, Mechanics' Institutes, public grounds and other charities and amenities. But the antidotes are frightfully inadequate, and the evil requires a deeper cure, which time and a simpler social organization must supply.¹ At present she does not rule her wealth. She is simply a good England, but no divinity, or wise and instructed soul. She too is in the stream of fate, one victim more in a common catastrophe.

But being in the fault, she has the misfortune of greatness to be held as the chief offender. England must be held responsible for the despotism of expense. Her prosperity, the splendor which so much manhood and talent and perseverance has thrown upon vulgar aims, is the very argument of materialism. Her success strengthens the hands of base wealth. Who can propose to youth poverty and wisdom, when mean gain has arrived at the conquest of letters and arts; when English success has grown out of the very renunciation of principles, and the dedication to outsides? A civility of trifles, of money and expense, an erudition of sensation takes place, and the putting as many impediments as we can between the man and his objects. Hardly the bravest among them have 'the manliness to resist it successfully. Hence it has come that not the aims of a manly life, but the means of meeting a certain ponderous expense, is that which is to be considered by a youth in England emerging from his minority. A large family is reckoned a misfortune. And it is a consolation in the death of the young, that a source of expense is closed.

CHAPTER XI

ARISTOCRACY

THE feudal character of the English state, now that it is getting obsolete, glares a little, in contrast with the democratic tendencies. The inequality of power and property shocks republican nerves. Palaces, halls, villas, walled parks, all over England, rival the splendor of royal seats. Many of the halls, like Haddon or Kedleston, are beautiful desolations. The proprietor never saw them, or never lived in them. Primogeniture built these sumptuous piles, and I suppose it is the sentiment of every traveller, as it was mine, It was well to come ere these were gone. Primogeniture is a cardinal rule of English property and institutions. Laws, customs, manners, the very persons and faces, affirm it.

The frame of society is aristocratic, the taste of the people is loyal. The estates, names and manners of the nobles flatter the fancy of the people and conciliate the necessary support. In spite of broken faith, stolen charters and the devastation of society by the profligacy of the court, we take sides as we read for the loyal

England and King Charles's "return to his
right" with his Cavaliers, — knowing what a
heartless trifler he is, and what a crew of God-
forsaken robbers they are. The people of England knew as much. But the fair idea of a
settled government connecting itself with heraldic
names, with the written and oral history of
Europe, and, at last, with the Hebrew religion
and the oldest traditions of the world, was too
pleasing a vision to be shattered by a few offensive realities and the politics of shoe-makers
and costermongers.' The hopes of the com-
moners take the same direction with the interest
of the patricians. Every man who becomes rich
buys land and does what he can to fortify the
nobility, into which he hopes to rise. The Anglican clergy are identified with the aristocracy.
Time and law have made the joining and mould-
ing perfect in every part. The Cathedrals, the
Universities, the national music, the popular
romances, conspire to uphold the heraldry which
the current politics of the day are sapping.'
The taste of the people is conservative. They
are proud of the castles, and of the language and
symbol of chivalry. Even the word *lord* is the
luckiest style that is used in any language to
designate a patrician. The superior education

and manners of the nobles recommend them to the country.

The Norwegian pirate got what he could and held it for his eldest son. The Norman noble, who was the Norwegian pirate baptized, did likewise. There was this advantage of Western over Oriental nobility, that this was recruited from below. English history is aristocracy with the doors open. Who has courage and faculty, let him come in. Of course the terms of admission to this club are hard and high. The selfishness of the nobles comes in aid of the interest of the nation to require signal merit. Piracy and war gave place to trade, politics and letters; the war-lord to the law-lord; the law-lord to the merchant and the mill-owner; but the privilege was kept, whilst the means of obtaining it were changed.

The foundations of these families lie deep in Norwegian exploits by sea and Saxon sturdiness on land. All nobility in its beginnings was somebody's natural superiority. The things these English have done were not done without peril of life, nor without wisdom and conduct; and the first hands, it may be presumed, were often challenged to show their right to their honors, or yield them to better men. " He that

will be a head, let him be a bridge," said the
Welsh chief Benegridran, when he carried all his
men over the river on his back. " He shall have
the book," said the mother of Alfred, "who can
read it ; " and Alfred won it by that title: and
I make no doubt that feudal tenure was no sine-
cure, but baron, knight and tenant often had
their memories refreshed, in regard to the service
by which they held their lands. The De Veres,
Bohuns, Mowbrays and Plantagenets were not
addicted to contemplation. The Middle Age
adorned itself with proofs of manhood and
devotion. Of Richard Beauchamp, Earl of
Warwick, the Emperor told Henry V. that no
Christian king had such another knight for wisdom, nurture and manhood, and caused him to
be named, " Father of curtesie." " Our success
in France," says the historian, " lived and died
with him." [1]

The war-lord earned his honors, and no do-
nation of land was large, as long as it brought
the duty of protecting it, hour by hour, against
a terrible enemy. In France and in England,
the nobles were, down to a late day, born and
bred to war: and the duel, which in peace still
held them to the risks of war, diminished the
envy that in trading and studious nations would

else have pried into their title. They were looked on as men who played high for a great stake.

Great estates are not sinecures, if they are to be kept great. A creative economy is the fuel of magnificence. In the same line of Warwick, the successor next but one to Beauchamp was the stout earl of Henry VI. and Edward IV. Few esteemed themselves in the mode, whose heads were not adorned with the black ragged staff, his badge.[1] At his house in London, six oxen were daily eaten at a breakfast, and every tavern was full of his meat, and who had any acquaintance in his family should have as much boiled and roast as he could carry on a long dagger.

The new age brings new qualities into request; the virtues of pirates gave way to those of planters, merchants, senators and scholars. Comity, social talent and fine manners, no doubt, have had their part also. I have met somewhere with a historiette, which, whether more or less true in its particulars, carries a general truth. "How came the Duke of Bedford by his great landed estates? His ancestor having travelled on the continent, a lively, pleasant man, became the companion of a foreign prince wrecked on the Dorsetshire coast, where Mr. Russell lived. The prince recommended him to Henry VIII., who, liking his company, gave him a large share of the plundered church lands."

The pretence is that the noble is of unbroken descent from the Norman, and has never worked for eight hundred years. But the fact is otherwise. Where is Bohun? where is De Vere? The lawyer, the farmer, the silk-mercer lies *perdu* under the coronet, and winks to the antiquary to say nothing; especially skilful lawyers, nobody's sons, who did some piece of work at a nice moment for government and were rewarded with ermine.

The national tastes of the English do not lead them to the life of the courtier, but to secure the comfort and independence of their homes. The aristocracy are marked by their predilection for country-life. They are called the county-families. They have often no residence in London and only go thither a short time, during the season, to see the opera; but they concentrate the love and labor of many generations on the building, planting and decoration of their homesteads. Some of them are too old and too proud to wear titles, or, as

Sheridan said of Coke, "disdain to hide their head in a coronet;" and some curious examples are cited to show the stability of English families. Their proverb is, that fifty miles from London, a family will last a hundred years; at a hundred miles, two hundred years; and so on; but I doubt that steam, the enemy of time as well as of space, will disturb these ancient rules. Sir Henry Wotton says of the first Duke of Buckingham, "He was born at Brookeby in Leicestershire, where his ancestors had chiefly continued about the space of four hundred years, rather without obscurity, than with any great lustre."[1] Wraxall says that in 1781, Lord Surrey, afterwards Duke of Norfolk, told him that when the year 1783 should arrive, he meant to give a grand festival to all the descendants of the body of Jockey of Norfolk,[2] to mark the day when the dukedom should have remained three hundred years in their house, since its creation by Richard III. Pepys tells us, in writing of an Earl Oxford, in 1666, that the honor had now remained in that name and blood six hundred years.

This long descent of families and this cleaving through ages to the same spot of ground, captivates the imagination.[3] It has too a connection with the names of the towns and districts of the country.

The names are excellent,—an atmosphere of legendary melody spread over the land. Older than all epics and histories which clothe a nation, this undershirt sits close to the body. What history too, and what stores of primitive and savage observation it infolds! Cambridge is the bridge of the Cam; Sheffield the field of the river Sheaf; Leicester the *castra*, or camp, of the Lear, or Leir (now Soar); Rochdale, of the Roch; Exeter or Excester, the *castra* of the Ex; Exmouth, Dartmouth, Sidmouth, Teignmouth, the mouths of the Ex, Dart, Sid and Teign rivers. Waltham is strong town; Radcliffe is red cliff; and so on:—a sincerity and use in naming very striking to an American, whose country is whitewashed all over by unmeaning names, the cast-off clothes of the country from which its emigrants came; or named at a pinch from a psalm-tune. But the English are those "barbarians" of Jamblichus,¹ who "are stable in their manners, and firmly continue to employ the same words, which also are dear to the gods."

'T is an old sneer that the Irish peerage drew their names from playbooks. The English lords do not call their lands after their own names, but call themselves after their lands, as if the man represented the country that bred him; and they rightly wear the token of the glebe that gave them birth, suggesting that the tie is not cut, but that there in London, — the crags of Argyle, the kail of Cornwall, the downs of Devon, the iron of Wales, the clays of Stafford are neither forgetting nor forgotten, but know the man who was born by them and who, like the long line of his fathers, has carried that crag, that shore, dale, fen, or woodland, in his blood and manners. It has, too, the advantage of suggesting responsibleness. A susceptible man could not wear a name which represented in a strict sense a city or a county of England, without hearing in it a challenge to duty and honor.

The predilection of the patricians for residence in the country, combined with the degree of liberty possessed by the peasant, makes the safety of the English hall. Mirabeau wrote prophetically from England, in 1784, " If revolution break out in France, I tremble for the aristocracy : their châteaux will be reduced to ashes and their blood be spilt in torrents. The English tenant would defend his lord to the last extremity." [1]   The English go to their estates

for grandeur. The French live at court, and
exile themselves to their estates for economy.
As they do not mean to live with their tenants,
they do not conciliate them, but wring from
them the last *sous*. Evelyn writes from Blois, in
1644: "The wolves are here in such numbers,
that they often come and take children out of
the streets; yet will not the Duke, who is sovereign here, permit them to be destroyed."

In evidence of the wealth amassed by ancient
families, the traveller is shown the palaces in
Piccadilly, Burlington House, Devonshire
House, Lansdowne House in Berkshire Square,
and lower down in the city, a few noble houses
which still withstand in all their amplitude the
encroachment of streets. The Duke of Bedford
includes or included a mile square in the heart
of London, where the British Museum, once
Montague House, now stands, and the land
occupied by Woburn Square, Bedford Square,
Russell Square. The Marquis of Westminster
built within a few years the series of squares
called Belgravia. Stafford House[1] is the noblest
palace in London. Northumberland House
holds its place by Charing Cross.[2] Chesterfield
House remains in Audley Street. Sion House
and Holland House are in the suburbs. But

most of the historical houses are masked or lost in the modern uses to which trade or charity has converted them. A multitude of town palaces contain inestimable galleries of art.

In the country, the size of private estates is more impressive. From Barnard Castle I rode on the highway twenty-three miles from High Force, a fall of the Tees, towards Darlington, past Raby Castle, through the estate of the Duke of Cleveland. The Marquis of Breadalbane rides out of his house a hundred miles in a straight line to the sea, on his own property. The Duke of Sutherland owns the County of Sutherland, stretching across Scotland from sea to sea. The Duke of Devonshire, besides his other estates, owns 96,000 acres in the County of Derby. The Duke of Richmond has 40,000 acres at Goodwood and 300,000 at Gordon Castle. The Duke of Norfolk's park in Sussex is fifteen miles in circuit. An agriculturist bought lately the island of Lewes, in Hebrides, containing 500,000 acres. The possessions of the Earl of Lonsdale gave him eight seats in Parliament. This is the Heptarchy again; and before the Reform of 1832, one hundred and fifty-four persons sent three hundred and seven members to Parliament. The borough-mongers governed England.

These large domains are growing larger. The great estates are absorbing the small freeholds. In 1786 the soil of England was owned by 250,000 corporations and proprietors; and in 1822, by 32,000. These broad estates find room in this narrow island. All over England, scattered at short intervals among ship-yards, mills, mines and forges, are the paradises of the nobles, where the livelong repose and refinement are heightened by the contrast with the roar of industry and necessity, out of which you have stepped aside.

I was surprised to observe the very small attendance usually in the House of Lords. Out of five hundred and seventy-three peers, on ordinary days only twenty or thirty. Where are they? I asked. "At home on their estates, devoured by *ennui*, or in the Alps, or up the Rhine, in the Harz Mountains, or in Egypt, or in India, on the Ghauts." But, with such interests at stake, how can these men afford to neglect them? "O," replied my friend, "why should they work for themselves, when every man in England works for them and will suffer before they come to harm?" The hardest radical instantly uncovers and changes his tone to a lord. It was remarked, on the 10th April, 1848 (the day of the Chartist demonstration), that the upper classes were for the first time actively interesting themselves in their own defence, and men of rank were sworn special constables with the rest. " Besides, why need they sit out the debate ? Has not the Duke of Wellington, at this moment, their proxies — the proxies of fifty peers — in his pocket, to vote for them if there be an emergency ? " [1]

It is however true that the existence of the House of Peers as a branch of the government entitles them to fill half the Cabinet ; and their weight of property and station gives them a vir- tual nomination of the other half ; whilst they have their share in the subordinate offices, as a school of training. This monopoly of political power has given them their intellectual and so- cial eminence in Europe. [2] A few law lords and a few political lords take the brunt of public business. In the army, the nobility fill a large part of the high commissions, and give to these a tone of expense and splendor and also of ex- clusiveness. [3] They have borne their full share of duty and danger in this service, and there are few noble families which have not paid, in some of their members, the debt of life or limb in the

sacrifices of the Russian war. For the rest, the
nobility have the lead in matters of state and of
expense; in questions of taste, in social usages,
in convivial and domestic hospitalities. In general, all that is required of them is to sit securely,
to preside at public meetings, to countenance
charities and to give the example of that decorum
so dear to the British heart.

If one asks, in the critical spirit of the day,
what service this class have rendered? — uses
appear, or they would have perished long ago.
Some of these are easily enumerated, others more
subtle make a part of unconscious history.[1] Their
institution is one step in the progress of society.
For a race yields a nobility in some form, however we name the lords, as surely as it yields
women.

The English nobles are high-spirited, active,
educated men, born to wealth and power, who
have run through every country and kept in
every country the best company, have seen every
secret of art and nature, and, when men of any
ability or ambition, have been consulted in the
conduct of every important action. You cannot
wield great agencies without lending yourself to
them, and when it happens that the spirit of the
earl meets his rank and duties, we have the best

examples of behavior. Power of any kind readily
appears in the manners ; and beneficent power,
le talent de bien faire, gives a majesty which cannot be concealed or resisted.

These people seem to gain as much as they lose
by their position. They survey society as from
the top of St. Paul's, and if they never hear plain
truth from men, they see the best of everything,
in every kind, and they see things so grouped
and amassed as to infer easily the sum and genius,
instead of tedious particularities. Their good behavior deserves all its fame, and they have that
simplicity and that air of repose which are the
finest ornament of greatness.[1]

The upper classes have only birth, say the
people here, and not thoughts. Yes, but they
have manners, and it is wonderful how much
talent runs into manners : — nowhere and never
so much as in England. They have the sense of
superiority, the absence of all the ambitious effort
which disgusts in the aspiring classes, a pure tone
of thought and feeling, and the power to command, among their other luxuries, the presence
of the most accomplished men in their festive
meetings.

Loyalty is in the English a sub-religion. They
wear the laws as ornaments, and walk by their

faith in their painted May-Fair as if among the forms of gods. The economist of 1855 who asks, Of what use are the lords? may learn of Franklin to ask, Of what use is a baby? They have been a social church proper to inspire sentiments mutually honoring the lover and the loved. Politeness is the ritual of society, as prayers are of the church, a school of manners, and a gentle blessing to the age in which it grew. 'T is a romance adorning English life with a larger horizon; a midway heaven, fulfilling to their sense their fairy tales and poetry. This, just as far as the breeding of the nobleman really made him brave, handsome, accomplished and great-hearted.

On general grounds, whatever tends to form manners or to finish men, has a great value. Every one who has tasted the delight of friendship will respect every social guard which our manners can establish, tending to secure from the intrusion of frivolous and distasteful people. The jealousy of every class to guard itself is a testimony to the reality they have found in life. When a man once knows that he has done justice to himself, let him dismiss all terrors of aristocracy as superstitions, so far as he is concerned. He who keeps the door of a mine, whether of cobalt, or mercury, or nickel, or plumbago, securely knows that the world cannot do without him. Everybody who is real is open and ready for that which is also real.

Besides, these are they who make England that strongbox and museum it is ; who gather and protect works of art, dragged from amidst burning cities and revolutionary countries, and brought hither out of all the world. I look with respect at houses six, seven, eight hundred, or, like Warwick Castle, nine hundred years old. I pardoned high park-fences, when I saw that besides does and pheasants, these have preserved Arundel marbles, Townley galleries, Howard and Spenserian libraries, Warwick and Portland vases, Saxon manuscripts, monastic architectures, millennial trees, and breeds of cattle elsewhere extinct. In these manors, after the frenzy of war and destruction subsides a little, the antiquary finds the frailest Roman jar or crumbling Egyptian mummy-case, without so much as a new layer of dust, keeping the series of history unbroken and waiting for its interpreter, who is sure to arrive. These lords are the treasurers and librarians of mankind, engaged by their pride and wealth to this function.

Yet there were other works for British dukes to do. George Loudon, Quintinye, Evelyn, had taught them to make gardens. Arthur Young, Bakewell and Mechi have made them agricultural.[1] Scotland was a camp until the day of Culloden. The Dukes of Athol, Sutherland, Buccleugh and the Marquis of Breadalbane have introduced the rape-culture, the sheep-farm, wheat, drainage, the plantation of forests, the artificial replenishment of lakes and ponds with fish, the renting of game-preserves. Against the cry of the old tenantry and the sympathetic cry of the English press, they have rooted out and planted anew, and now six millions of people live, and live better, on the same land that fed three millions.

The English barons, in every period, have been brave and great, after the estimate and opinion of their times. The grand old halls scattered up and down in England, are dumb vouchers to the state and broad hospitality of their ancient lords. Shakspeare's portraits of good Duke Humphrey, of Warwick, of Northumberland, of Talbot, were drawn in strict consonance with the traditions. A sketch of the Earl of Shrewsbury, from the pen of Queen Elizabeth's archbishop Parker;[2] Lord Herbert of Cherbury's autobiography;[3] the letters and essays of Sir Philip Sidney; the anecdotes pre-

served by the antiquaries Fuller and Collins;
some glimpses at the interiors of noble houses,
which we owe to Pepys and Evelyn; the details which Ben Jonson's masques (performed
at Kenilworth, Althorpe, Belvoir and other
noble houses), record or suggest; down to Aubrey's passages of the life of Hobbes in the
house of the Earl of Devon, are favorable pictures of a romantic style of manners. Penshurst
still shines for us, and its Christmas revels,
" where logs not burn, but men." At Wilton
House the "Arcadia" was written, amidst conversations with Fulke Greville, Lord Brooke,
a man of no vulgar mind, as his own poems
declare him.' I must hold Ludlow Castle an
honest house, for which Milton's "Comus"
was written, and the company nobly bred which
performed it with knowledge and sympathy.
In the roll of nobles are found poets, philosophers, chemists, astronomers, also men of solid
virtues and of lofty sentiments; often they
have been the friends and patrons of genius
and learning, and especially of the fine arts; and
at this moment, almost every great house has
its sumptuous picture-gallery.

Of course there is another side to this gor-
geous show. Every victory was the defeat of

a party only less worthy. Castles are proud things, but 't is safest to be outside of them. War is a foul game, and yet war is not the worst part of aristocratic history. In later times, when the baron, educated only for war, with his brains paralyzed by his stomach, found himself idle at home, he grew fat and wanton and a sorry brute.' Grammont, Pepys and Evelyn show the kennels to which the king and court went in quest of pleasure. Prostitutes taken from the theatres were made duchesses, their bastards dukes and earls. " The young men sat uppermost, the old serious lords were out of favor." The discourse that the king's companions had with him was "poor and frothy." No man who valued his head might do what these pot-companions familiarly did with the king. In logical sequence of these dignified revels, Pepys can tell the beggarly shifts to which the king was reduced, who could not find paper at his council table, and " no handkerchers " in his wardrobe, "and but three bands to his neck," and the linen-draper and the stationer were out of pocket and refusing to trust him, and the bakeı will not bring bread any longer. Meantime the English Channel was swept and London threatened by the Dutch fleet, manned too by Eng-

'ish sailors, who, having been cheated of their pay for years by the king, enlisted with the enemy.

The Selwyn[1] correspondence, in the reign of George III., discloses a rottenness in the aristocracy which threatened to decompose the state. The sycophancy and sale of votes and honor, for place and title; lewdness, gaming, smuggling, bribery and cheating; the sneer at the childish indiscretion of quarrelling with ten thousand a year; the want of ideas; the splendor of the titles, and the apathy of the nation, are instructive, and make the reader pause and explore the firm bounds which confined these vices to a handful of rich men. In the reign of the Fourth George, things do not seem to have mended, and the rotten debauchee let down from a window by an inclined plane into his coach to take the air, was a scandal to Europe which the ill fame of his queen and of his family did nothing to retrieve.

Under the present reign the perfect decorum of the Court is thought to have put a check on the gross vices of the aristocracy; yet gaming, racing, drinking and mistresses bring them down, and the democrat can still gather scandals, if he will. Dismal anecdotes abound, verifying the

gossip of the last generation, of dukes served
by bailiffs, with all their plate in pawn ; of great
lords living by the showing of their houses, and
of an old man wheeled in his chair from room
to room, whilst his chambers are exhibited to
the visitor for money ; of ruined dukes and earls
living in exile for debt. The historic names of
the Buckinghams, Beauforts, Marlboroughs and
Hertfords have gained no new lustre, and now
and then darker scandals break out, ominous
as the new chapters added under the Orleans
dynasty to the " Causes Célèbres " ¹ in France.
Even peers who are men of worth and public
spirit are overtaken and embarrassed by their
vast expense. The respectable Duke of Devonshire, willing to be the Mæcenas and Lucullus
of his island, is reported to have said that he
cannot live at Chatsworth but one month in the
year. Their many houses eat them up. They
cannot sell them, because they are entailed.
They will not let them, for pride's sake, but
keep them empty, aired, and the grounds mown
and dressed, at a cost of four or five thousand
pounds a year. The spending is for a great part
in servants, in many houses exceeding a hundred.

Most of them are only chargeable with idleness, which, because it squanders such vast

v

power of benefit, has the mischief of crime. "They might be little Providences on earth," said my friend, "and they are, for the most part, jockeys and fops." Campbell says, "Acquaintance with the nobility, I could never keep up. It requires a life of idleness, dressing and attendance on their parties." I suppose too that a feeling of self-respect is driving cultivated men out of this society, as if the noble were slow to receive the lessons of the times and had not learned to disguise his pride of place. A man of wit, who is also one of the celebrities of wealth and fashion, confessed to his friend that he could not enter their houses without being made to feel that they were great lords, and he a low plebeian. With the tribe of *artistes*, including the musical tribe, the patrician morgue keeps no terms, but excludes them. When Julia Grisi and Mario sang at the houses of the Duke of Wellington and other grandees, a cord was stretched between the singer and the company.

When every noble was a soldier, they were carefully bred to great personal prowess. The education of a soldier is a simpler affair than that of an earl in the nineteenth century. And this was very seriously pursued; they were ex-

pert in every species of equitation, to the most
dangerous practices, and this down to the accession of William of Orange. But graver men
appear to have trained their sons for civil affairs.
Elizabeth extended her thought to the future;
and Sir Philip Sidney in his letter to his brother,
and Milton and Evelyn, gave plain and hearty
counsel. Already too the English noble and
squire were preparing for the career of the
country-gentleman and his peaceable expense.
They went from city to city, learning receipts
to make perfumes, sweet powders, pomanders,
antidotes, gathering seeds, gems, coins and divers curiosities, preparing for a private life there-
after, in which they should take pleasure in these
recreations.

All advantages given to absolve the young
patrician from intellectual labor are of course
mistaken. " In the university, noblemen are
exempted from the public exercises for the degree, etc., by which they attain a degree called
honorary.[1] At the same time, the fees they have
to pay for matriculation, and on all other occasions, are much higher."[2] Fuller records " the
observation of foreigners, that Englishmen, by
making their children gentlemen before they are
men, cause they are so seldom wise men."[3]

This cockering justifies Dr. Johnson's bitter apology for primogeniture, that "it makes but one fool in a family."

The revolution in society has reached this class. The great powers of industrial art have no exclusion of name or blood. The tools of our time, namely steam, ships, printing, money and popular education, belong to those who can handle them; and their effect has been that advantages once confined to men of family are now open to the whole middle class. The road that grandeur levels for his coach, toil can travel in his cart.

This is more manifest every day, but I think it is true throughout English history. English history, wisely read, is the vindication of the brain of that people. Here at last were climate and condition friendly to the working faculty. Who now will work and dare, shall rule. This is the charter, or the chartism, which fogs and seas and rains proclaimed, — that intellect and personal force should make the law; that industry and administrative talent should administer; that work should wear the crown. I know that not this, but something else is pretended. The fiction with which the noble and the bystander equally please themselves is that the former is

of unbroken descent from the Norman, and so
has never worked for eight hundred years. All
the families are new, but the name is old, and
they have made a covenant with their memories
not to disturb it. But the analysis of the peerage and gentry shows the rapid decay and ex-
tinction of old families, the continual recruiting
of these from new blood.[1] The doors, though
ostentatiously guarded, are really open, and
hence the power of the bribe. All the barriers
to rank only whet the thirst and enhance the
prize. " Now," said Nelson, when clearing for
battle, " a peerage, or Westminster Abbey ! "
" I have no illusion left," said Sidney Smith,
" but the Archbishop of Canterbury." " The
lawyers," said Burke, " are only birds of passage
in this House of Commons," and then added,
with a new figure, " they have their best bower
anchor in the House of Lords."

Another stride that has been taken appears in
the perishing of heraldry. Whilst the privileges
of nobility are passing to the middle class, the
badge is discredited and the titles of lordship are
getting musty and cumbersome. I wonder that
sensible men have not been already impatient of
them. They belong, with wigs, powder and scar-
let coats, to an earlier age and may be advanta-

geously consigned, with paint and tattoo, to the dignitaries of Australia and Polynesia.

A multitude of English, educated at the universities, bred into their society with manners, ability and the gifts of fortune, are every day confronting the peers on a footing of equality, and outstripping them, as often, in the race of honor and influence. That cultivated class is large and ever enlarging. It is computed that, with titles and without, there are seventy thousand of these people coming and going in London, who make up what is called high society. They cannot shut their eyes to the fact that an untitled nobility possess all the power without the inconveniences that belong to rank, and the rich Englishman goes over the world at the present day, drawing more than all the advantages which the strongest of his kings could command.

CHAPTER XII

UNIVERSITIES

OF British universities, Cambridge has the most illustrious names on its list. At the present day too, it has the advantage of Oxford, counting in its *alumni* a greater number of distinguished scholars. I regret that I had but a single day wherein to see King's College Chapel, the beautiful lawns and gardens of the colleges, and a few of its gownsmen.

But I availed myself of some repeated invitations to Oxford, where I had introductions to Dr. Daubeny, Professor of Botany, and to the Regius Professor of Divinity, as well as to a valued friend, a Fellow of Oriel, and went thither on the last day of March, 1848. I was the guest of my friend in Oriel, was housed close upon that college, and I lived on college hospitalities.[1]

My new friends showed me their cloisters, the Bodleian Library, the Randolph Gallery, Merton Hall and the rest. I saw several faithful, high-minded young men, some of them in the mood of making sacrifices for peace of mind, — a topic, of course, on which I had no counsel to offer. Their affectionate and gregarious ways reminded me at once of the habits of *our* Cambridge men, though I imputed to these English an advantage in their secure and polished manners. The halls are rich with oaken wainscoting and ceiling. The pictures of the founders hang from the walls ; the tables glitter with plate. A youth came forward to the upper table and pronounced the ancient form of grace before meals, which, I suppose, has been in use here for ages, *Benedictus, benedicat ; benedicitur, benedicatur.*[1]

It is a curious proof of the English use and wont, or of their good nature, that these young men are locked up every night at nine o'clock, and the porter at each hall is required to give the name of any belated student who is admitted after that hour. Still more descriptive is the fact that out of twelve hundred young men, comprising the most spirited of the aristocracy, a duel has never occurred.

Oxford is old, even in England, and conservative. Its foundations date from Alfred and even from Arthur, if, as is alleged, the Pheryllt of the Druids had a seminary here. In the reign of Edward I., it is pretended, here were thirty thousand students ; and nineteen most noble foundations were then established. Chaucer found it as firm as if it had always stood ; and it is, in Brit-

ish story, rich with great names, the school of
the island and the link of England to the learned
of Europe. Hither came Erasmus, with delight,
in 1497.[1] Albericus Gentilis, in 1580, was re-
lieved and maintained by the university.[2] Albert
Alaskie, a noble Polonian, Prince of Sirad, who
visited England to admire the wisdom of Queen
Elizabeth, was entertained with stage-plays in
the Refectory of Christ-Church in 1583. Isaac
Casaubon, coming from Henri Quatre of France
by invitation of James I., was admitted to Christ-
Church, in July, 1613.[3] I saw the Ashmolean
Museum, whither Elias Ashmole in 1682 sent
twelve cart-loads of rarities. Here indeed was
the Olympia of all Antony Wood's and Aubrey's
games and heroes, and every inch of ground has
its lustre. For Wood's *Athenæ Oxonienses*, or
calendar of the writers of Oxford for two hundred years, is a lively record of English manners
and merits, and as much a national monument
as Purchas's Pilgrims or Hansard's Register.
On every side, Oxford is redolent of age and
authority. Its gates shut of themselves against
modern innovation.[4] It is still governed by the
statutes of Archbishop Laud. The books in
Merton Library are still chained to the wall.
Here, on August 27, 1660, John Milton's *Pro*

Populo Anglicano Defensio and *Iconoclastes* were
committed to the flames. I saw the school-court
or quadrangle where, in 1683, the Convocation
caused the Leviathan of Thomas Hobbes to be
publicly burnt.[1] I do not know whether this
learned body have yet heard of the Declaration
of American Independence, or whether the
Ptolemaic astronomy does not still hold its
ground against the novelties of Copernicus.

As many sons, almost so many benefactors.
It is usual for a nobleman, or indeed for almost
every wealthy student, on quitting college to
leave behind him some article of plate ; and gifts
of all values, from a hall or a fellowship or a
library, down to a picture or a spoon, are con-
tinually accruing, in the course of a century.
My friend Doctor J. gave me the following
anecdote. In Sir Thomas Lawrence's collection
at London were the cartoons of Raphael and
Michael Angelo. This inestimable prize was
offered to Oxford University for seven thousand
pounds. The offer was accepted, and the committee charged with the affair had collected three
thousand pounds, when, among other friends
they called on Lord Eldon. Instead of a hundred pounds, he surprised them by putting down
his name for three thousand pounds. They told

him they should now very easily raise the remainder. "No," he said, "your men have
probably already contributed all they can spare;
I can as well give the rest:" and he withdrew
his cheque for three thousand, and wrote four
thousand pounds. I saw the whole collection
in April, 1848.

In the Bodleian Library, Dr. Bandinel showed
me the manuscript Plato, of the date of A. D.
896, brought by Dr. Clarke from Egypt; a
manuscript Virgil of the same century; the first
Bible printed at Mentz (I believe in 1450); and
a duplicate of the same, which had been deficient
in about twenty leaves at the end. But one day,
being in Venice, he bought a room full of books
and manuscripts, — every scrap and fragment,
— for four thousand louis d'ors, and had the
doors locked and sealed by the consul. On pro-
ceeding afterwards to examine his purchase, he
found the twenty deficient pages of his Mentz
Bible, in perfect order; brought them to Oxford
with the rest of his purchase, and placed them
in the volume; but has too much awe for the
Providence that appears in bibliography also,
to suffer the reunited parts to be re-bound. The
oldest building here is two hundred years
younger than the frail manuscript brought by

Dr. Clarke from Egypt. No candle or fire is ever lighted in the Bodleian. Its catalogue is the standard catalogue on the desk of every library in Oxford. In each several college they underscore in red ink on this catalogue the titles of books contained in the library of that college, — the theory being that the Bodleian has all books. This rich library spent during the last year (1847), for the purchase of books, £1668.

The logical English train a scholar as they train an engineer. Oxford is a Greek factory, as Wilton mills weave carpet and Sheffield grinds steel. They know the use of a tutor, as they know the use of a horse; and they draw the greatest amount of benefit out of both. The reading men are kept, by hard walking, hard riding and measured eating and drinking, at the top of their condition, and two days before the examination, do no work, but lounge, ride, or run, to be fresh on the college doomsday. Seven years' residence is the theoretic period for a master's degree. In point of fact, it has long been three years' residence, and four years more of standing. This " three years " is about twenty-one months in all.[1]

" The whole expense," says Professor Sewel,

" of ordinary college tuition at Oxford, is about sixteen guineas a year." But this plausible statement may deceive a reader unacquainted with the fact that the principal teaching relied on is private tuition. And the expenses of private tuition are reckoned at from £50 to £70 a year, or $1000 for the whole course of three years and a half. At Cambridge, $750 a year is economical, and $1500 not extravagant.[1]

The number of students and of residents, the dignity of the authorities, the value of the foundations, the history and the architecture, the known sympathy of entire Britain in what is done there, justify a dedication to study in the undergraduate such as cannot easily be in America, where his college is half suspected by the Freshman to be insignificant in the scale beside trade and politics. Oxford is a little aristocracy in itself, numerous and dignified enough to rank with other estates in the realm; and where fame and secular promotion are to be had for study, and in a direction which has the unanimous respect of all cultivated nations.

This aristocracy, of course, repairs its own losses; fills places, as they fall vacant, from the body of students. The number of fellowships at Oxford is 540, averaging £200 a year, with lodging and diet at the college. If a young American, loving learning and hindered by poverty, were offered a home, a table, the walks and the library in one of these academical palaces, and a thousand dollars a year, as long as he chose to remain a bachelor, he would dance for joy. Yet these young men thus happily placed, and paid to read, are impatient of their few checks, and many of them preparing to resign their fellowships. They shuddered at the prospect of dying a Fellow, and they pointed out to me a paralytic old man, who was assisted into the hall. As the number of undergraduates at Oxford is only about 1200 or 1300, and many of these are never competitors, the chance of a fellowship is very great. The income of the nineteen colleges is conjectured at £150,000 a year.

The effect of this drill is the radical knowledge of Greek and Latin and of mathematics, and the solidity and taste of English criticism. Whatever luck there may be in this or that award, an Eton captain can write Latin longs and shorts, can turn the Court-Guide into hexameters, and it is certain that a Senior Classic can quote correctly from the *Corpus Poetarum* and is critically learned in all the humanities. Greek

erudition exists on the Isis and Cam, whether
the Maud man or the Brasenose man be properly ranked or not; the atmosphere is loaded
with Greek learning; the whole river has reached
a certain height, and kills all that growth of
weeds which this Castalian water kills. The
English nature takes culture kindly. So Milton thought. It refines the Norseman. Access
to the Greek mind lifts his standard of taste.
He has enough to think of, and, unless of an
impulsive nature, is indisposed from writing or
speaking, by the fulness of his mind and the
new severity of his taste. The great silent crowd
of thoroughbred Grecians always known to be
around him, the English writer cannot ignore.
They prune his orations and point his pen.
Hence the style and tone of English journalism.
The men have learned accuracy and compre-
hension, logic, and pace, or speed of working.
They have bottom, endurance, wind. When
born with good constitutions, they make those
eupeptic studying-mills, the cast-iron men, the
dura ilia, whose powers of performance compare
with ours as the steam-hammer with the music-
box;[1] — Cokes, Mansfields, Seldens and Bent-
leys, and when it happens that a superior brain
puts a rider on this admirable horse, we obtain

those masters of the world who combine the highest energy in affairs with a supreme culture.

It is contended by those who have been bred at Eton, Harrow, Rugby and Westminster, that the public sentiment within each of those schools is high-toned and manly ; that, in their playgrounds, courage is universally admired, meanness despised, manly feelings and generous conduct are encouraged : that an unwritten code of honor deals to the spoiled child of rank and to the child of upstart wealth, an even-handed justice, purges their nonsense out of both and does all that can be done to make them gentlemen.

Again, at the universities, it is urged that all goes to form what England values as the flower of its national life, — a well-educated gentleman. The German Huber, in describing to his countrymen the attributes of an English gentleman, frankly admits that " in Germany, we have nothing of the kind. A gentleman must possess a political character, an independent and public position, or at least the right of assuming it. He must have average opulence, either of his own, or in his family. He should also have bodily activity and strength, unattainable by our

sedentary life in public offices. The race of
English gentlemen presents an appearance of
manly vigor and form not elsewhere to be found
among an equal number of persons. No other
nation produces the stock. And in England, it
has deteriorated. The university is a decided
presumption in any man's favor. And so eminent are the members that a glance at the calendars will show that in all the world one cannot
be in better company than on the books of one
of the larger Oxford or Cambridge colleges." [1]

These seminaries are finishing schools for the
upper classes, and not for the poor. The useful is exploded. The definition of a public school
is "a school which excludes all that could fit a
man for standing behind a counter." [2]

No doubt, the foundations have been per-
verted. Oxford, which equals in wealth several of
the smaller European states, shuts up the lec-
tureships which were made " public for all men
thereunto to have concourse;" mis-spends the
revenues bestowed for such youths " as should be
most meet for towardness, poverty and painful-
ness;" there is gross favoritism; many chairs
and many fellowships are made beds of ease; and
it is likely that the university will know how to
resist and make inoperative the terrors of parlia-

v

mentary inquiry; no doubt their learning is grown obsolete;— but Oxford also has its merits, and I found here also proof of the national fidelity and thoroughness. Such knowledge as they prize they possess and impart. Whether in course or by indirection, whether by a cramming tutor or by examiners with prizes and foundational scholarships, education, according to the English notion of it, is arrived at. I looked over the Examination Papers of the year 1848, for the various scholarships and fellowships, the Lusby, the Hertford, the Dean-Ireland and the University (copies of which were kindly given me by a Greek professor), containing the tasks which many competitors had victoriously performed, and I believed they would prove too severe tests for the candidates for a Bachelor's degree in Yale or Harvard. And in general, here was proof of a more searching study in the appointed directions, and the knowledge pretended to be conveyed was conveyed. Oxford sends out yearly twenty or thirty very able men and three or four hundred well-educated men.

The diet and rough exercise secure a certain amount of old Norse power. A fop will fight, and in exigent circumstances will play the manly

part. In seeing these youths I believed I saw
already an advantage in vigor and color and
general habit, over their contemporaries in the
American colleges.[1] No doubt much of the
power and brilliancy of the reading-men is
merely constitutional or hygienic. With a hard-
ier habit and resolute gymnastics, with five miles
more walking, or five ounces less eating, or with
a saddle and gallop of twenty miles a day, with
skating and rowing-matches, the American would
arrive at as robust exegesis and cheery and hila-
rious tone. I should readily concede these
advantages, which it would be easy to acquire,
if I did not find also that they read better than
we, and write better.

English wealth falling on their school and university training, makes a systematic reading of
the best authors, and to the end of a knowledge
how the things whereof they treat really stand :
whilst pamphleteer or journalist, reading for an
argument for a party, or reading to write, or at
all events for some by-end imposed on them,
must read meanly and fragmentarily. Charles I.
said that he understood English law as well as
a gentleman ought to understand it.

Then they have access to books; the rich
libraries collected at every one of many thou-

sands of houses, give an advantage not to be attained by a youth in this country, when one thinks how much more and better may be learned by a scholar who, immediately on hearing of a book, can consult it, than by one who is on the quest, for years, and reads inferior books because he cannot find the best.

Again, the great number of cultivated men keep each other up to a high standard. The habit of meeting well-read and knowing men teaches the art of omission and selection.

Universities are of course hostile to geniuses, which, seeing and using ways of their own, discredit the routine: as churches and monasteries persecute youthful saints. Yet we all send our sons to college, and, though he be a genius, the youth must take his chance. The university must be retrospective. The gale that gives direction to the vanes on all its towers blows out of antiquity. Oxford is a library, and the professors must be librarians. And I should as soon think of quarrelling with the janitor for not magnifying his office by hostile sallies into the street, like the Governor of Kertch or Kinburn,' as of quarrelling with the professors for not admiring the young neologists who pluck the beards of Euclid and Aristotle, or for not attempting themselves to fill their vacant shelves as original writers.

It is easy to carp at colleges, and the college, if we will wait for it, will have its own turn. Genius exists there also, but will not answer a call of a committee of the House of Commons. It is rare, precarious, eccentric and darkling. England is the land of mixture and surprise, and when you have settled it that the universities are moribund, out comes a poetic influence from the heart of Oxford,[1] to mould the opinions of cities, to build their houses as simply as birds their nests, to give veracity to art and charm mankind, as an appeal to moral order always must. But besides this restorative genius, the best poetry of England of this age, in the old forms, comes from two graduates at Cambridge.[2]

CHAPTER XIII

RELIGION

NO people at the present day can be explained by their national religion. They do not feel responsible for it; it lies far outside of them. Their loyalty to truth and their labor and expenditure rest on real foundations, and not on a national church. And English life, it is evident, does not grow out of the Athanasian creed, or the Articles, or the Eucharist. It is with religion as with marriage. A youth marries in haste; afterwards, when his mind is opened to the reason of the conduct of life, he is asked what he thinks of the institution of marriage and of the right relations of the sexes? 'I should have much to say,' he might reply, 'if the question were open, but I have a wife and children, and all question is closed for me.' In the barbarous days of a nation, some *cultus* is formed or imported; altars are built, tithes are paid, priests ordained. The education and expenditure of the country take that direction, and when wealth, refinement, great men, and ties to the world supervene, its prudent men say, Why fight against Fate, or lift these absurdities which are

now mountainous? Better find some niche or
crevice in this mountain of stone which religious
ages have quarried and carved, wherein to bestow
yourself, than attempt anything ridiculously and
dangerously above your strength, like removing it.[1]

In seeing old castles and cathedrals, I sometimes say, as to-day in front of Dundee Church
tower, which is eight hundred years old, 'This
was built by another and a better race than any
that now look on it.'[2] And plainly there has
been great power of sentiment at work in this
island, of which these buildings are the proofs;
as volcanic basalts show the work of fire which
has been extinguished for ages. England felt
the full heat of the Christianity which fermented
Europe, and drew, like the chemistry of fire, a
firm line between barbarism and culture. The
power of the religious sentiment put an end to
human sacrifices, checked appetite, inspired the
crusades, inspired resistance to tyrants, inspired
self-respect, set bounds to serfdom and slavery,
founded liberty, created the religious architecture, — York, Newstead, Westminster, Fountains Abbey, Ripon, Beverley and Dundee, —
works to which the key is lost, with the sentiment which created them; inspired the English

Bible, the liturgy, the monkish histories, the chronicle of Richard of Devizes.' The priest translated the Vulgate, and translated the sanctities of old hagiology into English virtues on English ground. It was a certain affirmative or aggressive state of the Caucasian races. Man awoke refreshed by the sleep of ages. The violence of the northern savages exasperated Christianity into power. It lived by the love of the people. Bishop Wilfrid manumitted two hundred and fifty serfs, whom he found attached to the soil. The clergy obtained respite from labor for the boor on the Sabbath and on church festivals. "The lord who compelled his boor to labor between sunset on Saturday and sunset on Sunday, forfeited him altogether." The priest came out of the people and sympathized with his class. The church was the mediator, check and democratic principle, in Europe. Latimer, Wicliffe, Arundel, Cobham, Antony Parsons, Sir Harry Vane, George Fox, Penn, Bunyan are the democrats, as well as the saints of their times. The Catholic Church, thrown on this toiling, serious people, has made in fourteen centuries a massive system, close fitted to the manners and genius of the country, at once domestical and stately. In the long time, it has blended with

everything in heaven above and the earth beneath. It moves through a zodiac of feasts and
fasts, names every day of the year, every town
and market and headland and monument, and
has coupled itself with the almanac, that no court
can be held, no field ploughed, no horse shod,
without some leave from the church. All max-
ims of prudence or shop or farm are fixed and
dated by the church. Hence its strength in the
agricultural districts. The distribution of land
into parishes enforces a church sanction to every
civil privilege; and the gradation of the clergy,
— prelates for the rich and curates for the poor,
— with the fact that a classical education has
been secured to the clergyman, makes them
" the link which unites the sequestered peasantry
with the intellectual advancement of the age." [1]

The English Church has many certificates to
show of humble effective service in humanizing
the people, in cheering and refining men, feeding, healing and educating. It has the seal of
martyrs and confessors; the noblest books; a
sublime architecture; a ritual marked by the
same secular merits, nothing cheap or purchas-
able.

From this slow-grown church important re-
actions proceed; much for culture, much for

giving a direction to the nation's affection and will to-day. The carved and pictured chapel — its entire surface animated with image and emblem — made the parish-church a sort of book and Bible to the people's eye.

Then, when the Saxon instinct had secured a service in the vernacular tongue, it was the tutor and university of the people. In York minster, on the day of the enthronization of the new archbishop, I heard the service of evening prayer read and chanted in the choir. It was strange to hear the pretty pastoral of the betrothal of Rebecca and Isaac, in the morning of the world, read with circumstantiality in York minster, on the 13th January, 1848, to the decorous English audience, just fresh from the Times newspaper and their wine, and listening with all the devotion of national pride. That was binding old and new to some purpose. The reverence for the Scriptures is an element of civilization, for thus has the history of the world been preserved and is preserved. Here in England every day a chapter of Genesis, and a leader in the Times.

Another part of the same service on this occasion was not insignificant. Handel's coronation anthem, *God save the King*, was played by

Dr. Camidge on the organ, with sublime effect. The minster and the music were made for each other. It was a hint of the part the church plays as a political engine. From his infancy, every Englishman is accustomed to hear daily prayers for the Queen, for the royal family and the Parliament, by name; and this lifelong consecration cannot be without influence on his opinions.

The universities also are parcel of the ecclesiastical system, and their first design is to form the clergy. Thus the clergy for a thousand years have been the scholars of the nation.

The national temperament deeply enjoys the unbroken order and tradition of its church; the liturgy, ceremony, architecture; the sober grace, the good company, the connection with the throne and with history, which adorn it. And whilst it endears itself thus to men of more taste than activity, the stability of the English nation is passionately enlisted to its support, from its inextricable connection with the cause of public order, with politics and with the funds.[1]

Good churches are not built by bad men; at least there must be probity and enthusiasm somewhere in the society. These minsters were neither built nor filled by atheists. No church has had more learned, industrious or devoted men; plenty of "clerks and bishops, who, out of their gowns, would turn their backs on no man."[1] Their architecture still glows with faith in immortality. Heats and genial periods arrive in history, or, shall we say, plenitudes of Divine Presence, by which high tides are caused in the human spirit, and great virtues and talents appear, as in the eleventh, twelfth, thirteenth, and again in the sixteenth and seventeenth centuries, when the nation was full of genius and piety.

But the age of the Wicliffes, Cobhams, Arundels, Beckets; of the Latimers, Mores, Cranmers; of the Taylors, Leightons, Herberts; of the Sherlocks and Butlers, is gone. Silent revolutions in opinion have made it impossible that men like these should return, or find a place in their once sacred stalls. The spirit that dwelt in this church has glided away to animate other activities, and they who come to the old shrines find apes and players rustling the old garments.

The religion of England is part of good-breeding.[2] When you see on the continent the well-dressed Englishman come into his ambassador's chapel and put his face for silent prayer into his smooth-brushed hat, you cannot help

feeling how much national pride prays with
him, and the religion of a gentleman. So far is
he from attaching any meaning to the words,
that he believes himself to have done almost
the generous thing, and that it is very conde-
scending in him to pray to God. A great duke
said on the occasion of a victory, in the House
of Lords, that he thought the Almighty God
had not been well used by them, and that it
would become their magnanimity, after so great
successes, to take order that a proper acknowledgment be made. It is the church of the
gentry, but it is not the church of the poor.
The operatives do not own it, and gentlemen
lately testified in the House of Commons that
in their lives they never saw a poor man in a
ragged coat inside a church.

The torpidity on the side of religion of the
vigorous English understanding shows how
much wit and folly can agree in one brain.
Their religion is a quotation ; their church is a
doll ; and any examination is interdicted with
screams of terror. In good company you expect
them to laugh at the fanaticism of the vulgar ;
but they do not ; they are the vulgar.[1]

The English, in common perhaps with Chris-
tendom in the nineteenth century, do not respect

power, but only performance; value ideas only for an economic result. Wellington esteems a saint only as far as he can be an army chaplain: " Mr. Briscoll, by his admirable conduct and good sense, got the better of Methodism, which had appeared among the soldiers and once among the officers." They value a philosopher as they value an apothecary who brings bark or a drench; and inspiration is only some blow-pipe, or a finer mechanical aid.

I suspect that there is in an Englishman's brain a valve that can be closed at pleasure, as an engineer shuts off steam. The most sensible and well-informed men possess the power of thinking just so far as the bishop in religious matters, and as the chancellor of the exchequer in politics. They talk with courage and logic, and show you magnificent results, but the same men who have brought free trade or geology to their present standing, look grave and lofty and shut down their valve as soon as the conversation approaches the English Church. After that, you talk with a box-turtle.¹

The action of the university, both in what is taught and in the spirit of the place, is directed more on producing an English gentleman, than a saint or a psychologist. It ripens a bishop,

and extrudes a philosopher. I do not know
that there is more cabalism in the Anglican than
in other churches, but the Anglican clergy are
identified with the aristocracy. They say here,
that if you talk with a clergyman, you are sure
to find him well-bred, informed and candid: he
entertains your thought or your project with
sympathy and praise. But if a second clergyman come in, the sympathy is at an end: two
together are inaccessible to your thought, and
whenever it comes to action, the clergyman
invariably sides with his church.

The Anglican Church is marked by the grace
and good sense of its forms, by the manly
grace of its clergy. The gospel it preaches is
'By taste are ye saved.' It keeps the old structures in repair, spends a world of money in
music and building, and in buying Pugin ¹ and
architectural literature. It has a general good
name for amenity and mildness. It is not in
ordinary a persecuting church; it is not inquisi-
torial, not even inquisitive; is perfectly well-
bred, and can shut its eyes on all proper occasions. If you let it alone, it will let you alone.
But its instinct is hostile to all change in politics, literature, or social arts. The church has
not been the founder of the London University,

of the Mechanics' Institutes, of the Free School, of whatever aims at diffusion of knowledge. The Platonists of Oxford are as bitter against this heresy, as Thomas Taylor.[1]

The doctrine of the Old Testament is the religion of England.[2] The first leaf of the New Testament it does not open. It believes in a Providence which does not treat with levity a pound sterling. They are neither transcendentalists nor Christians. They put up no Socratic prayer, much less any saintly prayer for the Queen's mind; ask neither for light nor right, but say bluntly, " Grant her in health and wealth long to live." And one traces this Jewish prayer in all English private history, from the prayers of King Richard, in Richard of Devizes' Chronicle,[3] to those in the diaries of Sir Samuel Romilly and of Haydon the painter. " Abroad with my wife," writes Pepys piously, " the first time that ever I rode in my own coach; which do make my heart rejoice and praise God, and pray him to bless it to me, and continue it."[4] The bill for the naturalization of the Jews (in 1753) was resisted by petitions from all parts of the kingdom, and by petition from the city of London, reprobating this bill, as " tending extremely to the dishonor of the Christian religion, and extremely injurious to the interests and commerce of the kingdom in general, and of the city of London in particular." [1]

But they have not been able to congeal humanity by act of Parliament. "The heavens journey still and sojourn not," and arts, wars, discoveries and opinion go onward at their own pace. The new age has new desires, new enemies, new trades, new charities, and reads the Scriptures with new eyes. [2] The chatter of French politics, the steam-whistle, the hum of the mill and the noise of embarking emigrants had quite put most of the old legends out of mind; so that when you came to read the liturgy to a modern congregation, it was almost absurd in its unfitness, and suggested a masquerade of old costumes.

No chemist has prospered in the attempt to crystallize a religion. It is endogenous, like the skin and other vital organs. A new statement every day. The prophet and apostle knew this, and the nonconformist confutes the conformists, by quoting the texts they must allow. It is the condition of a religion to require religion for its expositor. Prophet and apostle can only be rightly understood by prophet and apostle. The statesman knows that the reli-

v

gious element will not fail, any more than the
supply of fibrine and chyle; but it is in its
nature constructive, and will organize such a
church as it wants. The wise legislator will
spend on temples, schools, libraries, colleges,
but will shun the enriching of priests. If in any
manner he can leave the election and paying of
the priest to the people, he will do well. Like
the Quakers, he may resist the separation of a
class of priests, and create opportunity and
expectation in the society to run to meet natural endowment in this kind. But when wealth
accrues to a chaplaincy, a bishopric, or rector-
ship, it requires moneyed men for its stewards,
who will give it another direction than to the
mystics of their day. Of course, money will do
after its kind, and will steadily work to unspir-
itualize and unchurch the people to whom it
was bequeathed. The class certain to be excluded from all preferment are the religious, —
and driven to other churches; which is nature's
vis medicatrix.

The curates are ill paid, and the prelates are
overpaid. This abuse draws into the church
the children of the nobility and other unfit
persons who have a taste for expense. Thus a
bishop is only a surpliced merchant. Through

his lawn I can see the bright buttons of the
shopman's coat glitter. A wealth like that of
Durham makes almost a premium on felony.
Brougham, in a speech in the House of Commons
on the Irish elective franchise, said, "How
will the reverend bishops of the other house be
able to express their due abhorrence of the
crime of perjury, who solemnly declare in the
presence of God that when they are called upon
to accept a living, perhaps of £4000 a year, at
that very instant they are moved by the Holy
Ghost to accept the office and administration
thereof, and for no other reason whatever?"
The modes of initiation are more damaging
than custom-house oaths. The Bishop is elected
by the Dean and Prebends of the cathedral.
The Queen sends these gentlemen a *congé
d'élire*, or leave to elect; but also sends them
the name of the person whom they are to elect.
They go into the cathedral, chant and pray and
beseech the Holy Ghost to assist them in their
choice; and, after these invocations, invariably
find that the dictates of the Holy Ghost agree
with the recommendations of the Queen.

But you must pay for conformity. All goes
well as long as you run with conformists. But
you, who are an honest man in other particu-

lars, know that there is alive somewhere a man whose honesty reaches to this point also that he shall not kneel to false gods, and on the day when you meet him, you sink into the class of counterfeits. Besides, this succumbing has grave penalties. If you take in a lie, you must take in all that belongs to it. England accepts this ornamented national church, and it glazes the eyes, bloats the flesh, gives the voice a stertorous clang, and clouds the understanding of the receivers.

The English Church, undermined by German criticism, had nothing left but tradition; and was led logically back to Romanism. But that was an element which only hot heads could breathe: in view of the educated class, generally, it was not a fact to front the sun; and the alienation of such men from the church became complete.[1]

Nature, to be sure, had her remedy. Religious persons are driven out of the Established Church into sects, which instantly rise to credit and hold the Establishment in check.[2] Nature has sharper remedies, also. The English, abhorring change in all things, abhorring it most in matters of religion, cling to the last rag of form, and are dreadfully given to cant. The

English (and I wish it were confined to them,
but 't is a taint in the Anglo-Saxon blood in
both hemispheres), — the English and the
Americans cant beyond all other nations. The
French relinquish all that industry to them.
What is so odious as the polite bows to God, in
our books and newspapers? The popular press
is flagitious in the exact measure of its sancti-
mony, and the religion of the day is a theatrical
Sinai, where the thunders are supplied by the
property-man. The fanaticism and hypocrisy
create satire. Punch finds an inexhaustible
material. Dickens writes novels on Exeter-Hall
humanity. Thackeray exposes the heartless
high life. Nature revenges herself more sum-
marily by the heathenism of the lower classes.
Lord Shaftesbury calls the poor thieves together
and reads sermons to them, and they call it
'gas.' George Borrow' summons the Gypsies
to hear his discourse on the Hebrews in Egypt,
and reads to them the Apostles' Creed in Romany. "When I had concluded," he says, "I
looked around me. The features of the assembly were twisted, and the eyes of all turned
upon me with a frightful squint; not an individual present but squinted; the genteel Pepa,
the good-humored Chicharona, the Cosdami,

all squinted; the Gypsy jockey squinted worst
of all."

The church at this moment is much to be
pitied.[1] She has nothing left but possession. If
a bishop meets an intelligent gentleman and
reads fatal interrogations in his eyes, he has
no resource but to take wine with him.[2] False
position introduces cant, perjury, simony and
ever a lower class of mind and character into
the clergy: and, when the hierarchy is afraid
of science and education, afraid of piety, afraid of
tradition and afraid of theology, there is nothing
left but to quit a church which is no longer
one.[3]

But the religion of England, — is it the Established Church? no; is it the sects? no; they
are only perpetuations of some private man's
dissent, and are to the Established Church as
cabs are to a coach, cheaper and more convenient, but really the same thing. Where dwells
the religion? Tell me first where dwells electricity, or motion, or thought, or gesture. They
do not dwell or stay at all. Electricity cannot
be made fast, mortared up and ended, like London Monument or the Tower, so that you shall
know where to find it, and keep it fixed, as the
English do with their things, forevermore; it is

passing, glancing, gesticular; it is a traveller, a newness, a surprise, a secret, which perplexes them and puts them out.[1] Yet, if religion be the doing of all good, and for its sake the suffering of all evil, *souffrir de tout le monde, et ne faire souffrir personne*, that divine secret has existed in England from the days of Alfred to those of Romilly, of Clarkson and of Florence Nightingale, and in thousands who have no fame.

CHAPTER XIV

LITERATURE[1]

A STRONG common sense, which it is not easy to unseat or disturb, marks the English mind for a thousand years: a rude strength newly applied to thought, as of sailors and soldiers who had lately learned to read. They have no fancy, and never are surprised into a covert or witty word, such as pleased the Athenians and Italians, and was convertible into a fable not long after; but they delight in strong earthy expression, not mistakable, coarsely true to the human body, and, though spoken among princes, equally fit and welcome to the mob. This homeliness, veracity and plain style appear in the earliest extant works and in the latest. It imports into songs and ballads the smell of the earth, the breath of cattle, and, like a Dutch painter, seeks a household charm, though by pails and pans. They ask their constitutional utility in verse. The kail and herrings are never out of sight. The poet nimbly recovers himself from every sally of the imagination. The English muse loves the farmyard, the lane and market. She says, with De Staël, "I tramp in the mire with wooden shoes, whenever they would force me into the clouds." For the Englishman has accurate perceptions ; takes hold of things by the right end, and there is no slipperiness in his grasp. He loves the axe, the spade, the oar, the gun, the steam-pipe : he has built the engine he uses. He is materialist, economical, mercantile.[1] He must be treated with sincerity and reality ; with muffins, and not the promise of muffins ; and prefers his hot chop, with perfect security and convenience in the eating of it, to the chances of the amplest and Frenchiest bill of fare, engraved on embossed paper. When he is intellectual, and a poet or a philosopher, he carries the same hard truth and the same keen machinery into the mental sphere. His mind must stand on a fact. He will not be baffled, or catch at clouds, but the mind must have a symbol palpable and resisting. What he relishes in Dante is the vise-like tenacity with which he holds a mental image before the eyes, as if it were a scutcheon painted on a shield. Byron " liked something craggy to break his mind upon." A taste for plain strong speech, what is called a biblical style, marks the English. It is in Alfred and the Saxon Chronicle and in the Sagas of the Northmen. Latimer was homely. Hobbes was

perfect in the "noble vulgar speech." Donne,
Bunyan, Milton, Taylor, Evelyn, Pepys,
Hooker, Cotton and the translators wrote it.
How realistic or materialistic in treatment of his
subject is Swift. He describes his fictitious persons as if for the police. Defoe has no insecurity
or choice. Hudibras has the same hard mental-
ity, — keeping the truth at once to the senses
and to the intellect.

It is not less seen in poetry. Chaucer's hard
painting of his Canterbury pilgrims satisfies the
senses. Shakspeare, Spenser and Milton, in
their loftiest ascents, have this national grip and
exactitude of mind. This mental materialism
makes the value of English transcendental genius; in these writers and in Herbert, Henry
More, Donne and Sir Thomas Browne. The
Saxon materialism and narrowness, exalted into
the sphere of intellect, makes the very genius
of Shakspeare and Milton. When it reaches
the pure element, it treads the clouds as securely
as the adamant. Even in its elevations materialistic, its poetry is common sense inspired ; or
iron raised to white heat.

The marriage of the two qualities is in their
speech. It is a tacit rule of the language to
make the frame or skeleton of Saxon words,

and, when elevation or ornament is sought, to
interweave Roman, but sparingly; nor is a
sentence made of Roman words alone, without
loss of strength. The children and laborers use
the Saxon unmixed. The Latin unmixed is
abandoned to the colleges and Parliament.
Mixture is a secret of the English island; and,
in their dialect, the male principle is the Saxon,
the female, the Latin; and they are combined
in every discourse. A good writer, if he has
indulged in a Roman roundness, makes haste
to chasten and nerve his period by English
monosyllables.[1]

When the Gothic nations came into Europe
they found it lighted with the sun and moon of
Hebrew and of Greek genius. The tablets of
their brain, long kept in the dark, were finely
sensible to the double glory. To the images
from this twin source (of Christianity and art),
the mind became fruitful as by the incubation
of the Holy Ghost. The English mind flow-
ered in every faculty. The common sense was
surprised and inspired. For two centuries England was philosophic, religious, poetic. The
mental furniture seemed of larger scale: the
memory capacious like the storehouse of the
rains. The ardor and endurance of study, the

boldness and facility of their mental construction, their fancy and imagination and easy spanning of vast distances of thought, the enterprise or accosting of new subjects, and, generally, the easy exertion of power, — astonish, like the legendary feats of Guy of Warwick. The union of Saxon precision and Oriental soaring, of which Shakspeare is the perfect example, is shared in less degree by the writers of two centuries. I find not only the great masters out of all rivalry and reach, but the whole writing of the time charged with a masculine force and freedom.

There is a hygienic simpleness, rough vigor and closeness to the matter in hand even in the second and third class of writers ; and, I think, in the common style of the people, as one finds it in the citation of wills, letters and public documents ; in proverbs and forms of speech. The more hearty and sturdy expression may indicate that the savageness of the Norseman was not all gone. Their dynamic brains hurled off their words as the revolving stone hurls off scraps of grit. I could cite from the seventeenth century sentences and phrases of edge not to be matched in the nineteenth. Their poets by simple force of mind equalized themselves with the accumu-

lated science of ours. The country gentlemen
had a posset or drink they called October; and
the poets, as if by this hint, knew how to distil
the whole season into their autumnal verses : and
as nature, to pique the more, sometimes works
up deformities into beauty in some rare Aspasia or Cleopatra ; and as the Greek art wrought
many a vase or column, in which too long or
too lithe, or nodes, or pits and flaws are made
a beauty of;— so these were so quick and vital
that they could charm and enrich by mean and
vulgar objects.

A man must think that age well taught and
thoughtful, by which masques and poems, like
those of Ben Jonson, full of heroic sentiment in
a manly style, were received with favor. The
unique fact in literary history, the unsurprised reception of Shakspeare; — the reception proved
by his making his fortune; and the apathy proved
by the absence of all contemporary panegyric,—
seems to demonstrate an elevation in the mind
of the people. Judge of the splendor of a nation by the insignificance of great individuals in
it.' The manner in which they learned Greek
and Latin, before our modern facilities were yet
ready; without dictionaries, grammars, or in-
dexes, by lectures of a professor, followed by

their own searchings, — required a more robust memory, and coöperation of all the faculties; and their scholars, Camden, Usher, Selden, Mede, Gataker, Hooker, Taylor, Burton, Bentley, Brian Walton, acquired the solidity and method of engineers.[1]

The influence of Plato tinges the British genius. Their minds loved analogy; were cognizant of resemblances, and climbers on the staircase of unity.[2] 'T is a very old strife between those who elect to see identity and those who elect to see discrepancies; and it renews itself in Britain. The poets, of course, are of one part; the men of the world, of the other. But Britain had many disciples of Plato; — More, Hooker, Bacon, Sidney, Lord Brooke, Herbert, Browne, Donne, Spenser, Chapman, Milton, Crashaw, Norris, Cudworth, Berkeley, Jeremy Taylor.

Lord Bacon has the English duality. His centuries of observations on useful science, and his experiments, I suppose, were worth nothing. One hint of Franklin, or Watt, or Dalton, or Davy, or any one who had a talent for experiment, was worth all his lifetime of exquisite trifles. But he drinks of a diviner stream, and marks the influx of idealism into England.[3]

Where that goes, is poetry, health and progress. The rules of its genesis or its diffusion are not known. That knowledge, if we had it, would supersede all that we call science of the mind. It seems an affair of race, or of meta-chemistry; —the vital point being, how far the sense of unity, or instinct of seeking resemblances, predominated. For wherever the mind takes a step, it is to put itself at one with a larger class, discerned beyond the lesser class with which it has been conversant. Hence, all poetry and all affirmative action comes.

Bacon, in the structure of his mind, held of the analogists, of the idealists, or (as we popularly say, naming from the best example) Platonists. Whoever discredits analogy and requires heaps of facts before any theories can be attempted, has no poetic power, and nothing original or beautiful will be produced by him. Locke is as surely the influx of decomposition and of prose, as Bacon and the Platonists of growth. The Platonic is the poetic tendency; the so-called scientific is the negative and poisonous. 'T is quite certain that Spenser, Burns, Byron and Wordsworth will be Platonists, and that the dull men will be Lockists. Then politics and commerce will absorb from the educated class men of talents without genius, precisely because such have no resistance.

Bacon, capable of ideas, yet devoted to ends, required in his map of the mind, first of all, universality, or *prima philosophia;* the receptacle for all such profitable observations and axioms as fall not within the compass of any of the special parts of philosophy, but are more common and of a higher stage.[1] He held this element essential: it is never out of mind: he never spares rebukes for such as neglect it; believing that no perfect discovery can be made in a flat or level, but you must ascend to a higher science. " If any man thinketh philosophy and universality to be idle studies, he doth not consider that all professions are from thence served and supplied; and this I take to be a great cause that has hindered the progression of learning, because these fundamental knowledges have been studied but in passage." He explained himself by giving various quaint examples of the summary or common laws of which each science has its own illustration. He complains that " he finds this part of learning very deficient, the profounder sort of wits drawing a bucket now and then for their own use, but the spring-head unvisited. This was the *dry light* which did scorch and

offend most men's watery natures."[1] Plato had
signified the same sense, when he said, "All the
great arts require a subtle and speculative research into the law of nature, since loftiness of
thought and perfect mastery over every subject
seem to be derived from some such source as this.
This Pericles had, in addition to a great natural
genius. For, meeting with Anaxagoras, who
was a person of this kind, he attached himself
to him, and nourished himself with sublime
speculations on the absolute intelligence; and
imported thence into the oratorical art whatever
could be useful to it."[2]

A few generalizations always circulate in the
world, whose authors we do not rightly know,
which astonish, and appear to be avenues to vast
kingdoms of thought, and these are in the world
constants, like the Copernican and Newtonian
theories in physics. In England these may be
traced usually to Shakspeare, Bacon, Milton,
or Hooker, even to Van Helmont[3] and Behmen,
and do all have a kind of filial retrospect to
Plato and the Greeks. Of this kind is Lord
Bacon's sentence, that " Nature is commanded
by obeying her; " his doctrine of poetry, which
"accommodates the shows of things to the desires
of the mind," or the Zoroastrian definition of

poetry, mystical, yet exact, " apparent pictures
of unapparent natures ; " [1] Spenser's creed that
" soul is form, and doth the body make ; " [2] the
theory of Berkeley, that we have no certain assurance of the existence of matter ; [3] Doctor
Samuel Clarke's argument for theism from the
nature of space and time ; Harrington's political
rule that power must rest on land, [4] — a rule
which requires to be liberally interpreted ; the
theory of Swedenborg, so cosmically applied by
him, that the man makes his heaven and hell ;
Hegel's study of civil history, as the conflict of
ideas and the victory of the deeper thought ; the
identity-philosophy of Schelling, couched in the
statement that "all difference is quantitative."
So the very announcement of the theory of gravitation, of Kepler's three harmonic laws, and even
of Dalton's doctrine of definite proportions, finds
a sudden response in the mind, which remains
a superior evidence to empirical demonstrations.
I cite these generalizations, some of which are
more recent, merely to indicate a class. Not
these particulars, but the mental plane or the
atmosphere from which they emanate was the
home and element of the writers and readers in
what we loosely call the Elizabethan age (say,
in literary history, the period from 1575 to

1625), yet a period almost short enough to justify Ben Jonson's remark on Lord Bacon, — "About his time, and within his view, were born all the wits that could honor a nation, or help study."

Such richness of genius had not existed more than once before. These heights could not be maintained. As we find stumps of vast trees in our exhausted soils, and have received traditions of their ancient fertility to tillage, so history reckons epochs in which the intellect of famed races became effete. So it fared with English genius. These heights were followed by a meanness and a descent of the mind into lower levels ; the loss of wings ; no high speculation. Locke, to whom the meaning of ideas was unknown, became the type of philosophy, and his " understanding " the measure, in all nations, of the English intellect. His countrymen forsook the lofty sides of Parnassus, on which they had once walked with echoing steps, and disused the studies once so beloved ; the powers of thought fell into neglect.[1] The later English want the faculty of Plato and Aristotle, of grouping men in natural classes by an insight of general laws, so deep that the rule is deduced with equal precision from few subjects, or from one, as from

multitudes of lives. Shakspeare is supreme in
that, as in all the great mental energies. The
Germans generalize : the English cannot inter-
pret the German mind.' German science com-
prehends the English. The absence of the faculty in England is shown by the timidity which
accumulates mountains of facts, as a bad general
wants myriads of men and miles of redoubts to
compensate the inspirations of courage and
conduct.

The English shrink from a generalization.
" They do not look abroad into universality, or
they draw only a bucketful at the fountain of the
First Philosophy for their occasion, and do not
go to the spring-head." Bacon, who said this,
is almost unique among his countrymen in that
faculty ; at least among the prose-writers. Milton, who was the stair or high table-land to let
down the English genius from the summits of
Shakspeare, used this privilege sometimes in
poetry, more rarely in prose. For a long interval afterwards, it is not found. Burke was addicted to generalizing, but his was a shorter line ;
as his thoughts have less depth, they have less
compass. Hume's abstractions are not deep or
wise. He owes his fame to one keen observation, that no copula had been detected between

any cause and effect, either in physics or in thought; that the term cause and effect was loosely or gratuitously applied to what we know only as consecutive, not at all as causal.[1] Doctor Johnson's written abstractions have little value; the tone of feeling in them makes their chief worth.

Mr. Hallam, a learned and elegant scholar, has written the history of European literature for three centuries, — a performance of great ambition, inasmuch as a judgment was to be attempted on every book. But his eye does not reach to the ideal standards: the verdicts are all dated from London; all new thought must be cast into the old moulds. The expansive element which creates literature is steadily denied. Plato is resisted, and his school. Hallam is uniformly polite, but with deficient sympathy; writes with resolute generosity, but is unconscious of the deep worth which lies in the mystics, and which often outvalues as a seed of power and a source of revolution all the correct writers and shining reputations of their day. He passes in silence, or dismisses with a kind of contempt, the profounder masters: a lover of ideas is not only uncongenial, but unintelligible.[2] Hallam inspires respect by his know-

ledge and fidelity, by his manifest love of good
books, and he lifts himself to own better than
almost any the greatness of Shakspeare, and
better than Johnson he appreciates Milton.
But in Hallam, or in the firmer intellectual
nerve of Mackintosh, one still finds the same
type of English genius. It is wise and rich, but
it lives on its capital. It is retrospective. How
can it discern and hail the new forms that are
looming up on the horizon, new and gigantic
thoughts which cannot dress themselves out of
any old wardrobe of the past?

The essays, the fiction and the poetry of the
day have the like municipal limits. Dickens,
with preternatural apprehension of the language
of manners and the varieties of street life; with
pathos and laughter, with patriotic and still
enlarging generosity, writes London tracts. He
is a painter of English details, like Hogarth;
local and temporary in his tints and style, and
local in his aims. Bulwer, an industrious writer,
with occasional ability, is distinguished for his
reverence of intellect as a temporality, and appeals to the worldly ambition of the student.
His romances tend to fan these low flames.
Their novelists despair of the heart. Thackeray
finds that God has made no allowance for the

poor thing in his universe, — more's the pity, he thinks, — but 't is not for us to be wiser; we must renounce ideals and accept London.[1]

The brilliant Macaulay, who expresses the tone of the English governing classes of the day, explicitly teaches that *good* means good to eat, good to wear, material commodity; that the glory of modern philosophy is its direction on "fruit;" to yield economical inventions; and that its merit is to avoid ideas and avoid morals.[2] He thinks it the distinctive merit of the Baconian philosophy in its triumph over the old Platonic, its disentangling the intellect from theories of the all-Fair and all-Good, and pinning it down to the making a better sick chair and a better wine-whey for an invalid; — this not ironically, but in good faith; — that, "solid advantage," as he calls it, meaning always sensual benefit, is the only good. The eminent benefit of astronomy is the better navigation it creates to enable the fruit-ships to bring home their lemons and wine to the London grocer. It was a curious result, in which the civility and religion of England for a thousand years ends in denying morals and reducing the intellect to a sauce-pan. The critic hides his skepticism under the English cant of practical. To convince the reason, to touch the conscience, is romantic pretension. The fine arts fall to the ground. Beauty, except as luxurious commodity, does not exist. It is very certain, I may say in passing, that if Lord Bacon had been only the sensualist his critic pretends, he would never have acquired the fame which now entitles him to this patronage. It is because he had imagination, the leisures of the spirit, and basked in an element of contemplation out of all modern English atmospheric gauges, that he is impressive to the imaginations of men and has become a potentate not to be ignored. Sir David Brewster [1] sees the high place of Bacon, without finding Newton indebted to him, and thinks it a mistake. Bacon occupies it by specific gravity or levity, not by any feat he did, or by any tutoring more or less of Newton, etc., but as an effect of the same cause which showed itself more pronounced afterwards in Hooke, Boyle and Halley.[2]

Coleridge, a catholic mind, with a hunger for ideas; with eyes looking before and after to the highest bards and sages, and who wrote and spoke the only high criticism in his time, is one of those who save England from the reproach of no longer possessing the capacity to appreciate what rarest wit the island has yielded. Yet the misfortune of his life, his vast attempts but most inadequate performings, failing to accomplish any one masterpiece, — seems to mark the closing of an era.[1] Even in him, the traditional Englishman was too strong for the philosopher, and he fell into *accommodations;* and as Burke had striven to idealize the English State, so Coleridge ' narrowed his mind' in the attempt to reconcile the Gothic rule and dogma of the Anglican Church, with eternal ideas. But for Coleridge, and a lurking taciturn minority uttering itself in occasional criticism, oftener in private discourse, one would say that in Germany and in America is the best mind in England rightly respected. It is the surest sign of national decay, when the Bramins can no longer read or understand the Braminical philosophy.

In the decomposition and asphyxia that followed all this materialism, Carlyle was driven by his disgust at the pettiness and the cant, into the preaching of Fate. In comparison with all this rottenness, any check, any cleansing, though by fire, seemed desirable and beautiful. He saw little difference in the gladiators, or "the causes " for which they combated ; the one comfort was, that they were all going speedily into the abyss together. And his imagination, finding no nutriment in any creation, avenged itself by celebrating the majestic beauty of the laws of decay. The necessities of mental structure force all minds into a few categories; and where impatience of the tricks of men makes Nemesis amiable, and builds altars to the negative Deity, the inevitable recoil is to heroism or the gallantry of the private heart, which decks its immolation with glory, in the unequal combat of will against fate.[1]

Wilkinson, the editor of Swedenborg, the annotator of Fourier and the champion of Hahnemann, has brought to metaphysics and to physiology a native vigor, with a catholic perception of relations, equal to the highest attempts, and a rhetoric like the armory of the invincible knights of old. There is in the action of his mind a long Atlantic roll not known except in deepest waters, and only lacking what ought to accompany such powers, a manifest centrality. If his mind does not rest in immovable biases, perhaps the orbit is larger and the return is not yet: but a master should inspire a confidence that he will adhere to his convictions and give his present studies always the same high place.[2]

It would be easy to add exceptions to the limitary tone of English thought, and much more easy to adduce examples of excellence in particular veins; and if, going out of the region of dogma, we pass into that of general culture, there is no end to the graces and amenities, wit, sensibility and erudition of the learned class. But the artificial succor which marks all English performance appears in letters also: much of their æsthetic production is antiquarian and manufactured, and literary reputations have been achieved by forcible men, whose relation to literature was purely accidental, but who were driven by tastes and modes they found in vogue into their several careers. So, at this moment, every ambitious young man studies geology: so members of Parliament are made, and churchmen.

The bias of Englishmen to practical skill has reacted on the national mind. They are incapable of an inutility, and respect the five mechanic powers even in their song.[1] The voice of their modern muse has a slight hint of the steamwhistle, and the poem is created as an ornament and finish of their monarchy, and by no means as the bird of a new morning which forgets the past world in the full enjoyment of that which is forming. They are with difficulty ideal ; they are the most conditioned men, as if, having the best conditions, they could not bring themselves to forfeit them. Every one of them is a thousand years old and lives by his memory : and when you say this, they accept it as praise.

Nothing comes to the book-shops but politics, travels, statistics, tabulation and engineering; and even what is called philosophy and letters is mechanical in its structure, as if inspiration had ceased, as if no vast hope, no religion, no song of joy, no wisdom, no analogy existed any more. The tone of colleges and of scholars and of literary society has this mortal air. I seem to walk on a marble floor, where nothing will grow. They exert every variety of talent on a lower ground and may be said to live and act in a sub-mind. They have lost all commanding views in literature, philosophy and science.[1] A good Englishman shuts himself out of three fourths of his mind and confines himself to one fourth. He has learning, good sense, power of labor, and logic ; but a faith in the laws of the mind like that of Archimedes ; a belief like that of Euler and Kepler, that experience must follow and not lead the laws of the mind ; a devotion to the theory of politics like that of

Hooker and Milton and Harrington, the modern English mind repudiates.

I fear the same fàult lies in their science, since they have known how to make it repulsive and bereave nature of its charm; — though perhaps the complaint flies wider, and the vice attaches to many more than to British physicists. The eye of the naturalist must have a scope like nature itself, a susceptibility to all impressions, alive to the heart as well as to the logic of creation. But English science puts humanity to the door. It wants the connection which is the test of genius. The science is false by not being poetic. It isolates the reptile or mollusk it assumes to explain; whilst reptile or mollusk only exists in system, in relation. The poet only sees it as an inevitable step in the path of the Creator. But, in England, one hermit finds this fact, and another finds that, and lives and dies ignorant of its value. There are great exceptions, of John Hunter, a man of ideas; perhaps of Robert Brown, the botanist; and of Richard Owen, who has imported into Britain the German homologies, and enriched science with contributions of his own, adding sometimes the divination of the old masters to the unbroken power of labor in the English mind. But for the most part the natural science in England is out of its loyal alliance with morals, and is as void of imagination and free play of thought as conveyancing. It stands in strong contrast with the genius of the Germans, those semi-Greeks, who love analogy, and, by means of their height of view, preserve their enthusiasm and think for Europe.[1]

No hope, no sublime augury cheers the student, no secure striding from experiment onward to a foreseen law, but only a casual dipping here and there, like diggers in California " prospecting for a placer " that will pay.[2] A horizon of brass of the diameter of his umbrella shuts down around his senses. Squalid contentment with conventions, satire at the names of philosophy and religion, parochial and shop-till politics, and idolatry of usage, betray the ebb of life and spirit. As they trample on nationalities to reproduce London and Londoners in Europe and Asia, so they fear the hostility of ideas, of poetry, of religion, — ghosts which they cannot lay ; and, having attempted to domesticate and dress the Blessed Soul itself in English broadcloth and gaiters, they are tormented with fear that herein lurks a force that will sweep their system away. The artists say, " Nature puts them out ; " the scholars have become unideal.

They parry earnest speech with banter and
levity; they laugh you down, or they change
the subject. "The fact is," say they over their
wine, "all that about liberty, and so forth, is
gone by; it won't do any longer." The practical and comfortable oppress them with inexorable claims, and the smallest fraction of power
remains for heroism and poetry. No poet dares
murmur of beauty out of the precinct of his
rhymes. No priest dares hint at a Providence
which does not respect English utility. The
island is a roaring volcano of fate, of material
values, of tariffs and laws of repression, glutted
markets and low prices.

In the absence of the highest aims, of the
pure love of knowledge and the surrender to
nature, there is the suppression of the imagination, the priapism of the senses and the understanding; we have the factitious instead of the
natural; tasteless expense, arts of comfort, and
the rewarding as an illustrious inventor who-
soever will contrive one impediment more to
interpose between the man and his objects.[1]

Thus poetry is degraded and made ornamen-
tal. Pope and his school wrote poetry fit to put
round frosted cake. What did Walter Scott
write without stint? a rhymed traveller's guide

to Scotland.¹ And the libraries of verses they
print have this Birmingham character. How
many volumes of well-bred metre we must jin-
gle through, before we can be filled, taught, renewed! We want the miraculous; the beauty
which we can manufacture at no mill, — can
give no account of; the beauty of which Chaucer
and Chapman had the secret. The poetry of
course is low and prosaic; only now and then,
as in Wordsworth, conscientious; or in Byron,
passional; or in Tennyson, factitious. But if
I should count the poets who have contributed
to the Bible of existing England sentences of
guidance and consolation which are still glow-
ing and effective, — how few! Shall I find my
heavenly bread in the reigning poets? Where
is great design in modern English poetry? The
English have lost sight of the fact that poetry
exists to speak the spiritual law, and that no
wealth of description or of fancy is yet essen-
tially new and out of the limits of prose, until
this condition is reached. Therefore the grave
old poets, like the Greek artists, heeded their
designs, and less considered the finish. It was
their office to lead to the divine sources, out of
which all this, and much more, readily springs;
and, if this religion is in the poetry, it raises us

to some purpose and we can well afford some staidness or hardness, or want of popular tune in the verses.

The exceptional fact of the period is the genius of Wordsworth. He had no master but nature and solitude. " He wrote a poem," says Landor, " without the aid of war." His verse is the voice of sanity in a worldly and ambitious age. One regrets that his temperament was not more liquid and musical. He has written longer than he was inspired. But for the rest, he has no competitor.'

Tennyson is endowed precisely in points where Wordsworth wanted. There is no finer ear, nor more command of the keys of language. Color, like the dawn, flows over the horizon from his pencil, in waves so rich that we do not miss the central form. Through all his refinements, too, he has reached the public, — a certificate of good sense and general power, since he who aspires to be the English poet must be as large as London, not in the same kind as London, but in his own kind. But he wants a subject, and climbs no mount of vision to bring its secrets to the people. He contents himself with describing the Englishman as he is, and proposes no better. There are all degrees in poetry and we must be thankful for every beautiful talent. But it is only a first success, when the ear is gained. The best office of the best poets has been to show how low and uninspired was their general style, and that only once or twice they have struck the high chord.[1]

That expansiveness which is the essence of the poetic element, they have not. It was no Oxonian, but Hafiz, who said, " Let us be crowned with roses, let us drink wine, and break up the tiresome old roof of heaven into new forms." A stanza of the song of nature the Oxonian has no ear for, and he does not value the salient and curative influence of intellectual action, studious of truth without a by-end.

By the law of contraries, I look for an irresistible taste for Orientalism in Britain. For a self-conceited modish life, made up of trifles, clinging to a corporeal civilization, hating ideas, there is no remedy like the Oriental largeness. That astonishes and disconcerts English decorum. For once, there is thunder it never heard, light it never saw, and power which trifles with time and space. I am not surprised then to find an Englishman like Warren Hastings, who had been struck with the grand style of thinking in the Indian writings, deprecating

the prejudices of his countrymen while offering
them a translation of the Bhagvat. "Might I,
an unlettered man, venture to prescribe bounds
to the latitude of criticism, I should exclude, in
estimating the merit of such a production, all
rules drawn from the ancient or modern literature of Europe, all references to such sentiments or manners as are become the standards
of propriety for opinion and action in our own
modes, and, equally, all appeals to our revealed
tenets of religion and moral duty." [1] He goes
to bespeak indulgence to " ornaments of fancy
unsuited to our taste, and passages elevated to
a tract of sublimity into which our habits of
judgment will find it difficult to pursue them."
Meantime, I know that a retrieving power
lies in the English race which seems to make
any recoil possible ; in other words, there is at
all times a minority of profound minds existing
in the nation, capable of appreciating every
soaring of intellect and every hint of tendency.
While the constructive talent seems dwarfed
and superficial, the criticism is often in the
noblest tone and suggests the presence of the
invisible gods. I can well believe what I have
often heard, that there are two nations in England ; but it is not the Poor and the Rich, nor

is it the Normans and Saxons, nor the Celt and the Goth. These are each always becoming the other; for Robert Owen does not exaggerate the power of circumstance. But the two complex–ions, or two styles of mind, — the perceptive class, and the practical finality class, — are ever in counterpoise, interacting mutually: one in hopeless minorities; the other in huge masses; one studious, contemplative, experimenting; the other, the ungrateful pupil, scornful of the source whilst availing itself of the knowledge for gain; these two nations, of genius and of animal force, though the first consist of only a dozen souls [1] and the second of twenty millions, forever by their discord and their accord yield the power of the English State.

CHAPTER XV

THE TIMES

THE power of the newspaper is familiar in America and in accordance with our political system. In England, it stands in antagonism with the feudal institutions, and it is all the more beneficent succor against the secretive tendencies of a monarchy. The celebrated Lord Somers [1] " knew of no good law proposed and passed in his time, to which the public papers had not directed his attention." There is no corner and no night. A relentless inquisition drags every secret to the day, turns the glare of this solar microscope on every malfaisance, so as to make the public a more terrible spy than any foreigner; and no weakness can be taken advantage of by an enemy, since the whole people are already forewarned. Thus England rids herself of those incrustations which have been the ruin of old states. Of course, this inspection is feared. No antique privilege, no comfortable monopoly, but sees surely that its days are counted; the people are familiarized with the reason of reform, and, one by one, take away every argument of the obstructives. " So your

grace likes the comfort of reading the newspapers," said Lord Mansfield to the Duke of
Northumberland; "mark my words; you and
I shall not live to see it, but this young gentleman (Lord Eldon) may, or it may be a little
later; but a little sooner or later, these newspapers will most assuredly write the dukes of
Northumberland out of their titles and possessions, and the country out of its king." The
tendency in England towards social and political
institutions like those of America, is inevitable,
and the ability of its journals is the driving force.

England is full of manly, clever, well-bred
men who possess the talent of writing off-hand
pungent paragraphs, expressing with clearness
and courage their opinion on any person or performance. Valuable or not, it is a skill that is
rarely found, out of the English journals. The
English do this, as they write poetry, as they ride
and box, by being educated to it. Hundreds
of clever Praeds and Freres and Froudes and
Hoods and Hooks and Maginns and Mills and
Macaulays, make poems, or short essays for a
journal, as they make speeches in Parliament
and on the hustings, or as they shoot and ride.[1]
It is a quite accidental and arbitrary direction
of their general ability. Rude health and spirits,

an Oxford education and the habits of society
are implied, but not a ray of genius. It comes
of the crowded state of the professions, the
violent interest which all men take in politics,
the facility of experimenting in the journals, and
high pay.

The most conspicuous result of this talent
is the Times newspaper. No power in England is more felt, more feared, or more obeyed.
What you read in the morning in that journal,
you shall hear in the evening in all society.
It has ears everywhere, and its information is
earliest, completest and surest. It has risen,
year by year, and victory by victory, to its present authority. I asked one of its old contributors whether it had once been abler than it is
now? "Never," he said; "these are its palmiest
days." It has shown those qualities which are
dear to Englishmen, unflinching adherence to its
objects, prodigal intellectual ability and a tower-
ing assurance, backed by the perfect organization
in its printing-house and its world-wide network
of correspondence and reports. It has its own
history and famous trophies. In 1820, it adopted
the cause of Queen Caroline, and carried it
against the king. It adopted a poor-law system, and almost alone lifted it through. When

Lord Brougham was in power, it decided against him, and pulled him down. It declared war against Ireland, and conquered it. It adopted the League against the Corn Laws, and, when Cobden had begun to despair, it announced his triumph. It denounced and discredited the French Republic of 1848, and checked every sympathy with it in England, until it had enrolled 200,000 special constables to watch the Chartists and make them ridiculous on the 10th April. It first denounced and then adopted the new French Empire, and urged the French Alliance and its results.[1] It has entered into each municipal, literary and social question, almost with a controlling voice. It has done bold and seasonable service in exposing frauds which threatened the commercial community. Meantime, it attacks its rivals by perfecting its printing machinery, and will drive them out of circulation : for the only limit to the circulation of The Times is the impossibility of printing copies fast enough ; since a daily paper can only be new and seasonable for a few hours. It will kill all but that paper which is diametrically in opposition ; since many papers, first and last, have lived by their attacks on the leading journal.

The late Mr. Walter was printer of The

Times, and had gradually arranged the whole *matériel* of it in perfect system. It is told that when he demanded a small share in the proprietary and was refused, he said, "As you please, gentlemen; and you may take away The Times from this office when you will; I shall publish The New Times next Monday morning." The proprietors, who had already complained that his charges for printing were excessive, found that they were in his power, and gave him whatever he wished.

I went one day with a good friend to The Times office, which was entered through a pretty garden-yard in Printing-House Square. We walked with some circumspection, as if we were entering a powder-mill; but the door was opened by a mild old woman, and, by dint of some transmission of cards, we were at last conducted into the parlor of Mr. Morris, a very gentle person, with no hostile appearances. The statistics are now quite out of date, but I remember he told us that the daily printing was then 35,000 copies; that on the 1st March, 1848, the greatest number ever printed — 54,000 — were issued; that, since February, the daily circulation had increased by 8000 copies. The old press they were then using printed five or six thousand

sheets per hour; the new machine, for which they
were then building an engine, would print twelve
thousand per hour. Our entertainer confided us
to a courteous assistant to show us the establishment, in which, I think, they employed a hundred and twenty men. I remember I saw the reporters' room, in which they redact their hasty
stenographs, but the editor's room, and who is
in it, I did not see, though I shared the curiosity
of mankind respecting it.

The staff of The Times has always been made
up of able men. Old Walter, Sterling, Bacon,
Barnes, Alsiger, Horace Twiss, Jones Lloyd,
John Oxenford, Mr. Mosely, Mr. Bailey, have
contributed to its renown in their special departments.[1] But it has never wanted the first pens
for occasional assistance. Its private information
is inexplicable, and recalls the stories of Fouché's
police, whose omniscience made it believed that
the Empress Josephine must be in his pay. It
has mercantile and political correspondents in
every foreign city, and its expresses outrun the
despatches of the government. One hears anecdotes of the rise of its servants, as of the func-
tionaries of the India House. I was told of the
dexterity of one of its reporters, who, finding himself, on one occasion, where the magistrates had

strictly forbidden reporters, put his hands into
his coat-pocket, and with pencil in one hand and
tablet in the other, did his work.

The influence of this journal is a recognized
power in Europe, and, of course, none is more
conscious of it than its conductors. The tone of
its articles has often been the occasion of comment from the official organs of the continental
courts, and sometimes the ground of diplomatic
complaint. 'What would The Times say?' is
a terror in Paris, in Berlin, in Vienna, in Copenhagen and in Nepaul. Its consummate dis-
cretion and success exhibit the English skill of
combination. The daily paper is the work of
many hands, chiefly, it is said, of young men recently from the University, and perhaps reading
law in chambers in London. Hence the aca-
demic elegance and classic allusion which adorns
its columns. Hence, too, the heat and gallantry
of its onset. But the steadiness of the aim suggests the belief that this fire is directed and fed by
older engineers; as if persons of exact information, and with settled views of policy, supplied
the writers with the basis of fact and the object
to be attained, and availed themselves of their
younger energy and eloquence to plead the cause.
Both the council and the executive departments

gain by this division. Of two men of equal ability, the one who does not write but keeps his eye
on the course of public affairs, will have the
higher judicial wisdom. But the parts are kept
in concert, all the articles appear to proceed from
a single will. The Times never disapproves of
what itself has said, or cripples itself by apology for the absence of the editor, or the indiscretion of him who held the pen. It speaks out bluff
and bold, and sticks to what it says. It draws
from any number of learned and skilful contributors; but a more learned and skilful person su-
pervises, corrects, and co-ordinates. Of this
closet, the secret does not transpire. No writer
is suffered to claim the authorship of any paper;
everything good, from whatever quarter, comes
out editorially; and thus, by making the paper
everything and those who write it nothing, the
character and the awe of the journal gain.

The English like it for its complete information. A statement of fact in The Times is as
reliable as a citation from Hansard.[1] Then they
like its independence; they do not know, when
they take it up, what their paper is going to say:
but, above all, for the nationality and confidence
of its tone. It thinks for them all; it is their
understanding and day's ideal daguerreotyped.

When I see them reading its columns, they seem to me becoming every moment more British. It has the national courage, not rash and petulant, but considerate and determined. No dignity or wealth is a shield from its assault. It attacks a duke as readily as a policeman, and with the most provoking airs of condescension. It makes rude work with the Board of Admiralty. The Bench of Bishops is still less safe. One bishop fares badly for his rapacity, and another for his bigotry, and a third for his courtliness. It addresses occasionally a hint to Majesty itself, and sometimes a hint which is taken. There is an air of freedom even in their advertising columns, which speaks well for England to a foreigner. On the days when I arrived in London in 1847, I read, among the daily announcements, one offering a reward of fifty pounds to any person who would put a nobleman, described by name and title, late a member of Parliament, into any county jail in England, he having been convicted of obtaining money under false pretences.

Was never such arrogancy as the tone of this paper. Every slip of an Oxonian or Cantabrigian who writes his first leader assumes that we subdued the earth before we sat down to write this particular Times. One would think the

world was on its knees to The Times office for
its daily breakfast. But this arrogance is calculated. Who would care for it, if it "surmised,"
or "dared to confess," or "ventured to predict,"
etc.? No; *it is so*, and so it shall be.

The morality and patriotism of The Times
claim only to be representative, and by no means
ideal. It gives the argument, not of the majority, but of the commanding class. Its editors
know better than to defend Russia, or Austria,
or English vested rights, on abstract grounds.
But they give a voice to the class who at the
moment take the lead; and they have an instinct
for finding where the power now lies, which is
eternally shifting its banks. Sympathizing with,
and speaking for the class that rules the hour,
yet being apprised of every ground-swell, every
Chartist resolution, every Church squabble, every
strike in the mills, they detect the first trem-
blings of change. They watch the hard and
bitter struggles of the authors of each liberal
movement, year by year; watching them only
to taunt and obstruct them,—until, at last, when
they see that these have established their fact,
that power is on the point of passing to them,
they strike in with the voice of a monarch, astonish those whom they succor as much as those

whom they desert, and make victory sure. Of
course the aspirants see that The Times is one
of the goods of fortune, not to be won but by
winning their cause.

Punch is equally an expression of English
good sense, as the London Times. It is the
comic version of the same sense. Many of its
caricatures are equal to the best pamphlets, and
will convey to the eye in an instant the popular
view which was taken of each turn of public affairs. Its sketches are usually made by masterly
hands, and sometimes with genius; the delight
of every class, because uniformly guided by that
taste which is tyrannical in England. It is a new
trait of the nineteenth century, that the wit and
humor of England — as in Punch, so in the
humorists, Jerrold, Dickens, Thackeray, Hood
— have taken the direction of humanity and
freedom.[1]

The Times, like every important institution, shows the way to a better. It is a living
index of the colossal British power. Its existence honors the people who dare to print all
they know, dare to know all the facts and do
not wish to be flattered by hiding the extent of
the public disaster.[2] There is always safety in
valor. I wish I could add that this journal as-

pired to deserve the power it wields, by guidance of the public sentiment to the right. It is usually pretended, in Parliament and elsewhere, that the English press has a high tone, — which it has not. It has an imperial tone, as of a powerful and independent nation. But, as with other empires, its tone is prone to be official, and even officinal. The Times shares all the limitations of the governing classes, and wishes never to be in a minority. If only it dared to cleave to the right, to show the right to be the only expedient, and feed its batteries from the central heart of humanity, it might not have so many men of rank among its contributors, but genius would be its cordial and invincible ally ; it might now and then bear the brunt of formidable combinations, but no journal is ruined by wise courage. It would be the natural leader of British reform ; its proud function, that of being the voice of Europe, the defender of the exile and patriot against despots, would be more effectually discharged ; it would have the authority which is claimed for that dream of good men not yet come to pass, an International Congress ; and the least of its victories would be to give to England a new millennium of beneficent power.'

CHAPTER XVI

STONEHENGE

IT had been agreed between my friend Mr.
Carlyle and me, that before I left England we
should make an excursion together to Stonehenge, which neither of us had seen; and the project pleased my fancy with the double attraction
of the monument and the companion. It seemed
a bringing together of extreme points, to visit
the oldest religious monument in Britain in
company with her latest thinker, and one whose
influence may be traced in every contemporary
book. I was glad to sum up a little my experiences, and to exchange a few reasonable words
on the aspects of England with a man on whose
genius I set a very high value, and who had as
much penetration and as severe a theory of duty
as any person in it. On Friday, 7th July, we
took the South Western Railway through
Hampshire to Salisbury, where we found a carriage to convey us to Amesbury. The fine
weather and my friend's local knowledge of
Hampshire, in which he is wont to spend a part
of every summer, made the way short. There
was much to say, too, of the travelling Ameri-

v

cans and their usual objects in London. I
thought it natural that they should give some
time to works of art collected here which they
cannot find at home, and a little to scientific
clubs and museums, which, at this moment,
make London very attractive. But my philosopher was not contented. Art and ' high art ' is
a favorite target for his wit. "Yes, *Kunst* is a
great delusion, and Goethe and Schiller wasted
a great deal of good time on it : " — and he
thinks he discovers that old Goethe found this
out, and, in his later writings, changed his tone.
As soon as men begin to talk of art, architecture
and antiquities, nothing good comes of it.
He wishes to go through the British Museum
in silence, and thinks a sincere man will see
something and say nothing. In these days, he
thought, it would become an architect to consult
only the grim necessity, and say, ' I can build
you a coffin for such dead persons as you are,
and for such dead purposes as you have, but
you shall have no ornament.' ¹ For the science,
he had if possible even less tolerance, and compared the *savans* of Somerset House to the boy
who asked Confucius "how many stars in the
sky ? " Confucius replied, "he minded things
near him : " then said the boy, "how many

hairs are there in your eyebrows?" Confucius said, "he did n't know and did n't care."

Still speaking of the Americans, Carlyle complained that they dislike the coldness and exclusiveness of the English, and run away to France and go with their countrymen and are amused, instead of manfully staying in London, and confronting Englishmen and acquiring their culture, who really have much to teach them.

I told Carlyle that I was easily dazzled, and was accustomed to concede readily all that an Englishman would ask; I saw everywhere in the country proofs of sense and spirit, and success of every sort: I like the people; they are as good as they are handsome; they have everything and can do everything; but meantime, I surely know that as soon as I return to Massachusetts I shall lapse at once into the feeling, which the geography of America inevitably inspires, that we play the game with immense advantage; that there and not here is the seat and centre of the British race; and that no skill or activity can long compete with the prodigious natural advantages of that country, in the hands of the same race; and that England, an old and exhausted island, must one day be contented, like other parents to be strong only in her children. But this was a proposition which no Englishman of whatever condition can easily entertain.[1]

We left the train at Salisbury and took a carriage to Amesbury, passing by Old Sarum, a bare, treeless hill, once containing the town which sent two members to Parliament, — now, not a hut ; and, arriving at Amesbury, stopped at the George Inn. After dinner we walked to Salisbury Plain. On the broad downs, under the gray sky, not a house was visible, nothing but Stonehenge, which looked like a group of brown dwarfs in the wide expanse, — Stonehenge and the barrows, which rose like green bosses about the plain, and a few hayricks. On the top of a mountain, the old temple would not be more impressive. Far and wide a few shepherds with their flocks sprinkled the plain, and a bagman drove along the road. It looked as if the wide margin given in this crowded isle to this primeval temple were accorded by the veneration of the British race to the old egg out of which all their ecclesiastical structures and history had proceeded. Stonehenge is a circular colonnade with a diameter of a hundred feet, and enclosing a second and a third colonnade within. We walked round the stones and clambered over them, to wont ourselves with their strange aspect and groupings, and found a nook sheltered from the wind among them, where Carlyle lighted his cigar. It was pleasant to see that just this simplest of all simple structures — two upright stones and a lintel laid across — had long out-stood all later churches and all history, and were like what is most permanent on the face of the planet: these, and the barrows, — mere mounds (of which there are a hundred and sixty within a circle of three miles about Stonehenge), like the same mound on the plain of Troy, which still makes good to the passing mariner on Hellespont, the vaunt of Homer and the fame of Achilles. Within the enclosure grow butter-cups, nettles, and all around, wild thyme, daisy, meadowsweet, goldenrod, thistle and the carpet-ing grass. Over us, larks were soaring and sing-ing; — as my friend said, " the larks which were hatched last year, and the wind which was hatched many thousand years ago." We counted and measured by paces the biggest stones, and soon knew as much as any man can suddenly know of the inscrutable temple. There are ninety-four stones, and there were once probably one hun-dred and sixty. The temple is circular and un-covered, and the situation fixed astronomically,

— the grand entrances, here and at Abury, being placed exactly northeast, " as all the gates of the old cavern temples are." How came the stones here ? for these *sarsens,* or Druidical sandstones, are not found in this neighborhood. The *sacrificial stone,* as it is called, is the only one in all these blocks that can resist the action of fire, and as I read in the books, must have been brought one hundred and fifty miles.

On almost every stone we found the marks of the mineralogist's hammer and chisel. The nineteen smaller stones of the inner circle are of granite. I, who had just come from Professor Sedgwick's Cambridge Museum of megatheria and mastodons, was ready to maintain that some cleverer elephants or mylodonta had borne off and laid these rocks one on another. Only the good beasts must have known how to cut a well-wrought tenon and mortise, and to smooth the surface of some of the stones. The chief mystery is, that any mystery should have been allowed to settle on so remarkable a monument, in a country on which all the muses have kept their eyes now for eighteen hundred years. We are not yet too late to learn much more than is known of this structure. Some diligent Fellowes or Layard will arrive, stone by stone, at the whole history, by that exhaustive British sense and perseverance, so whimsical in its choice of objects, which leaves its own Stonehenge or Choir Gaur ' to the rabbits, whilst it opens pyramids and uncovers Nineveh. Stonehenge, in virtue of the simplicity of its plan and its good preservation, is as if new and recent; and, a thousand years hence, men will thank this age for the accurate history. We walked in and out and took again and again a fresh look at the uncanny stones. The old sphinx put our petty differences of nationality out of sight. To these conscious stones we two pilgrims were alike known and near. We could equally well revere their old British meaning. My philosopher was subdued and gentle. In this quiet house of destiny he happened to say, " I plant cypresses wherever I go, and if I am in search of pain, I cannot go wrong." The spot, the gray blocks and their rude order, which refuses to be disposed of, suggested to him the flight of ages and the succession of religions. The old times of England impress Carlyle much : he reads little, he says, in these last years, but *Acta Sanctorum;* the fifty-three volumes of which are in the London Library. He finds all English history therein. He can see, as he reads, the old Saint of Iona sitting there and writing, a man to men.' The *Acta Sanctorum* show plainly that the men of those times believed in God and in the immortality of the soul, as their abbeys and cathedrals testify: now, even the puritanism is all gone. London is pagan. He fancied that greater men had lived in England than any of her writers; and, in fact, about the time when those writers appeared, the last of these were already gone.

We left the mound in the twilight, with the design to return the next morning, and coming back two miles to our inn we were met by little showers, and late as it was, men and women were out attempting to protect their spread windrows. The grass grows rank and dark in the showery England. At the inn, there was only milk for one cup of tea. When we called for more, the girl brought us three drops. My friend was annoyed, who stood for the credit of an English inn, and still more the next morning, by the dog-cart, sole procurable vehicle, in which we were to be sent to Wilton. I engaged the local antiquary, Mr. Brown, to go with us to Stonehenge, on our way, and show us what he knew of the "astronomical" and "sacrificial" stones. I stood on the last, and he pointed to the upright, or rather, inclined stone, called the "astro-

nomical," and bade me notice that its top ranged
with the sky-line. "Yes." Very well. Now, at
the summer solstice, the sun rises exactly over
the top of that stone, and, at the Druidical temple at Abury, there is also an astronomical stone,
in the same relative position.

In the silence of tradition, this one relation
to science becomes an important clew; but we
were content to leave the problem with the rocks.
Was this the "Giants' Dance," which Merlin
brought from Killaraus, in Ireland, to be Uther
Pendragon's monument to the British nobles
whom Hengist slaughtered here, as Geoffrey of
Monmouth relates?[1] or was it a Roman work,
as Inigo Jones explained to King James; or
identical in design and style with the East Indian
temples of the sun, as Davies in the Celtic Researches maintains? Of all the writers, Stukeley
is the best. The heroic antiquary, charmed with
the geometric perfections of his ruin, connects
it with the oldest monuments and religion of the
world, and with the courage of his tribe, does
not stick to say, "the Deity who made the world
by the scheme of Stonehenge." He finds that
the *cursus*[2] on Salisbury Plain stretches across
the downs like a line of latitude upon the globe,
and the meridian line of Stonehenge passes

exactly through the middle of this *cursus*. But
here is the high point of the theory : the Druids
had the magnet; laid their courses by it; their
cardinal points in Stonehenge, Ambresbury,' and
elsewhere, which vary a little from true east and
west, followed the variations of the compass.
The Druids were Phœnicians. The name of
the magnet is *lapis Heracleus*, and Hercules was
the god of the Phœnicians. Hercules, in the
legend, drew his bow at the sun, and the sun-
god gave him a golden cup, with which he sailed
over the ocean. What was this, but a compass-
box? This cup or little boat, in which the magnet was made to float on water and so show the
north, was probably its first form, before it was
suspended on a pin. But science was an *arcanum*, and, as Britain was a Phœnician secret, so
they kept their compass a secret, and it was lost
with the Tyrian commerce. The golden fleece
again, of Jason, was the compass, — a bit of
loadstone, easily supposed to be the only one in
the world, and therefore naturally awakening the
cupidity and ambition of the young heroes of a
maritime nation to join in an expedition to obtain possession of this wise stone. Hence the
fable that the ship Argo was loquacious and
oracular. There is also some curious coincidence

in the names. Apollodorus makes *Magnes* the
son of *Æolus*, who married *Nais*. On hints like
these, Stukeley builds again the grand colonnade
into historic harmony, and computing backward
by the known variations of the compass, bravely
assigns the year 406 before Christ for the date
of the temple.

For the difficulty of handling and carrying
stones of this size, the like is done in all cities,
every day, with no other aid than horse-power.
I chanced to see, a year ago, men at work on
the substructure of a house in Bowdoin Square,
in Boston, swinging a block of granite of the
size of the largest of the Stonehenge columns,
with an ordinary derrick. The men were common masons, with paddies to help, nor did they
think they were doing anything remarkable. I
suppose there were as good men a thousand
years ago. And we wonder how Stonehenge was
built and forgotten. After spending half an hour
on the spot, we set forth in our dog-cart over
the downs for Wilton, Carlyle not suppressing
some threats and evil omens on the proprietors,
for keeping these broad plains a wretched sheep-
walk when so many thousands of English men
were hungry and wanted labor. But I heard
afterwards that it is not an economy to cultivate

this land, which only yields one crop on being broken up, and is then spoiled.

We came to Wilton and to Wilton Hall, — the renowned seat of the Earls of Pembroke, a house known to Shakspeare and Massinger, the frequent home of Sir Philip Sidney, where he wrote the Arcadia; where he conversed with Lord Brooke, a man of deep thought, and a poet, who caused to be engraved on his tomb-stone, " Here lies Fulke Greville, Lord Brooke, the friend of Sir Philip Sidney." It is now the property of the Earl of Pembroke, and the residence of his brother, Sidney Herbert, Esq., and is esteemed a noble specimen of the English manor-hall. My friend had a letter from Mr. Herbert to his housekeeper, and the house was shown. The state drawing-room is a double cube, 30 feet high, by 30 feet wide, by 60 feet long : the adjoining room is a single cube, of 30 feet every way. Although these apartments and the long library were full of good family portraits, Vandykes and other; and though there were some good pictures, and a quadrangle cloister full of antique and modern statuary, — to which Carlyle, catalogue in hand, did all too much justice, — yet the eye was still drawn to the windows, to a magnificent lawn, on

which grew the finest cedars in England. I had
not seen more charming grounds. We went out,
and walked over the estate. We crossed a bridge
built by Inigo Jones, over a stream of which
the gardener did not know the name (*Qu.*
Alph?)[1]; watched the deer; climbed to the
lonely sculptured summer-house, on a hill
backed by a wood; came down into the Italian
garden and into a French pavilion garnished
with French busts; and so again to the house,
where we found a table laid for us with bread,
meats, peaches, grapes and wine.

On leaving Wilton House, we took the
coach for Salisbury. The Cathedral, which was
finished six hundred years ago, has even a spruce
and modern air, and its spire is the highest in
England. I know not why, but I had been
more struck with one of no fame, at Coventry,
which rises three hundred feet from the ground,
with the lightness of a mullein plant, and not at
all implicated with the church. Salisbury is now
esteemed the culmination of the Gothic art in
England, as the buttresses are fully unmasked
and honestly detailed from the sides of the pile.
The interior of the Cathedral is obstructed by
the organ in the middle, acting like a screen. I
know not why in real architecture the hunger

of the eye for length of line is so rarely gratified. The rule of art is that a colonnade is more
beautiful the longer it is, and that *ad infinitum*.
And the nave of a church is seldom so long that
it need be divided by a screen.

We loitered in the church, outside the choir,
whilst service was said. Whilst we listened to
the organ, my friend remarked, the music is
good, and yet not quite religious, but somewhat
as if a monk were panting to some fine Queen
of Heaven. Carlyle was unwilling, and we did
not ask to have the choir shown us, but returned
to our inn, after seeing another old church of
the place.¹ We passed in the train Clarendon
Park, but could see little but the edge of a
wood, though Carlyle had wished to pay closer
attention to the birthplace of the Decrees of
Clarendon. At Bishopstoke we stopped, and
found Mr. H., who received us in his carriage, and took us to his house at Bishops
Waltham.²

On Sunday we had much discourse, on a
very rainy day. My friends asked, whether
there were any Americans?—any with an
American idea,—any theory of the right future
of that country? Thus challenged, I bethought
myself neither of caucuses nor congress, neither

of presidents nor of cabinet-ministers, nor of such
as would make of America another Europe. I
thought only of the simplest and purest minds;
I said, " Certainly yes; — but those who hold
it are fanatics of a dream which I should hardly
care to relate to your English ears, to which it
might be only ridiculous, — and yet it is the
only true." So I opened the dogma of no-
government and non-resistance, and anticipated
the objections and the fun, and procured a kind
of hearing for it. I said, it is true ·that I have
never seen in any country a man of sufficient
valor to stand for this truth, and yet it is plain
to me that no less valor than this can command
my respect. I can easily see the bankruptcy of
the vulgar musket-worship, — though great
men be musket-worshippers ; — and 't is certain
as God liveth, the gun that does not need another gun, the law of love and justice alone, can
effect a clean revolution. I fancied that one or
two of my anecdotes made some impression on
Carlyle, and I insisted that the manifest absurdity of the view to English feasibility could
make no difference to a gentleman ; that as to
our secure tenure of our mutton-chop and spin-
ach in London or in Boston, the soul might
quote Talleyrand, " *Monsieur, je n'en vois pas*

la nécessité." As I had thus taken in the conversation the saint's part, when dinner was announced, Carlyle refused to go out before me,
— " he was altogether too wicked." I planted
my back against the wall, and our host wittily
rescued us from the dilemma, by saying he was
the wickedest and would walk out first, then
Carlyle followed, and I went last.'

On the way to Winchester, whither our host
accompanied us in the afternoon, my friends
asked many questions respecting American
landscape, forests, houses, — my house, for example. It is not easy to answer these queries
well. There, I thought, in America, lies nature
sleeping, overgrowing, almost conscious, too
much by half for man in the picture, and so
giving a certain *tristesse*, like the rank vegetation of swamps and forests seen at night, steeped
in dews and rains, which it loves ; and on it
man seems not able to make much impression.
There, in that great sloven continent, in high
Alleghany pastures, in the sea-wide sky-skirted
prairie, still sleeps and murmurs and hides the
great mother, long since driven away from the
trim hedge-rows and over-cultivated garden of
England. And, in England, I am quite too
sensible of this. Every one is on his good be-

havior and must be dressed for dinner at six. So I put off my friends with very inadequate details, as best I could.

Just before entering Winchester we stopped at the Church of Saint Cross, and after looking though the quaint antiquity, we demanded a piece of bread and a draught of beer, which the founder, Henry de Blois, in 1136, commanded should be given to every one who should ask it at the gate. We had both, from the old couple who take care of the church. Some twenty people every day, they said, make the same demand. This hospitality of seven hundred years' standing did not hinder Carlyle from pronouncing a malediction on the priest who receives £2000 a year, that were meant for the poor, and spends a pittance on this small-beer and crumbs.

In the Cathedral I was gratified, at least by the ample dimensions. The length of line exceeds that of any other English church; being 556 feet, by 250 in breadth of transept. I think I prefer this church to all I have seen, except Westminster and York. Here was Canute buried, and here Alfred the Great was crowned and buried, and here the Saxon kings; and, later, in his own church, William of Wykeham.

v

It is very old : part of the crypt into which we went down and saw the Saxon and Norman arches of the old church on which the present stands, was built fourteen or fifteen hundred years ago. Sharon Turner, in his History of the Anglo-Saxons, says, " Alfred was buried at Winchester, in the Abbey he had founded there, but his remains were removed by Henry I. to the new Abbey in the meadows at Hyde, on the northern quarter of the city, and laid under the high altar. The building was destroyed at the Reformation, and what is left of Alfred's body now lies covered by modern buildings, or buried in the ruins of the old." William of Wykeham's shrine tomb was unlocked for us, and Carlyle took hold of the recumbent statue's marble hands and patted them affectionately, for he rightly values the brave man who built Windsor and this Cathedral and the School here and New College at Oxford. But it was growing late in the afternoon. Slowly we left the old house, and parting with our host, we took the train for London.

CHAPTER XVII

PERSONAL

IN these comments on an old journey, now revised after seven busy years have much changed men and things in England, I have abstained from reference to persons, except in the last chapter and in one or two cases where the fame of the parties seemed to have given the public a property in all that concerned them. I must further allow myself a few notices, if only as an acknowledgment of debts that cannot be paid. My journeys were cheered by so much kindness from new friends, that my impression of the island is bright with agreeable memories both of public societies and of households : and, what is nowhere better found than in England, a cultivated person fitly surrounded by a happy home, with

"Honor, love, obedience, troops of friends,"[1]

is of all institutions the best. At the landing in Liverpool I found my Manchester correspondent awaiting me, a gentleman whose kind reception was followed by a train of friendly and effective attentions which never rested whilst I remained in the country. A man of sense and of letters, the editor of a powerful local journal, he added to solid virtues an infinite sweetness and *bonhommie*. There seemed a pool of honey about his heart which lubricated all his speech and action with fine jets of mead. An equal good fortune attended many later accidents of my journey, until the sincerity of English kindness ceased to surprise. My visit fell in the fortunate days when Mr. Bancroft was the American Minister in London, and at his house, or through his good offices, I had easy access to excellent persons and to privileged places. At the house of Mr. Carlyle, I met persons eminent in society and in letters. The privileges of the Athenæum and of the Reform Clubs were hospitably opened to me, and I found much advantage in the circles of the "Geologic," the "Antiquarian" and the "Royal" Societies. Every day in London gave me new opportunities of meeting men and women who give splendor to society. I saw Rogers, Hallam, Macaulay, Milnes, Milman, Barry Cornwall, Dickens, Thackeray, Tennyson, Leigh Hunt, D'Israeli, Helps, Wilkinson, Bailey, Kenyon and Forster: the younger poets, Clough, Arnold and Patmore ; and among the men of science, Robert Brown, Owen, Sedg-

wick, Faraday, Buckland, Lyell, De la Beche,
Hooker, Carpenter, Babbage and Edward
Forbes.[1] It was my privilege also to converse
with Miss Baillie, with Lady Morgan, with Mrs.
Jameson and Mrs. Somerville.[2] A finer hospitality made many private houses not less known
and dear. It is not in distinguished circles that
wisdom and elevated characters are usually found,
or, if found, they are not confined thereto; and
my recollections of the best hours go back to
private conversations in different parts of the
kingdom, with persons little known. Nor am I
insensible to the courtesy which frankly opened
to me some noble mansions, if I do not adorn
my page with their names. Among the privileges
of London, I recall with pleasure two or three
signal days, one at Kew, where Sir William
Hooker showed me all the riches of the vast
botanic garden; one at the Museum, where Sir
Charles Fellowes explained in detail the history
of his Ionic trophy-monument; and still another,
on which Mr. Owen accompanied my country-
man Mr. H. and myself through the Hunterian
Museum.

The like frank hospitality, bent on real service, I found among the great and the humble,
wherever I went; in Birmingham, in Oxford, in

Leicester, in Nottingham, in Sheffield, in Manchester, in Liverpool. At Edinburgh, through the kindness of Dr. Samuel Brown, I made the acquaintance of De Quincey, of Lord Jeffrey, of Wilson, of Mrs. Crowe, of the Messrs. Chambers, and of a man of high character and genius, the short-lived painter, David Scott.

At Ambleside in March, 1848, I was for a couple of days the guest of Miss Martineau, then newly returned from her Egyptian tour. On Sunday afternoon I accompanied her to Rydal Mount. And as I have recorded a visit to Wordsworth, many years before, I must not forget this second interview. We found Mr. Wordsworth asleep on the sofa. He was at first silent and indisposed, as an old man suddenly waked before he had ended his nap; but soon became full of talk on the French news. He was nationally bitter on the French; bitter on Scotchmen, too. No Scotchman, he said, can write English. He detailed the two models, on one or the other of which all the sentences of the historian Robertson are framed. Nor could Jeffrey, nor the Edinburgh Reviewers write English, nor can * * *, who is a pest to the English tongue.¹ Incidentally he added, Gibbon cannot write English. The Edinburgh

Review wrote what would tell and what would sell. It had however changed the tone of its literary criticism from the time when a certain letter was written to the editor by Coleridge. Mrs. W. had the Editor's answer in her possession. Tennyson he thinks a right poetic genius, though with some affectation. He had thought an elder brother of Tennyson at first the better poet, but must now reckon Alfred the true one. . . . In speaking of I know not what style, he said, " to be sure, it was the manner, but then you know the matter always comes out of the manner." . ∴. He thought Rio Janeiro the best place in the world for a great capital city. . . . We talked of English national character. I told him it was not creditable that no one in all the country knew anything of Thomas Taylor, the Platonist, whilst in every American library his translations are found. I said, If Plato's Republic were published in England as a new book to-day, do you think it would find any readers ? — he confessed it would not : " And yet," he added after a pause, with that complacency which never deserts a true-born Englishman, " and yet we have embodied it all." [1]

His opinions of French, English, Irish and

Scotch, seemed rashly formulized from little anecdotes of what had befallen himself and members of his family, in a diligence or stage-coach. His face sometimes lighted up, but his conversation was not marked by special force or elevation. Yet perhaps it is a high compliment to the cultivation of the English generally, when we find such a man not distinguished. He had a healthy look, with a weather-beaten face, his face corrugated, especially the large nose.

Miss Martineau, who lived near him, praised him to me not for his poetry, but for thrift and economy; for having afforded to his country-neighbors an example of a modest household where comfort and culture were secured without any display. She said that in his early house-keeping at the cottage where he first lived, he was accustomed to offer his friends bread and plainest fare; if they wanted anything more, they must pay him for their board. It was the rule of the house. I replied that it evinced English pluck more than any anecdote I knew. A gentleman in the neighborhood told the story of Walter Scott's staying once for a week with Wordsworth, and slipping out every day, under pretence of a walk, to the Swan Inn for a cold cut and porter; and one day passing with Words-

worth the inn, he was betrayed by the landlord's
asking him if he had come for his porter. Of
course this trait would have another look in
London, and there you will hear from different
literary men that Wordsworth had no personal
friend, that he was not amiable, that he was
parsimonious, etc. Landor, always generous,
says that he never praised anybody. A gentleman in London showed me a watch that once
belonged to Milton, whose initials are engraved
on its face. He said he once showed this to
Wordsworth, who took it in one hand, then
drew out his own watch and held it up with the
other, before the company, but no one making
the expected remark, he put back his own in
silence. I do not attach much importance to
the disparagement of Wordsworth among London scholars. Who reads him well will know
that in following the strong bent of his genius,
he was careless of the many, careless also of the
few, self-assured that he should " create the taste
by which he is to be enjoyed." He lived long
enough to witness the revolution he had wrought,
and to " see what he foresaw." [1] There are torpid
places in his mind, there is something hard and
sterile in his poetry, want of grace and variety,
want of due catholicity and cosmopolitan scope :

he had conformities to English politics and traditions ; he had egotistic puerilities in the choice
and treatment of his subjects ; but let us say of
him that, alone in his time, he treated the human mind well, and with an absolute trust. His
adherence to his poetic creed rested on real
inspirations. The Ode on Immortality is the
high-water mark which the intellect has reached
in this age. New means were employed, and
new realms added to the empire of the muse,
by his courage.[1]

CHAPTER XVIII

RESULT

ENGLAND is the best of actual nations. It is no ideal framework, it is an old pile built in different ages, with repairs, additions and makeshifts; but you see the poor best you have got. London is the epitome of our times, and the Rome of to-day. Broad-fronted, broad-bottomed Teutons, they stand in solid phalanx foursquare to the points of compass; they constitute the modern world, they have earned their vantage ground and held it through ages of adverse possession. They are well marked and differing from other leading races. England is tender-hearted. Rome was not. England is not so public in its bias; private life is its place of honor. Truth in private life, untruth in public, marks these home-loving men. Their political conduct is not decided by general views, but by internal intrigues and personal and family interest. They cannot readily see beyond England. The history of Rome and Greece, when written by their scholars, degenerates into English party pamphlets. They cannot see beyond England, nor in England can they transcend the interests of the governing classes. "English principles" mean a primary regard to the interests of property.' England, Scotland and Ireland combine to check the colonies. England and Scotland combine to check Irish manufactures and trade. England rallies at home to check Scotland. In England, the strong classes check the weaker. In the home population of near thirty millions, there are but one million voters. The Church punishes dissent, punishes education. Down to a late day, marriages performed by dissenters were illegal. A bitter class-legislation gives power to those who are rich enough to buy a law. The game-laws are a proverb of oppression. Pauperism incrusts and clogs the state, and in hard times becomes hideous. In bad seasons, the porridge was diluted. Multitudes lived miserably by shell-fish and sea-ware. In cities, the children are trained to beg, until they shall be old enough to rob. Men and women were convicted of poisoning scores of children for burial-fees. In Irish districts, men deteriorated in size and shape, the nose sunk, the gums were exposed, with diminished brain and brutal form. During the Australian emigration, multitudes were rejected by the commissioners as being too emaciated for useful colonists. During the Russian war, few of those that offered as recruits were found up to the medical standard, though it had been reduced.

The foreign policy of England, though ambitious and lavish of money, has not often been generous or just. It has a principal regard, to the interest of trade, checked however by the aristocratic bias of the ambassador, which usually puts him in sympathy with the continental Courts. It sanctioned the partition of Poland, it betrayed Genoa, Sicily, Parma, Greece, Turkey, Rome and Hungary.[1]

Some public regards they have. They have abolished slavery in the West Indies and put an end to human sacrifices in the East. At home they have a certain statute hospitality. England keeps open doors, as a trading country must, to all nations. It is one of their fixed ideas, and wrathfully supported by their laws in unbroken sequence for a thousand years. In *Magna Charta* it was ordained that all " merchants shall have safe and secure conduct to go out and come into England, and to stay there, and to pass as well by land as by water, to buy and sell by the ancient allowed customs, without any evil toll, except in time of war, or when they shall be of any nation at war with us." It is a statute and obliged hospitality and peremptorily maintained. But this shop-rule had one magnificent effect. It extends its cold unalterable courtesy to political exiles of every opinion, and is a fact which might give additional light to that portion of the planet seen from the farthest star. But this perfunctory hospitality puts no sweetness into their unaccommodating manners, no check on that puissant nationality which makes their existence incompatible with all that is not English.

What we must say about a nation is a superficial dealing with symptoms. We cannot go deep enough into the biography of the spirit who never throws himself entire into one hero, but delegates his energy in parts or spasms to vicious and defective individuals. But the wealth of the source is seen in the plenitude of English nature. What variety of power and talent; what facility and plenteousness of knighthood, lordship, ladyship, royalty, loyalty; what a proud chivalry is indicated in "Collins's Peerage," through eight hundred years! What dignity resting on what reality and stoutness! What courage in war, what sinew in labor, what cunning workmen, what inventors and engineers, what seamen and pilots, what clerks and scholars! No one man

and no few men can represent them. It is a
people of myriad personalities. Their many-
headedness is owing to the advantageous position of the middle class, who are always the source
of letters and science. Hence the vast plenty of
their æsthetic production. As they are many-
headed, so they are many-nationed: their colonization annexes archipelagoes and continents,
and their speech seems destined to be the universal language of men. I have noted the reserve
of power in the English temperament. In the
island, they never let out all the length of all
the reins, there is no Berserker rage, no aban-
donment or ecstasy of will or intellect, like that
of the Arabs in the time of Mahomet, or like
that which intoxicated France in 1789. But
who would see the uncoiling of that tremendous
spring, the explosion of their well-husbanded
forces, must follow the swarms which pouring
now for two hundred years from the British
islands, have sailed and rode and traded and
planted through all climates, mainly following
the belt of empire, the temperate zones, carrying the Saxon seed, with its instinct for liberty
and law, for arts and for thought, — acquiring
under some skies a more electric energy than
the native air allows, — to the conquest of the

globe. Their colonial policy, obeying the necessities of a vast empire, has become liberal.
Canada and Australia have been contented with
substantial independence. They are expiating
the wrongs of India by benefits; first, in works
for the irrigation of the peninsula, and roads, and
telegraphs; and secondly, in the instruction of
the people, to qualify them for self-government,
when the British power shall be finally called
home.

Their mind is in a state of arrested develop-
ment,[1] — a divine cripple like Vulcan; a blind
savant like Huber[2] and Sanderson. They do
not occupy themselves on matters of general and
lasting import, but on a corporeal civilization,
on goods that perish in the using. But they read
with good intent, and what they learn they in-
carnate. The English mind turns every abstrac-
tion it can receive into a portable utensil, or a
working institution. Such is their tenacity and
such their practical turn, that they hold all they
gain. Hence we say that only the English race
can be trusted with freedom, — freedom which
is double-edged and dangerous to any but
the wise and robust. The English designate the
kingdoms emulous of free institutions, as the
sentimental nations. Their culture is not an

outside varnish, but is thorough and secular in
families and the race. They are oppressive with
their temperament, and all the more that they
are refined. I have sometimes seen them walk
with my countrymen when I was forced to allow
them every advantage, and their companions
seemed bags of bones.

There is cramp limitation in their habit of
thought, sleepy routine, and a tortoise's instinct
to hold hard to the ground with his claws, lest
he should be thrown on his back. There is a
drag of inertia which resists reform in every
shape;—law-reform, army-reform, extension of
suffrage, Jewish franchise, Catholic emancipation,—the abolition of slavery, of impressment,
penal code and entails. They praise this drag,
under the formula that it is the excellence of the
British constitution that no law can anticipate
the public opinion. These poor tortoises must
hold hard, for they feel no wings sprouting at
their shoulders. Yet somewhat divine warms
at their heart and waits a happier hour. It hides
in their sturdy will. "Will," said the old philosophy, "is the measure of power," and personality is the token of this race. *Quid vult
valde vult.* What they do they do with a will.
You cannot account for their success by their

v

Christianity, commerce, charter, common law,
Parliament, or letters, but by the contumacious
sharp-tongued energy of English *naturel*, with
a poise impossible to disturb, which makes all
these its instruments. They are slow and reti-
cent, and are like a dull good horse which lets
every nag pass him, but with whip and spur
will run down every racer in the field. They
are right in their feeling, though wrong in their
speculation.

The feudal system survives in the steep inequality of property and privilege, in the limited
franchise, in the social barriers which confine
patronage and promotion to a caste, and still
more in the submissive ideas pervading these
people. The fagging of the schools is repeated
in the social classes. An Englishman shows no
mercy to those below him in the social scale, as
he looks for none from those above him; any
forbearance from his superiors surprises him,
and they suffer in his good opinion. But the
feudal system can be seen with less pain on
large historical grounds. It was pleaded in
mitigation of the rotten borough, that it worked
well, that substantial justice was done. Fox,
Burke, Pitt, Erskine, Wilberforce, Sheridan,
Romilly, or whatever national man, were by

this means sent to Parliament, when their return by large constituencies would have been
doubtful. So now we say that the right measures of England are the men it bred; that it
has yielded more able men in five hundred years
than any other nation; and, though we must
not play Providence and balance the chances of
producing ten great men against the comfort
of ten thousand mean men, yet retrospectively,
we may strike the balance and prefer one Alfred,
one Shakspeare, one Milton, one Sidney, one
Raleigh, one Wellington, to a million foolish
democrats.

The American system is more democratic,
more humane; yet the American people do not
yield better or more able men, or more inventions or books or benefits than the English.
Congress is not wiser or better than Parliament.
France has abolished its suffocating old *régime*,
but is not recently marked by any more wisdom
or virtue.

The power of performance has not been exceeded, — the creation of value. The English
have given importance to individuals, a principal end and fruit of every society. Every man
is allowed and encouraged to be what he is,
and is guarded in the indulgence of his whim.

" Magna Charta," said Rushworth, " is such a fellow that he will have no sovereign." By this general activity and by this sacredness of individuals, they have in seven hundred years evolved the principles of freedom. It is the land of patriots, martyrs, sages and bards, and if the ocean out of which it emerged should wash it away, it will be remembered as an island famous for immortal laws, for the announcements of original right which make the stone tables of liberty.

CHAPTER XIX

SPEECH AT MANCHESTER

A FEW days after my arrival at Manchester, in November, 1847, the Manchester Athenæum gave its annual Banquet in the Free-Trade Hall. With other guests, I was invited to be present and to address the company. In looking over recently a newspaper-report of my remarks, I incline to reprint it, as fitly expressing the feeling with which I entered England, and which agrees well enough with the more deliberate results of better acquaintance recorded in the foregoing pages. Sir Archibald Alison, the historian, presided, and opened the meeting with a speech. He was followed by Mr. Cobden, Lord Brackley and others, among whom was Mr. Cruikshank, one of the contributors to Punch.' Mr. Dickens's letter of apology for his absence was read. Mr. Jerrold, who had been announced, did not appear. On being introduced to the meeting I said: —

Mr. Chairman and Gentlemen: It is pleasant to me to meet this great and brilliant company, and doubly pleasant to see the faces of so many distinguished persons on this platform.

But I have known all these persons already.
When I was at home, they were as near to me as
they are to you. The arguments of the League
and its leader are known to all the friends of
free trade. The gayeties and genius, the political, the social, the parietal wit of Punch go duly
every fortnight to every boy and girl in Boston
and New York. Sir, when I came to sea, I found
the History of Europe, by Sir A. Alison, on the
ship's cabin table, the property of the captain;
— a sort of programme or play-bill to tell the
seafaring New Englander what he shall find
on his landing here. And as for Dombey, sir,
there is no land where paper exists to print on,
where it is not found; no man who can read,
that does not read it, and, if he cannot, he
finds some charitable pair of eyes that can, and
hears it.

But these things are not for me to say; these
compliments, though true, would better come
from one who felt and understood these merits
more. I am not here to exchange civilities with
you, but rather to speak of that which I am sure
interests these gentlemen more than their own
praises; of that which is good in holidays and
working-days, the same in one century and in
another century. That which lures a solitary

American in the woods with the wish to see England, is the moral peculiarity of the Saxon race, — its commanding sense of right and wrong, the love and devotion to that, — this is the imperial trait, which arms them with the sceptre of the globe.[1] It is this which lies at the foundation of that aristocratic character, which certainly wanders into strange vagaries, so that its origin is often lost sight of, but which, if it should lose this, would find itself paralyzed ; and in trade and in the mechanic's shop, gives that honesty in performance, that thoroughness and solidity of work which is a national characteristic. This conscience is one element, and the other is that loyal adhesion, that habit of friendship, that homage of man to man, running through all classes, — the electing of worthy persons to a certain fraternity, to acts of kindness and warm and stanch support, from year to year, from youth to age, — which is alike lovely and honorable to those who render and those who receive it ; which stands in strong contrast with the superficial attachments of other races, their excessive courtesy and short-lived connection.

You will think me very pedantic, gentlemen, but holiday though it be, I have not the smallest interest in any holiday except as it celebrates real and not pretended joys;¹ and I think it just, in this time of gloom and commercial disaster, of affliction and beggary in these districts, that, on these very accounts I speak of, you should not fail to keep your literary anniversary. I seem to hear you say, that for all that is come and gone yet, we will not reduce by one chaplet or one oak-leaf the braveries of our annual feast. For I must tell you, I was given to understand in my childhood that the British island from which my forefathers came was no lotus-garden, no paradise of serene sky and roses and music and merriment all the year round, no, but a cold, foggy, mournful country, where nothing grew well in the open air but robust men and virtuous women, and these of a wonderful fibre and endurance; that their best parts were slowly revealed; their virtues did not come out until they quarrelled; they did not strike twelve the first time; good lovers, good haters, and you could know little about them till you had seen them long, and little good of them till you had seen them in action; that in prosperity they were moody and dumpish, but in adversity they were grand. Is it not true, sir, that the wise ancients did not praise the ship parting with flying colors from the port, but only that

brave sailor which came back with torn sheets
and battered sides, stript of her banners, but
having ridden out the storm? And so, gentlemen, I feel in regard to this aged England, with
the possessions, honors and trophies, and also
with the infirmities of a thousand years gathering around her, irretrievably committed as she
now is to many old customs which cannot be
suddenly changed; pressed upon by the trans-
itions of trade and new and all incalculable
modes, fabrics, arts, machines and competing
populations. I see her not dispirited, not weak,
but well remembering that she has seen dark
days before; — indeed with a kind of instinct
that she sees a little better in a cloudy day, and
that in storm of battle and calamity she has a
secret vigor and a pulse like a cannon. I see
her in her old age, not decrepit, but young and
still daring to believe in her power of endurance
and expansion. Seeing this, I say, All hail!
mother of nations, mother of heroes, with
strength still equal to the time; still wise to
entertain and swift to execute the policy which
the mind and heart of mankind requires in the
present hour, and thus only hospitable to the
foreigner and truly a home to the thoughtful
and generous who are born in the soil. So be

it! so let it be! If it be not so, if the courage of England goes with the chances of a commercial crisis, I will go back to the capes of Massachusetts and my own Indian stream, and say to my countrymen, the old race are all gone, and the elasticity and hope of mankind must henceforth remain on the Alleghany ranges, or nowhere.[1]

NOTES

NOTES

ENGLISH TRAITS

WHEN Mr. Emerson first sailed for Europe he was, no doubt, urged by physicians to the measure to restore his shattered health, and by his friends, that his mind might be diverted by the scenes rich in beauty and association, and by the treasuries of art. Then and through life he cared little for travel for amusement; he had all the beauty and the facts that he wanted in the home horizon; but previous experience had shown him that even a rough sea-voyage was helpful, and this trip involved two, in sailing vessels. More than that, he had left his old life behind and now had opportunity to think out alone the plan of the life about to begin. Two or three men lived in Europe the courage and freshness of whose thoughts had cheered and helped him. In his sadder hours he almost wished to find a helpful Master, but his heart told him that this could not be, and thus answered the wish of his weakness: —

Journal, Rome, April 22, 1833. "Our stern experience replies with the tongue of all its days. Son of Man! it saith, all giving and receiving is reciprocal; you entertain angels unawares, but they cannot impart more or higher things than you are in a state to receive, but every step of your progress affects the intercourse you hold with all others; elevates its tone, deepens its meaning, sanctifies its spirit."

But, in the loneliness of an ancient city, and beset with sad memories of home, he felt assurance of helpful and strengthening friendship soon to come. He was to find that friend in Carlyle.

The verses "In Naples" are sad; the last lines of those "Written at Rome" (see Appendix to the *Poems*) show hope reviving with health: —

> Generously trust
> Thy fortune's web to the beneficent hand
> That until now has put his world in fee
> To thee. He watches for thee still. His love
> Broods over thee, and as God lives in heaven,
> However long thou walkest solitary,
> The hour of heaven shall come, the man appear.

Six months before, he had written in his journal: "I am cheered and instructed by this paper on Corn Law Rhymes in the *Edinburgh* by my Germanick new-light writer, whoever he be. He gives us confidence in our principles. He assures the truth-lover everywhere of sympathy. Blessed art that makes books, and so joins me to that stranger by this perfect railroad."

A few weeks later, having found the name of the unknown champion, he writes, — his sickness showing in the shade of doubt: —

"If Carlyle knew what an interest I have in his persistent Goodness, would it not be worth one effort more, one prayer, one mediation. But will he resist the deluge of bad example in England? One manifestation of goodness in a noble soul brings him in debt to all the beholders that he shall not betray their love and trust which he has awakened."

During his short stay in France on his way northward, of which there is no mention in *English Traits*, he made this entry: —

"Thus shall I write memoirs? A man who was no courtier, but loved men, went to Rome and there lived with boys.

He came to France and in Paris lives alone, and in Paris seldom speaks. If he do not see Carlyle in Edinburgh, he may go to America without saying anything in earnest except to Cranch and to Landor."

In lonely Nithsdale he found the friend he was seeking, not the teacher, and found also, as the Spirit had said, that, even with angels found unawares, all giving and receiving is reciprocal.

"That man came to see me," said Carlyle to Richard Monckton Milnes. "I don't know what brought him, and we kept him one night and then he left us. I saw him go up the hill; I did n't go with him to see him descend. I preferred to watch him mount and vanish like an angel."

But it was the Carlyle that God meant, that Emerson loved, and through all the years of their lives — fortunately with the ocean between — it was this Carlyle that he regarded and addressed, not the sad prophet denouncing the world of his day.

More contemporary side-lights will be given in the notes to the pages describing their intercourse.

The young man's wish to see Wordsworth and Coleridge was gratified, but little was gained by the sight at near range of these masters of poetry and philosophy.

Journal, September,'1833. "It occurs forcibly, yea, somewhat pathetically, that he who visits a man of genius out of admiration for his parts should treat him tenderly. 'T is odds but he will be disappointed. That is not the man of genius's fault, — he was honest and human, but the fault of his [the visitor's] own ignorance of the limits of human excellence. Let him feel then that his visit was unwelcome, and that he is indebted to the tolerance and good nature of his idol, and so spare him the abuse of his own reacting feelings, — the backstroke."

At the time of his first visit to England Mr. Emerson had published nothing and of course was entirely unknown. It is said that he preached once or twice in London; if so, of course at Unitarian chapels, but of this I find no authentic record. His friend, Mr. Alexander Ireland, then of Edinburgh, to whose charge Dr. Samuel Brown, "the chemical philosopher," had committed him, says in his memoirs,[1] that he heard him deliver a discourse in the Unitarian Chapel in that city, and tells of the effect produced on his hearers. "It is almost needless to say that nothing like it had ever been heard by them before, and many of them did not know what to make of it. The originality of his thoughts, the consummate beauty of the language in which they were clothed, the calm dignity of his bearing . . . and the singular directness and simplicity of his manner, free from the least shadow of dogmatic assumption, made a deep impression upon me."

The second visit to England was made under quite other conditions. *Nature* and the two volumes of *Essays*, sent at first to a few friends, had found readers in England enough to warrant publication of editions there. Mr. Emerson's friends, those who knew him personally and those whom his writings had won him, wished to see him and hear his thoughts from his own lips. Mr. Ireland made Mr. William Lloyd Garrison, then returning to Boston, the bearer of a generous and urgent invitation to consider the project of a lengthened visit to England and the delivery of lectures in the chief towns, Mr. Ireland himself assuming the burden of the necessary correspondence and business arrangements. The proposal was seconded by friendly and hospitable letters from Carlyle.

He urged Mr. Emerson's coming on another score. "Un-

[1] *Ralph Waldo Emerson, his Life, Genius and Writings; A Biographical Sketch.* London: Simpkin, Marshall & Co., 1882.

questionably you would get an immense quantity of food for ideas, though perhaps not at all in the way you anticipate, in looking about among us: nay, if you even thought us *stupid*, there is something in the godlike indifference with which London will accept and sanction even that verdict — something highly instructive at least.''

Learning from a delayed letter that Emerson was actually on the seas, Carlyle sent with all urgency a letter to meet him on landing, saying, '' Know then, my Friend, that in verity your home is *here* . . . and here surely, if anywhere in the wide earth, there ought to be a brother's welcome and kind home waiting you! Yes, by Allah!''

He landed in the end of October, 1847. After a short visit to Carlyle, he returned to Manchester, where lived Mr. Ireland, of whom he said, '' he approves himself the king of all friends and helpful agents . . . active, unweariable, imperturbable.'' Thanks to his zeal and influence through his paper, the *Manchester Examiner*, Mr. Emerson found arrangements made for courses in Liverpool and Manchester, and lectures in the important towns in the midland and northern counties, which occupied him until February. Mechanics' institutes afforded him many of his audiences, in some respects like those of country Lyceums at home, and quite as agreeable to him as the gathering of more aristocratic hearers in London.

In February he went to Edinburgh. Mr. Ireland says, '' His four lectures created a great sensation in the Scottish metropolis and stirred the hearts of many independent thinkers. The orthodox of that firm stronghold of religious formalism were grieved and shocked, although Emerson, knowing the tone of feeling there, had, with the utmost delicacy, avoided such subjects as might bring him into direct contact with it.''

v

He quotes a hearer as saying, "What a quiet, calm conversation it is! It is not the seraph or burning one you see; it is the cherubic reason thinking aloud before you. It is a soul totally unsheathed you have to do with, and you ask, Is this a spirit's tongue sounding on its way? so solitary and severe seems its harmony."

During this visit to Edinburgh, David Scott, the painter, whom Mr. Emerson describes as "a noble Stoic sitting apart here among his rainbow allegories," insisted on his sitting for his portrait. This picture was bought, after Mr. Emerson's death, by near friends, who considered the expression and attitude to be characteristic of him when lecturing, and was given to the Concord Public Library. Its somewhat hard drawing and coloring is offset in a measure by the insight of the painter, in placing the rainbow behind the figure of the apostle of hope.

In the Spring Mr. Emerson went to London and there stayed through March and April, seeing many interesting and notable people and receiving much friendly hospitality, of which much is told by Mr. Ireland in his book, and in Mr. Emerson's own letters home included in Mr. Cabot's Memoir. This was the stormy period of Chartist demonstrations in England, and of actual revolution in France. Though warned of possible danger, Mr. Emerson crossed the Channel and spent most of May in Paris, then in full ferment, with his friend Arthur Hugh Clough, a fellow of Oxford and author of *The Bothie of Tober-na-Vuolich* and other poems. He returned to London and gave, at the Portman Square Literary and Scientific Institute, a course of six lectures. Mr. Ireland speaks of the audience as "the élite of the social and literary world of the Metropolis. Mr. and Mrs. Carlyle, the Duchess of Sutherland, Lady Byron and her daughter Ada (Lady Love-

lace), the Duke of Argyll, Dr. John Carlyle, William and
Mary Howitt, Douglas Jerrold, Mr. John Forster, Thackeray
and many other distinguished persons were among his hearers.
. . . During the delivery of this course a letter appeared in
the *London Examiner* urging a repetition of it at a price sufficiently low to admit of poor literary men hearing Emerson."
The writer of this letter, on behalf of "poets, critics, philosophers, historians, scholars, and the other divine paupers of
that class," urged that this be done "because Emerson is a
phenomenon whose like is not in the world, and to miss him
is to lose an important part out of the nineteenth century."
Mr. Emerson met this demand. He wrote home, "I must
make amends for my aristocratic lecturing in Edwards St. at
prices which exclude all *my* public by reading three of my
old chapters in Exeter Hall to a city association." This done,
he gladly sailed for home in July.

"I leave England," he wrote to Miss Margaret Fuller,
"with an increased respect for the Englishman. His stuff or
substance seems to be the best of the world. I forgive him his
pride. My respect is the more generous that I have no sympathy with him, only an admiration."

This was no doubt a true and concise statement of his feeling about the race of modern Englishmen as he met them.
He admired their comeliness and strength, as fine animals,
their executive ability and prowess at home and abroad; he
had experienced their open hospitality. Above all, he respected their honesty and their courage, physical and moral —
but he found few idealists. The remarkable honor and esteem in which he held the English has another reason. He
had been from childhood their debtor. When he thought of
the English it was the English from Alfred's time onward.
In books he had found his friends and his delight, and there

were almost no American books. In the nursery he began
with Miss Edgeworth and Bunyan, went on to Shakspeare,
Milton, and Spenser, knew Homer through Chapman and
Pope, owed Montaigne to Cotton's racy English; Scott and
Byron had carried him into realms of romance ; as a boy he
had rejoiced in Berkeley's idealism, and the poems of the holy
Herbert. Gibbon's majestic chapters and the eloquence of
Burke had stirred him. Bacon and Newton aroused his admiration, Coleridge had enlightened him, and, last, in Wordsworth, Landor, and especially Carlyle he had found thought
and stimulus and advancing courage.

The English authors represented England for him, and
through them he knew of their men of action, whether Warwick or Drake, Strafford or Cromwell or Hastings.

After Mr. Emerson's return, while preparing *Representative Men* for the press, he was reading lectures on " England," " Anglo-Saxon," " Norseman and English Influence
on Modern Civilization,", " English Poetry," " France or
Urbanity," " The Anglo-American," and thus gradually
brought his new material into shape for publication in *English
Traits.*

The book appeared in 1856. Carlyle thus welcomed it:
" I got your Book by post in the Highlands ; and had such
a day over it as falls rarely to my lot! Not for seven years
and more have I got hold of such a Book; — Book by a real
man, with eyes in his head; nobleness, wisdom, humor, and
many other things in the heart of him. Such Books do not
turn up often in the decade, in the century. In fact I believe
it to be worth all the Books ever written by New England
upon Old. Franklin might have written such a thing (in his
own way); no other since! We do very well with it here,
and the wise part of us *best.*"

Page 3, note 1. Mr. Wall, a young artist of New Bedford, with whom he had crossed the Simplon from Italy. The copy of Michael Angelo's Fates, which always hung in Mr. Emerson's study, was painted by Mr. Wall.

Page 4, note 1. Scott and Mackintosh had died in the previous year, and apparently not until his visit in 1847 did he meet Jeffrey, De Quincey, or Hallam. In the letters quoted in Mr. Cabot's *Memoir of Emerson*, the interesting account of his meeting with the first two is given. De Quincey, then over sixty years of age, "with a very handsome face, . . . a very gentle old man speaking with the greatest deliberation and softness, and so refined in speech and manners as to make one quite indifferent to his extremely plain and poor dress," came, wet through and muddy, having walked ten miles in the storm, to dine with Mr. Emerson at the invitation of Mrs. Crowe. He later invited Mr. Emerson to dine with him and his daughters, and attended his lecture.

Page 4, note 2. William Wilberforce, the friend and helper of Pitt, a member of Parliament from Hull. He introduced the bill for the abolition of the slave trade, and for years championed the measure against the planters and merchants until its final success.

Page 5, note 1. Horatio Greenough was born in Boston in 1805. His fine personality and his high thought interested Mr. Emerson when they met in Italy and through the sculptor's short life. He made the statue of Washington in front of the National Capitol and many other good works of sculpture, and also designed Bunker Hill Monument.

Page 8, note 1. Pierre Charron (1514–1603), a French philosopher of note and a Roman Catholic theologian. He wrote the *Traité des Trois Vérités* and the *Traité de la Sagesse*. Mr. Emerson's journals in 1830 show that he had been looking up the beliefs of Heracleitus, Xenophanes, Empedocles, and other ancient philosophers in De Gérando's *Histoire Comparée des Systèmes de Philosophie*. Richard Lucas, D. D. (1648–1715), wrote "Enquiry after Happiness" and "Practical Christianity, or an Account of the Holiness which the Gospel enjoins."

Page 8, note 2. A friend informs me that the following hexameters of Julius Cæsar, the only specimen of his verse that we have, are found in an extract from the life of Terentius by Suetonius, preserved by Donatus in the introduction to his commentary on this poet. (*Deperditorum Librorum Reliquiæ.*)

Tu quoque, tu in summis, o dimidiate Menander,
Poneris, et merito, puri sermonis amator.
Lenibus atque utinam scriptis adjuncta foret vis
Comica, ut æquato virtus polleret honore
Cum Græcis, neve hac despectus parte jaceres!
Unum hoc mæror ac doleo tibi deesse, Terenti.

Thou also art placed, and rightly, among the highest, O halved Menander,[1] lover of clear language, and oh that the comic gift had been added to thy graceful writing, so that thy power might be held in honor equal to the Greek, nor thou lie neglected on this account. This one thing I regret, and mourn thy lack in it, O Terence.

Page 10, note 1. It is fair to remember that fifty years ago there seemed small chance that an American book would find many readers in England, and also that the American public for whom it was written was a small number of persons, re-

[1] *Dimidiate* is difficult to render in English. It may mean *diminished*, or *in miniature*, or refer to the fact that Terence borrowed freely from Menander.

verent towards English writers. The book, however, reached
Landor twenty-three years after the conversation reported, and
he published a commentary entitled "An Open Letter from
W. S. Landor to R. W. Emerson" (printed at Bath),[1] some
of the corrections in which of Mr. Emerson's statements it is
proper to give below. The whole pamphlet is very entertain-
ing in its radical and revolutionary vehemence, yet, consider-
ing the temper of the man, singularly respectful and friendly.

In a letter to Carlyle in 1841 Mr. Emerson spoke thus of
his value of Landor: —

"Many years ago I have read a hundred fine memorable
things in the *Imaginary Conversations*, though I knew well
the faults of that book, and the *Pericles and Aspasia* within
two years has given me delight. I was introduced to the Man
in Florence . . . and his speech I remember was below his
writing. I love the rich variety of his mind, his proud tastes,
his penetrating glances, and the poetic loftiness of his sentiment, which rises now and then to the meridian, though with
the flight, I own, rather of the rocket than an orb, and ter-
minates sometimes by a sudden tumble."

In the following extracts are the more important corrections
and comments which Landor made on Mr. Emerson's report,
in the "Open Letter": —

MY DEAR SIR: —

Your *English Traits* have given me great pleasure ; and
they would have done so, even if I had been treated by
you with less favour. The short conversations we held at

---

[1] This pamphlet of twenty pages of comment on some five pages of *Eng-
lish Traits* may be found reprinted in *Literary Anecdotes of the Nineteenth
Century*, vol. ii., edited by W. Robertson Nicoll, M. A., LL. D., and
Thomas J. Wise. London, 1896.

my Tuscan Villa were insufficient for an estimate of my character and opinions. A few of these and only a few, of the least important, I may have modified since. Let me run briefly over them as I find them stated in your pages. Twenty-three years have not obliterated from my memory the traces of your visit, in company with that intelligent man and glorious sculptor, who was delegated to erect a statue in your capitol to the tutelary genius of America.

Speaking of Michael Angelo, he says, —

"I confess I have no relish for his prodigious *giblet pie* in the Capella Sistina, known throughout the world as his Last Judgment. Grand in architecture, he was no ordinary poet, no lukewarm patriot."

He says of Raffaelle, "The cartoons are his noblest works: they place him as high as is Correggio in the dome of Parma: nothing has been, or is likely to be, higher. . . . Let me say, before we go farther, that I do not think ' the Greek historians the only good ones.' "

He then praises Davila, Machiavelli, Voltaire, Michelet, Gibbon, Napier.

"Is it certain that I am indiscriminating in my judgment on Charron ? Never have I compared him with Montaigne ; but there is much of wisdom, and, what is remarkable in the earlier French authors, much of sincerity in him.

"I am sorry to have ' *pestered you with Southey*,' and to have excited the enquiry, ' *Who is Southey ?* ' I will answer the question. Southey is the poet who has written the most imaginative poem of any in our own times, English or Continental ; such is the *Curse of Kehama*. Southey is the proseman who has written the purest prose ; Southey is the critic, is the most cordial and the least invidious. Show me another of any note, without captiousness, without arrogance and without malignity.

> ' Slow rises worth by poverty depressed.'

But Southey raised it."

Speaking of his early poem " Gebir," he says that in an English journal " on the strength of this poem I am compared and preferred to Göthe. I am not too much elated. Neither in my youthful days, nor in any other have I thrown upon the world such trash as ' Werther ' and ' Wilhelm Meister,' nor flavored my poetry with the corrugated spicery of metaphysics. Nor could he have written in a lifetime any twenty, in a hundred or thereabout, of my Imaginary Conversations. My poetry I throw to the Scotch terriers growling at my feet. Fifty pages of Shelley contain more of pure poetry than a hundred of Göthe.

. . . .

" I do not ' undervalue Socrates.' Being the cleverest of the Sophists, he turned the fraternity into ridicule: he eluded the grasp of his antagonist by anointing with the oil of quibble all that was tangible and prominent. To compare his philosophy (if indeed you can catch it) with the philosophy of Epicurus and Epictetus, whose systems meet, is insanity.

" I do not ' despise entomology.' I am ignorant of it; as indeed of almost all science.

" I love also flowers and plants; but I know less about them than is known by a beetle or a butterfly.

" I must have been misunderstood, or have been culpably inattentive, if I said, ' I knew not Herschell [sic] by name.' The father's I knew well, from his giving to a star the baptismal one of that pernicious madman who tore America from England."

Mr. Emerson published in the *Dial* in 1841 a paper on Landor which is now included in the volume *Natural History of Intellect.*

Page 10, note 2. In his chapter on "Boston" in *Natural History of Intellect* Mr. Emerson says that amid the laborious and economical population of New England you may often find "that refinement which no education and no habit of society can bestow; . . . which unites itself by natural affinity to the highest minds of the world; . . . and . . . gave a hospitality in this country to the spirit of Coleridge and Wordsworth, and to the music of Beethoven, before yet their genius had found a hearty welcome in Great Britain." There is evidence that at the age of twenty-three Mr. Emerson had been interested in Coleridge, and by him in German thought. In 1829, in a letter to his Aunt Mary Emerson, he speaks of his pleasure in Coleridge's "Friend" and says, "He has a tone a little lower than greatness, but what a living soul, what a universal knowledge!" and speaks of him as one "whose philosophy compares with others much as astronomy with the other sciences; taking post at the centre, and, as from a specular mount, sending sovereign glances to the circumference of things." [1]

John Sterling in a letter to Emerson in 1841,[2] says: "In my boyhood, twenty years ago, I well remember that, with quite insignificant exceptions, all the active and daring minds which would not take for granted the Thirty-nine Articles and the Quarterly Review took refuge with teachers like Mackintosh and Jeffrey, or at highest Madame de Staël. Wordsworth and Coleridge were mystagogues lurking in

[1] For the whole passage on Coleridge, see Mr. Cabot's *Memoir of Emerson,* p. 161.

[2] *A Correspondence between John Sterling and Ralph Waldo Emerson.*

caverns, and German literature was thought of with a good deal less favour than we are now disposed to show towards that of China.''

In the last lecture of the course on English Literature given in the winter of 1835–36 before the Society for the Diffusion of Useful Knowledge, Mr. Emerson said that Coleridge's true merit was not that of a philosopher or of a poet, but of a critic. He praised his '' subtlety of discrimination, surpassing all men in the fineness of his distinctions,'' and added, '' He has taken the widest survey of the moral, intellectual, and social world. His *Biographia Literaria* is the best book of criticism in the English language ; nay, I do not know any to which a modern scholar can be so much indebted. His works are of very unequal interest.''

Page 10, note 3. Daniel Waterland, arch-deacon of Middlesex early in the eighteenth century, published polemical treatises against Arians and Deists.

Page 14, note 1. Mr. Emerson said to Mr. Ireland of Wordsworth and Carlyle: '' Am I, who have hung over their works in my chamber at home, not to see these men in the flesh, and thank them and interchange some thoughts with them, when I am passing their very doors ?''

Page 15, note 1. From Mr. Emerson's notebook : —

CARLISLE IN CUMBERLAND, AUG. 26 (1853).

I am just arrived in merry Carlisle from Dumfries. A white day in my years. I found the youth I sought in Scotland, and good and wise and pleasant he seems to me. Thomas Carlyle lives in the parish of Dunscore, sixteen miles from Dumfries, amid wild and desolate heathery hills and without a single companion in this region out of his own house. There he has his wife, a most accomplished and agreeable woman. Truth and peace and faith dwell with them and beautify

them. I never saw more amiableness than is in his countenance. He speaks broad Scotch with evident relish—'in London yonder;' I liked well 'aboot it,' 'Ay, Ay,' etc. Nothing can be better than his stories, — the philosophic
phrase, etc.

Page 15, note 2. Mr. John Albee in his *Remembrances*
speaks of Mr. Emerson's remarks on the daguerreotype of
Carlyle (profile) which he showed him. "He spoke of his
physiognomy, his heavy eyebrows and projecting base of the
forehead, underset by the heavy lower jaw and lip, between
which as millstones, he said, every humbug was sure to be
pulverized."

Page 16, note 1. "Tunc uno quoque hinc inde instante,
ut quam primum se impendentibus contumeliis eriperet, scrobem
coram fieri imperavit, dimensus ad corporis sui modulum,
componique simul, si qua invenirentur, frusta marmoris, et
aquam simul et ligna conferri curando mox cadaveri, flens ad
singula atqui identidem dictitans ; — *Qualis artifex pereo!*"
— Suetonius, *De Vita Cæsarum*, Liber VI., 49.

Which passage may be thus rendered: "Then with some
one on each side urging him to save himself as soon as possible from the impending indignities, he commanded that a
grave be made, in his presence, to his measure, and bits of
marble, if any could be there found, be put together, and also
water and wood to be brought for the disposing of the corpse
soon to be, weeping at everything that was done and repeatedly exclaiming, 'What an artificer dies in me.' "

Page 18, note 1. Of this visit, from a man then totally
unknown, to him "the solitariest, stranded, most helpless
creature that I have been for many years," his work rejected
by publishers, and apparently by the world, Carlyle wrote two
years afterwards: "Long shall we remember that Autumn

Sunday that landed him (out of Infinite Space) on the Craigen-
puttock wilderness, *not* to leave us as he found us." And
Mrs. Carlyle wrote: " Friend, who, years ago, in the Desert
descended upon us out of the clouds, as it were, and made one
day there look like enchantment or us, and left me weeping
that it was only one day."

Page 19, note 1. " John S[tuart] Mill, the best mind he
knows, — more purity, more force ; has worked himself clear
of Benthamism." — Journal.

Page 21, note 1. Mr. Landor in the " Open Letter "
rudely comments on this preference, " More fool he ! "

Page 23, note 1. Literally, *a gain forever*.

Page 24, note 1. In a letter to Mr. Ireland, Mr. Emerson thus spoke of this visit to Ambleside: " I spent a valuable
hour, and perhaps a half more, with Mr. Wordsworth, who
is in sound health at seventy-seven years and was full of talk.
He would even have walked with me on my way to Miss
Martineau's, but it began to rain, and I would not suffer it."

But he felt of Wordsworth and the lights of Edinburgh, as
he said in another of his letters: "They have nothing half
so good to give you near, as they had at a distance."

Miss Martineau had written of Mr. Emerson as she saw
him in America in 1836 : " There is a remarkable man in
the United States, without knowing whom it is not too much
to say that the United States cannot be fully known. I mean
by this, not only that he has powers and worth which constitute him an element in the estimate which is to be formed of
his country, but that his intellect and his character are the
opposite of those which the influences of his country and his
time are supposed almost necessarily to form. Great things are
expected of him."

Page 26, note 1. In answering Mr. Ireland's kindly

urged proposal, Mr. Emerson had said: "I feel no call to make a visit of literary propagandism in England. All my impulses of that kind would rather employ me at home." Yet he felt that the stimulus would be good for him, and writing later to Carlyle, whom he wished to see again, said: "I should find my account in the strong inducement of a new audience to finish pieces which have lain waiting with little hope for months and years. Ah then, if I dared, I should be glad to add some golden hours to my life in seeing you, now all full-grown and acknowledged amidst your own people, — to hear and speak is so little, yet so much."

Page 31, note 1. The voyage in a small coaster to Charleston and St. Augustine, which threatenings in his lungs obliged him to take in the winter of 1827.

Page 34, note 1. Count Vittorio Alfieri of Asti in Piedmont (1749–1803), an author of note, and especially a tragic dramatist.

Page 35, note 1. In his lecture "Boston" (printed in *Natural History of Intellect*) he says that those Englishmen who planted New England "were precisely the idealists of England," and Mr. Lowell in the Ode which he recited at the Old North Bridge on the One Hundredth Anniversary of Concord Fight, thus stated the issue : —

"Here English law and English thought
Against the might of England fought."

Page 36, note 1. This was William Chambers of Edinburgh.

Page 37, note 1. At that time the eager American students of philosophy and theology were going to Göttingen, Jena, and Leipsic, while the young doctors and scientific students flocked to the Sorbonne and the hospitals of Paris.

Page 37, note 2.   Add South Carolina, and you have more than an equivalent for the area of Scotland. — Mr. Emerson's note in First Edition.

Page 39, note 1.   Mr. Emerson had full knowledge of the dismal conditions of life described, for he spent his first two months in lecturing and visiting in "The Black Country."

Page 41, note 1.   "Et penitus, toto divisos orbe Britannos. (And within it [the ocean], the Britons, cut off from all the world.") — Virgil, *Æneid* I., 67.

Page 43, note 1.

   " Thank Him who isled us here, and roughly set
   His Briton in blown seas and storming showers."
Tennyson's " Ode on the Death of the Duke of Wellington."

   Mr. Emerson wrote that an Englishman said to the Persian Ambassador in London, " I am told that in your country you worship the sun." " So would you, if you ever saw him," replied the Persian.

Page 44, note 1.   *The Races, A Fragment,* by Robert Knox, M. D., London, 1850; republished in fuller form in 1862: *The Races of Men, A Philosophical Inquiry into the Influence of Race over the Destinies of Nations.*

Page 44, note 2.   Charles Pickering, naturalist to the exploring expedition sent out by the United States in 1838, under Commodore Wilkes ; author of *Races of Man* and works on the geographical distribution of animals and plants.

Page 48, note 1.   Mr. Emerson had read Lyell and heard of Lamarck's teachings through him and others, and on his second visit to England had taken great interest in the conversation of the men of science.

   That the imperative needs brought about by emigration, or other radical change of conditions, wrought variations in species, was the argument brought up by Lamarck against those who

pointed to Egyptian sculpture as showing the absolute persist-
ence of race-type in men and animals. The conditions in
Egypt, being constant, did not provoke variation.

Page 49, note 1. J. R. Green, in his *Short History of
the English People*, says that even in the reign of Richard II.
strikes and combinations became frequent among the lower
craftsmen in the towns.

Page 49, note 2.

> Roomy Eternity
> Casts her schemes rarely,
> And an æon allows
> For each quality and part
> Of the multitudinous
> And many-chambered heart.
>
> " Fragments on Life," *Poems*, Appendix.

Mr. Emerson took great interest in his pear orchard, which
he set out soon after settling in Concord, and every morning
in good weather, before going to his study, visited, to prune,
watch for caterpillars and borers, or gather the fruit. He had
Downing's book on Fruits. A few pages in this gave him
especial pleasure; namely, the account of the theory and successful experiments in the amelioration of fruits, by Dr. Van
Mons, professor at Louvain in the Netherlands. All through
Mr. Emerson's works crop out allusions to this hopeful theory
of Amelioration, to him symbolic.

This theory, full of parables, might be thus stated in very
condensed form: —

The aim of nature in the wild fruit-tree is only to produce
a vigorous tree, and perfect seeds for continuing the species.

The object of culture is to subdue excess of vegetation,
lessen coarseness of tree, reduce size of seeds, and increase the
pulp of the fruit.

There is always a tendency of improved fruits to return by seeds to the wild state, especially in seeds borne by old fruit-trees, yet they never quite return.

But the seeds of a young tree of a good sort, being itself in a state of amelioration, have the least tendency to retrograde, and are most likely to produce improved sorts.

There is a limit to perfection in fruits. When this is reached, the next generation will more probably produce bad fruit than if raised from seeds of an indifferent sort in the course of amelioration. Seeds of the oldest good fruits usually produce inferior sorts; those from *recent varieties* of bad fruit, if reproduced uninterruptedly under good conditions for several generations, will certainly yield good fruit.

Van Mons was constantly on the watch for trees in a *state of variation* for his experiments. In the fifth generation his seedlings mostly gave excellent fruit and bore in the third year.

In 1823 Van Mons's nurseries contained two thousand seedlings of merit.

To his teachings and work should be credited a share in strengthening Mr. Emerson's faith in Compensation and in Ascension.

Page 50, note 1. " *La Nature aime les croisements* " is a quotation appearing in the journals.

Page 53, note 1. In spite of his praise for Plato, argument was not only disagreeable to Mr. Emerson, but he felt that the heat engendered burned up the perception. " Truth ceases to be truth when polemically stated," he said.

Page 55, note 1. In his boyhood Mr. Emerson delighted in Ossian and later in the genuine remains of the British bards, Taliessin, Llewarch Hen, and the others. We are apt to think and speak of the Scotch as one people, but the difference is striking between the religion of the Saxon Lowlander, fanatic-

v

ally wedded to his Kirk's dour dogma, and delighting in argumentative theology, and the Celtic Highlander's faith in Spirit, associated with wild, free Nature and almost ancestor-worship.

Page 55, note 2. "It was in the consulship of Cæcilius Metellus and Papirius Carbo, six hundred and forty years after the founding of Rome, that we first heard the clash of the Cimbrian arms. From that date, reckoning down to the second consulship of the Emperor Trajan, gives an interval of some two hundred and ten years. Our conquest of Germany is taking us a long time.

"And during the process we have had many hard blows in return. Not the Samnites, nor the Carthaginians, nor the Spaniards, nor the Gauls, nor even the Parthians themselves, have oftener given us a lesson. The freemen of Germany are more spirited antagonists than all the subjects of King Arsaces." [1]

Tacitus then enumerates the disastrous defeats of Roman armies in Germany, ending with the crushing blow when Varus lost three legions, and thus ends : " Nec impune Caius Marius in Italia, divus Julius in Gallia, Drusus ac Nero et Germanicus in suis eos sedibus perculerunt."

Page 56, note 1.

> The gale that wrecked you on the sand,
> It helped my rowers to row;
> The storm is my best galley-hand
> And drives me where I go.
>
> "Northman," Quatrains, *Poems.*

Page 57, note 1. Heimskringla, or The Sea-Kings of

---

[1] From the *Germania* of Tacitus (xxxvii.), translated by R. B. Townshend, M. A. London, 1894.

Norway, translated and edited by Samuel Laing. London, 1844.

Page 60, note 1. This story, one of those which Mr. Emerson liked to read to his children, is in Laing's *Sea-Kings of Norway*, above mentioned.

Page 61, note 1. Throughout *English Traits* it appears that Mr. Emerson had been carried along in the tide of historical reaction that set in in the first half of the century. The merits of the Anglo-Saxon then shone out after long eclipse by Norman glory, — much as " Cromwell damned to everlasting fame " was established as the hero of England by Carlyle. The tendency of many books of that day showed a democratic recoil from aristocratic feudalism,. and withal the dislike of France by English writers told to the disadvantage of the vikings who had really been much civilized by French residence. So, as was natural, the pendulum of opinion for the time went to the Saxon extreme. Yet with regard to the Saxon conquest of Britain, Tennyson's picture —

> " Last, a heathen horde,
> Reddening the sky with fire and earth with blood,
> And on the spear which pierced the mother's heart
> Spitting the babe, brake over sea " —

is borne out by Freeman and Green in their histories, and the Norman Conquest was gentle and beneficent beside that of the exterminating Saxon. Freeman writes: " The English wiped out everything Celtic and everything Roman. . . . A more fearful blow never fell on any nation than the landing of the Angles and Saxons was to the Celt of Britain. But we may now be thankful for the barbarism and ferocity of our forefathers."

Of the Norseman settled on the Seine he says: " The

Scandinavians in Gaul embraced the creed, the language and the manners of their French neighbors, without losing a whit of their old Scandinavian vigor and love of adventure. The people thus formed became the foremost apostles alike of French Chivalry and Latin Christianity. . . . To free England he (the Norman) gave a line of tyrants. . . . But to England he gave also a conquering nobility which in a few years became as truly English in England, as it had become French in Normandy. . . . In a word, the indomitable vigor of the Scandinavian, joined to the buoyant vivacity of the Gaul, produced the conquering and ruling race of Europe. And yet that race, as a race, has vanished. It has everywhere been absorbed by the races which it has conquered.''

Page 62, note 1. In one of the lectures on England Mr. Emerson said: "Then came the Gothic nations, Belgian, Saxon, Dane, Northman. The Emperor Charles V. said that ' all the nobility of Europe came out of Scandia and from the stock of the Goths.' ''

Page 64, note 1. Sir Samuel Romilly (1757–1818), of Huguenot descent, was solicitor-general under the Grenville administration in 1806. In Parliament he bravely advocated political reform, abolition of the slave trade, Catholic emancipation, and mitigation of the criminal code. The success of the last measure did not come until after his death by his own hand while suffering from melancholia.

Page 64, note 2. Charles Reade's story, *It is Never too Late to Mend,* was an important tract in arousing public attention in England to these outrages. It may be interesting to mention that one of Mr. Emerson's friends and neighbors, John S. Keyes, sheriff of Middlesex, was greatly moved by this book, and gave copies of it to the officers of the county jail at East Cambridge.

Page 70, note 1. I think this phrase was Lord Palmerston's, when asked how he could carry the load of care and labor that rested on him when he was Premier: " By putting a solid bar of eight hours' sleep between day and day."

Page 72, note 1. In the *Achievements of Cavalry* by General Sir Evelyn Wood, V. C., G. C. B., etc., in which six brilliant actions of cavalry in Europe in the last hundred years are selected, two are credited to the English service : 1st, at *Villars en Couchées* in Brittany in 1793, the breaking of a square of French infantry protected by artillery and cavalry by the Fifteenth Light Dragoons ; 2d, at *Garcia Hernandez* in the Peninsular War, where five "British" squadrons (*but Hanoverians, of the King's German Legion*) attacked the rear guard of a French division, broke two squares, and captured a general and one thousand prisoners. The French commander praised the gallantry of their action in the highest terms, and the Duke of Wellington said he had never seen so gallant a charge.

The English cavalry certainly distinguished themselves at the end of the day at Waterloo, and at Balaclava in the Crimea the superb courage and steadiness of Scarlett's Heavy Brigade in the morning, and the unquestioning gallantry of the hopeless charge of the Light Brigade under Lord Cardigan in the afternoon, demonstrated the individual prowess and admirable discipline of the British cavalryman, even when ill managed.

Page 76, note 1. Of George Stephenson, the introducer of the locomotive engine for railway use, and Chief Engineer of the Liverpool and Manchester Railway, Mr. Emerson writes in his journal : " At Chesterfield I dined in company with Stephenson, the old engineer, who built the first locomotive, and who is, in every way, one of the most remarkable men I have seen in England. I do not know but that I shall accept some day his reiterated invitation to 'go to his house and stay a few days and see Chatsworth and other things.'" His son, Robert Stephenson, was exactly Mr. Emerson's age. The tubular bridge over the Menai Straits was among his great engineering works.

Isambard Brunel, son of the constructor of the Thames tunnel, took part in floating and raising the Conway and Britannia tubular bridges.

Page 77, note 1. Henry de Bratton, or Bracton, in the thirteenth century, an ecclesiastic and jurist, and Chancellor of the Exchequer, wrote *De Legibus et Consuetudinibus Angliæ,* which is said to be " the first attempt to treat the whole extent of the English Law in a manner at once systematic and practical."

William Camden (1551–1623), the historian and antiquary, author of *Britannia* and of the *Annals of the Reign of Queen Elizabeth.* The Camden Society, for publication of valuable literary and antiquarian matter, takes its name from him.

Sir William Dugdale (1605–86), antiquarian and historian of extraordinary industry, to whom credit is due for his preservation of a vast amount of valuable and interesting records of the past legal, ecclesiastic, genealogical, artistic and heraldic.

John Selden (1584–1654), jurist, antiquarian, orientalist and author.

James Brindley (1716–72), a remarkable engineer who united the rivers of England — Mersey, Trent, Humber, Thames and Severn — by canals, and tunnelled Harecastle Hill.

Josiah Wedgwood (1730–95), whose studies of the antique " raised British pottery to the level of a fine art."

Page 79, note 1. Antony à Wood's *Athenæ Oxoniensis.*

Carlyle presented these two fine folio volumes to Emerson in 1848.

Page 79, note 2. *Man's Soule,* p. 29.

Page 82, note 1. Philip de Comines (1445–1509), whose abilities, and residence near Burgundy, necessarily deeply involved him in the political struggles between its duke and the king of France, each of whom he served in turn. His *Memoirs* are an important authority on the period, and to them is due much of the knowledge of the character of Louis XI. (portrayed by Sir Walter Scott in *Quentin Durward*).

Page 83, note 1. Mr. Emerson's friend, Professor Charles Eliot Norton, tells the story of an occurrence during their homeward voyage together from England in 1873. They were in the middle of the Atlantic, and in their talk the daring of Columbus was spoken of in his sailing on westward, week after week, without sight of land. Mr. Emerson said, "But Columbus had the compass. That was enough for a man of his quality." Then, producing from his pocket a small compass, he said, "I always carry this with me. I like to hold the god in my hand."

Page 85, note 1. In a lecture on the Anglo-American, contrasting the hurry and daring shiftiness of the Western pioneer with the cautious thoroughness of the Briton, Mr. Emerson said, "The engine is built in the boat, which does not commend it to the Englishman. The knees, instead of grand old oak, are sawed out of refuse sapling."

Page 86, note 1. John Clerk, a merchant of Eldin, near Edinburgh, wrote "An Essay on Naval Tactics" in 1790 (2d and 3d parts in 1797), which gave rise to a controversy due to the claim of Clerk, supported by others, that his plans, which had been circulated in manuscript before publication, had been adopted by Admiral Rodney at Dominica in April, 1782.

Page 87, note 1. In his *History of the War in the Peninsula* Napier says that "in the beginning of each war England has to seek in blood the knowledge necessary to insure success; and, like the fiend's progress towards Eden, her conquering course is through chaos followed by death."

Page 87, note 2. In his indignation at the cold and threatening attitude of aristocratic and official England towards our country in the first years of the Civil War, Mr. Emerson wrote thus: "England has no higher worship than Fate. . . . Never a lofty sentiment, never a Duty to Civilization, never a generosity, a moral self-restraint. In sight of a commodity, her religion, her morals are forgotten. Why need we be religious? Have I not bishops and clergy at home punctually praying, and sanctimonious from head to foot? Have they not been paid their last year's salary?"

Of course, in thus saying, he would have fully admitted what he said in his journal of 1849: "There are two or three Englands, and it is difficult to speak emphatically of England without finding that we are saying that which is true of only one of these — false of the others."

Page 89, note 1. In the Norse mythology of the *Edda.*

Page 90, note 1. Luke Hansard's *Journal of the House of Commons from 1774.*

Page 91, note 1. Sir Charles Fellowes on his travels discovered Xanthos, the capital of ancient Lycia, in 1838. His description of the remarkable architectural and sculptured remains there induced the British government to obtain permission for their excavation and removal to the British Museum. Mr. Emerson there saw with delight these treasures, under the guidance of Sir Charles Fellowes; especially the triumphal temple with the statues in honor of the twelve cities which sent aid to Harpagus in his reduction of Ionian cities. Mr. Emerson calls the Greek sculpture in the Museum the " Illustration of Homer and Herodotus," and adds, " England holds these things for mankind, and holds them well. Conservative, she is Conservator."

Page 92, note 1. Of the race, sifted by conscience and endurance, building their New Commonwealth in New England, he said: —

> The men of yore were stout and poor,
> And sailed for bread to every shore.
> And where they went on trade intent
>   They did what freemen can,
> Their dauntless ways did all men praise,
>   The merchant was a man.
> The world was made for honest trade, —
> To plant and eat be none afraid.
>
> " Boston," *Poems.*

Page 93, note 1. The Banshee in Irish legend was a familiar spirit of a household, whose cries prophesied their weal or woe.

Page 94, note 1. Pope's " Windsor Forest," quoted by Mr. Emerson from memory and differing slightly from the original lines.

Page 97, note 1. Mr. Emerson in a note to the earlier editions refers on this subject to the *Memorial of Horatio Greenough* (p. 66), published in New York in 1853.

Page 97, note 2. In the chapter on " Aristocracy " in this volume it is stated that the possessions of the Earl of Lonsdale gave him eight seats in Parliament and that " before the Reform of 1832 one hundred and fifty-four persons sent three hundred and seven members to Parliament. The borough-mongers governed England."

The Reform Bill, passed in June of that year (which by its

defeat the year before had occasioned terrible agitation throughout England, accompanied by riots), took away the right of
representation from fifty-six "rotten boroughs," and gave the
one hundred and forty-three members it gained to counties
or large towns which as yet sent no members to Parliament.

Page 97, note 3. Mr. Emerson here noted that "Sir
Samuel Romilly, purest of English patriots, decided that the
only independent mode of entering Parliament was to buy a
seat, and he bought Horsham." See a passage with regard to
this action in the end of the chapter "Results" in this volume.

Page 97, note 4. John Scott, Earl of Eldon (1751–1838),
the distinguished jurist, and Lord Chancellor of England for
twenty-eight years. He was a stanch Tory and earnestly
opposed Catholic emancipation and Parliamentary reform and
all liberal measures.

Page 98, note 1. Mr. Emerson used to read to his children for its pathetic eloquence a passage in which Coleridge
related the words of an old shepherd on the recent cruel
depopulation of the Highlands of Scotland by absentee chiefs
and lairds. The old man, after describing the brave and self-
respecting population of the strath in his youth, cries out,
"And what is here now but a shepherd and an underling or
two, and, it may be, a pair of small lads, — and a many,
many *sheep!*" He tells of the laird who "raised a company to go to the battles overseas for the love that was borne
to his name, and gained high preferment in consequence.
And what were the thanks that the folks had for those that
came back, some blind and more in danger of blindness, and
for those that perished in the hospitals or fell in battle fighting
before or beside him? Why, that their fathers were all turned
out of their farms before the year was over, or sent to wander
like so many gypsies, unless they would consent to shed their

gray hairs at ten-pence a day over the new canals! Had there been a price set on his head, he needed but have whistled and a hundred brave lads would have made a wall of flame around him with the flash of their broad-swords. Now, if the French should come among us, let him whistle to his sheep and see if *they* will fight for him!''

Page 100, note 1. Adam Gottlieb Oehlenschläger, for the reason given in the text, went to Germany and there became eminent as a writer of tragedies. He later went to Paris. *Hakon Jarl, Correggio,* and *Land Lost and Found* are among his pieces, the last based on the Norsemen's discovery of America.

Page 100, note 2. James Hutton, a man of wide education and of versatile gifts, turned his attention to geology, and wrote a *Theory of the Earth,* assuming that heat was the main agent in its changes.

Page 108, note 1. The devoted wife of Colonel John Hutchinson, one of the Parliamentary leaders in the civil war, and member of the high court of judiciary which condemned Charles I. to death. After the Restoration he was accused of conspiracy and died in prison. His wife wrote his Memoir, which was first published in 1806.

Lady Rachel Russell, daughter of the Earl of Southampton. Her husband, William Lord Russell, sentenced on a false charge of conspiracy against Charles II., was beheaded. His wife helped him during his defence, in which he was not allowed counsel.

Page 111, note 1. Contrast with this picture of the handsome but case-hardened beings whom he met, that which he drew, using the same image, of the advancing soul. ''Every soul is by this intrinsic necessity quitting its whole system of things and home and laws and faith, as the shell-fish crawls out of its beautiful but stony case, because it no longer admits of its growth, and slowly forms a new house." ("Compensation," *Essays, First Series.*)

The description in the text of the hard enamel, varnishing the Englishman, is, in Mr. Emerson's journal, followed by his adducing Pope, Swift, Johnson, Gibbon, Goldsmith and Gray, as instances. He goes on: "We get good men sometimes in this country; but Everett and Irving are the only persons I think of who have pretensions to finish, and their enamel will not rival the British. It seems an indemnity to the Briton for his precocious maturity. He has no generous daring in this age; the Platonism died in the Elizabethan; he is shut up in French limits; the practical, the comfortable oppress him with inexorable claims, so that the smallest fraction of power remains for poetry. But Birmingham comes in, and says, 'Never mind; I have some patent lustre that defies criticism!' and Moore made his whole fabric of the 'lustre,' and Tennyson supplied defects with it. Only Wordsworth bought none."

Page 113, note 1. From *A Relation, or rather a True Account of the Island of England,* by a Venetian Traveller (about A. D. 1500). Printed by the Camden Society, no. xxxvii. 1847.

Page 113, note 2. Mr. Emerson made this a household word, telling his children when unusually late to a meal, "Nothing but death or mutilation will hold as an excuse."

Page 116, note 1. Mr. Joshua Bates, the American member of the firm of Messrs. Baring Brothers of London, said to Mr. Emerson, "I have been here thirty years and nobody has ever attempted to cheat me."

Page 117, note 1. The above passage recalls some "Pythagorean opinions," copied by Mr. Emerson in the "Blotting

Book" of 1830, in which he took pleasure because they recognized the "Universal Mind" even in animals.

"Man has some affinity, not only with gods, but with animals; one mind runs through the universe. The soul breathes the representations of the images of things as a sort of air."

Page 118, note 1. A good instance of the Englishman's caution in "checking himself in compliments" is in the introduction to his audience of a lecturer by the presiding clergyman or squire, who takes pleasure "in calling your attention to the — er — *doubtless* very interesting remarks we are about to hear," etc.

Page 119, note 1. The Worthies of England, by Thomas Fuller (1608–61).

Page 120, note 1.

> " Truth-teller was our England's Alfred named;
> Truth-lover was our English duke;
> Whatever record leap to light,
> He never shall be shamed."

Tennyson's " Ode on the Death of the Duke of Wellington."

Page 120, note 2.

> " Round affrighted Lisbon drew
> The treble works, the vast designs
> Of his labored rampart-lines:
> Where he greatly stood at bay,
> Whence he issued forth anew,
> And ever great and greater grew,
> Beating from the wasted vines
> Back to France her banded swarms,
>
> . . . .
>
> Till o'er the hills her eagles flew."
>
> Tennyson's " Ode."

Page 122, note 1. A notable instance is that of George Stephenson, the great engineer, who, beginning life as a fireman in a colliery, and unable to read at eighteen, rose by his extraordinary achievements to wealth and consideration, but declined the offer of knighthood.

Page 123, note 1. Wellington, then Lieutenant-General Wellesley, in command of the first expedition to Portugal, had landed his forces, August 1, 1808, and soon after defeated Laborde and repulsed Junot. Sir Hugh Dalrymple, the English commissioner, made an agreement with the latter in a convention at Cintra by which the French were not only permitted to leave Portugal, but were conveyed to France with their arms and property.

Page 123, note 2. Lord Eldon's stanch Tory opposition to all reforms was not pursued in ignorance of the increasing unpopularity of his course; for Mr. Emerson notes that he said in his old age that, " were he to begin life again, he would be damned but he would begin as an agitator."

Page 123, note 3. Mr. Emerson made the following note in modification of the above passage, written several years before the book was published: —

" It is an unlucky moment to remember these sparkles of solitary virtue in the face of the honors lately paid in England to the Emperor Louis Napoleon. I am sure that no Englishman that I had the happiness to know, consented, when the aristocracy and the commons of London cringed like a Neapolitan rabble, before a successful thief. But, — how to resist one step, though odious, in a linked series of state necessities ? Governments must always learn too late that the use of dishonest agents is as ruinous for nations as for single men."

Page 124, note 1. The " spiritual" manifestations that began to attract attention in America about the year 1850 were first called " Rochester knockings " because they occurred in the family of John D. Fox of that city.

Page 126, note 1. From Daniel Defoe's *True-Born Englishman*, Part II.

Tacitus writes of the ancient Germans : " It is generally at their drinking-bouts that they discuss " all important matters of a public or private nature. " Not being a crafty or a cunning race, they furthermore disclose their secret thoughts in the freedom of the feast, and so the minds of all lie open and discovered. On the morrow the matter is debated again and the double process justifies itself. They discuss when disguise is impossible, they decide when too sober to blunder." (*Germania*, XXII.)

Page 128, note 1. Jehan Froissart, Canon of Chimay in Flanders (1337–1410), in his *Chroniques de France, d' Angleterre, d' Ecosse, d' Espagne, de Bretagne, de Gascogne, Flandres et lieux d' alentour.* Mr. Emerson used often to quote the remark of Grahame of Claverhouse to his prisoner, Morton, in Scott's *Old Mortality,* about the glorious old chronicler of chivalry: "I have half a mind to contrive you should have six months' imprisonment in order to procure you that pleasure. His chapters inspire me with more enthusiasm than even poetry itself."

Page 131, note 1. Shakspeare, *Henry IV.,* Part II., Act I., Scene 1.

Page 135, note 1. Milton, *L' Allegro.*

Page 135, note 2. It is of course Turner that is here referred to. In his journal Mr. Emerson tells of going with Mr. Stanfield, the painter, and another gentleman, to see Mr. Windus's large collection of Turner's pictures and drawings at Tottenham. Later Mr. Richard Owen, the anatomist, " carried us to Turner's studio, but Turner, though he had written him a note to announce his visit, was gone. So he [Owen] showed us the pictures. In his earlier pictures, he said, Turner painted conventionally, painted what he knew was there, finished the coat and buttons ; in the later he paints only what the eye really sees, and gives the genius of the city or landscape. He was engaged to paint a whale-ship, and he came one day to see Mr. Owen and asked to see a mullet (?) [Agassiz said a Clio][1] and begged him to explain to him from the beginning the natural history of the creature ; which he did ; Turner followed him with great accuracy. In process of time the picture was painted and Owen went there to see his mullet. ‘ I could not find it,’ he said, ‘ in the picture, but I doubt not it is all there.’ ”

The painter out of kindness to whom he smudged his own picture with water-color was Lawrence.

Mr. Emerson notes, “ Turner told Stanfield he will not suffer any portrait to be taken of him, for nobody would ever believe that such an ugly fellow made such beautiful things.”

Page 135, note 3.

> “ But I will wear my heart upon my sleeve
>   For daws to peck at.”

Shakspeare, *Othello*, Act I., Scene 1.

Page 139, note 1. Fuller’s *Worthies of England.*

Page 140, note 1. *Heimskringla*, Laing’s translation, vol. iii. p. 37.

Page 144, note 1. “ Humorist ” in the Elizabethan sense of indulging his humor or whim. In his notes on England

---

[1] This anecdote I copy from a book in which Mr. Emerson wrote out the story more fully than in the little notebook. The comment of Agassiz was evidently added later, inserted with a caret. It seems very possible that it was not a “ whale-ship,” but the “ Slave Ship ” now in the Boston Museum of Fine Arts.

Mr. Emerson quotes from Dr. A. Carlyle's *Autobiography*: "The humorist prevails more in England than in any country because liberty has long been universal there and wealth very general, which I hold to be the father and mother of the humorist."

Page 144, note 2. In 1844 Mr. R. H. Gurney, a banker of Norwich, said on his cross-examination before a railway committee, "I have never travelled by rails. I am an enemy to them. I have opposed the Norwich Railway. I have left a sum of money in my will to oppose railroads."

Page 145, note 1. Mr. Emerson in a lecture called "France; or, Urbanity," delivered soon after his return from this visit abroad, and often in his allusion to the French, shows something of the same tendency to "use France as a blackboard." It should be remembered that his experience of France was only in Paris, and mostly for a few weeks during the Revolution of 1848, a time which brought out the excitability of the French, a trait always disturbing to his serene mind.

Page 146, note 1. One brilliant exception to this rough British propagandism has been recently shown by Sir Andrew Clarke, whose wise humanity and consideration for the traditions and feelings of the fierce Malay race, with whom he had to deal, has been so successful in producing peace and prosperity, with almost no military backing, in the Straits Settlement.

Page 149, note 1. In some loose sheets of notes written in 1848 this plan is more fully stated.

"There is also this use to be made of brag, that men show their cards in that. Humor them by all means. Do not check the speaker by so much as a look; he is unconsciously telling you his idea of what he ought to do. Draw it all out, and

v

then hold him to it. Hold the Frenchman to his. He that is the liberator of the universe: he that has the most civilized of civilizations : France it is to which all nations sitting in darkness look with hope and all despots with despair. My best of human beings! I am delighted to hear you. And this is the mission of France. And France will suffer nobody nor any mad neighbour to do the like by Poland, Hungary or Turkey. Least of all to impede the liberty of the press or of speech in France. Take down the words, and give me your signature to this in black and white. Surely you do not hesitate !

"Well, but here are English, and I remember that the English say that the French are a little given — the least in the world — to rhodomontade — but that English speak what they think, and their word is as good as their bond. Well, these, then, we can hold to their boast : England is the refuge of freedom, English press is the public opinion of Europe, asylum of the oppressed, bulwark of freedom against the despotism. We will remember all this ; and see how well her actions bear it out in the approaching crisis."

Page 150, note 1. William Spence, principally known by his work on entomology, written in conjunction with the Rev. William Kirby. He was for a time a member of Parliament.

Page 150, note 2. The general distress among the poorer classes in England continuing after the passage of the Reform Bill in 1832 led to agitation and even riots on behalf of "The People's Charter" in 1839. The "six points" of Chartism were : Universal suffrage, vote by ballot, annual Parliaments, equal electoral districts, no property qualification for members, and payment for their services. Most of these points have been substantially won. Some Chartist demonstrations were broken up by the military arm of the government, and leading agitators imprisoned or transported. The last serious demonstrations were during the time of Mr. Emerson's stay in England, and gave rise to the more alarm because of the revolution then going on in France.

9 March, 1848. "I attended a Chartist Meeting in National Hall, Holburn. It was called to hear the report of the Deputation who had returned after carrying congratulations to the French Republic. The *Marseillaise* was sung by a party of men and women on the platform and chorused by the whole assembly: then the *Girondins*. The leaders appeared to be grave men intent on keeping a character for order and moral tone, but the great body of the meeting liked best the sentiment, ' Every man a ballot and every man a musket.' "

Mr. Emerson's comment is, " England a little top-heavy still, though she keeps her feet much better since the Cornlaws were thrown overboard."

Page 152, note 1. Mr. Emerson adopted the account of St. George given by Gibbon. The weight of evidence of the various chronicles now seems to show that the real St. George was not George the Arian, of Cappadocia, described in the text, but another who died two generations earlier.

It is said that Constantine the Great dedicated a church to the martyred St. George in Constantinople more than forty years before the killing of George the Arian, which occurred in A. D. 361. Eusebius relates that St. George, a man of no mean origin and highly esteemed for his temporal dignities, publicly tore down the edict against the Christians of the Emperor Diocletian, who was then in the city, and " after enduring what was likely to follow an act so daring, preserved his mind calm and serene until the moment his spirit fled."

Other authors tell of the prolonging of the tortures for ten days, the saint recovering and performing miracles in the intervals.

In the opinion of to-day the case of Amerigo Vespucci appears in a better light than that here presented. Although his statement that he was concerned in the voyage to the New World in 1497 is held to be false, he appears to have taken part in one or two expeditions which later reached the South American coast. A writer in the *American Encyclopædia* says that it does not appear that Vespucci himself had any intention of taking the honor of the discovery from Columbus.

Page 153, note 1. Benjamin Robert Haydon, the painter and writer on art, whose life was a struggle with poverty, and who was himself imprisoned for debt. In his bitterness he wrote : —

"The greatest curse that can befall a father in England is to have a son gifted with a passion and a genius for high art." (*Life of Haydon.*)

Page 155, note 1. The misery in the streets of the English cities, especially of women and children, distressed Mr. Emerson. In a letter to his wife soon after arriving in Manchester he said, referring to his youngest daughter: "My dear little Edie, to tell you the truth, costs me many a penny, day by day. I cannot go up the street but I shall see some woman in rags, with a little creature just of Edie's size and age, but in coarsest ragged clothes, and barefooted, stepping beside her; and I look curiously into *her* Edie's face with some terror lest it should resemble *mine*, and the far-off Edie wins from me the half-pence for this near one." For more to this purpose, see Mr. Cabot's Memoir, vol. ii., pp. 506, 507.

Page 156, note 1. Lord Bacon in his essay *On Expense* gave the like counsel: "Certainly, if a man will keep but of even hand, his ordinary expenses ought to be but half of his receipts; and, if he thinks to wax rich, but to the third part."

Page 161, note 1. In the Norse mythology, the Fenris wolf, son of Loki, was bound on Nifiheim, but steadily frays his bond, which will at last break, and in the Day of Doom he will swallow the Sun.

Page 162, note 1. Mr. Emerson's residence and visitings in the great industrial towns of Yorkshire and Lancashire, where he met manufacturers and operatives at the mechanics' institutes before which he lectured, gave him remarkable opportunities to see the huge material activities and their products ; also their social and economic results. Soon after landing he wrote that he had an invitation from a "Mr. Crawshay, who refused the tests at Cambridge after reading my essays! as he writes me. And so with small wisdom the world is moved as of old." He accepted, and soon after wrote: "I find here at Newcastle a most accomplished gentleman in Mr. Crawshay, at whose counting-room in his iron works I am now sitting after much conference on many and useful arts." It was his six-ton trip-hammer that suggested Thor's Miöllnir. Mr. Crawshay showed how it would fall close down to his silk hat and spare it, and then reduce a workman's borrowed hat to atoms.

Page 163, note 1. It will be remembered that John Evelyn, the well-known author of the *Diary*, wrote, at the instance of the Royal Society, when there was panic lest ship-timber should fail in England, his *Sylva, or Forest Trees*, which induced the planting of oaks that furnished the ship-yards of the next century.

Passing over the two poet-gardeners mentioned, Robert Brown, who accompanied the Australasian expedition in 1801 and described the flora of the Southern Hemisphere, was called by Humboldt the greatest botanist of the age. John Claudius Loudon, impelled by a love for agriculture and landscape-gardening, left Scotland and opened an agricultural school in England, and wrote the *Arboretum et Fruticetum Britanni-cum,* as well as encyclopædias of agriculture, gardening, plants, and cottage, farm and villa architecture. Joseph Paxton, the gardener of the Duke of Devonshire, by his skill made Chatsworth the most celebrated country seat of England, and in 1851 planned and superintended the erection of the Crystal Palace, for which service he was knighted.

Page 166, note 1. The English brag to this effect, in contrast to poor Scotland, comes out in the ballad of *Chevy-Chase:* King James, when the news of the death of Earl Douglas reaches him, exclaims in despair, —

> " ' I have not any captaine more
>   Of such account as hee.' "

But on the other side of the Border

> " Like tydings to King Henry came,
>   Within as short a space
>   That Percy of Northumberland
>   Was slaine in Chevy-Chase.
>   ' Now God be with him,' said our King,
>   ' Sith it will noe better bee ;
>   I trust I have within my realme
>   Five hundred as good as he.' "

Page 167, note 1.

> The horseman serves the horse,
> The neatherd serves the neat,
> The merchant serves the purse,
> The eater serves his meat;

'T is the day of the chattel,
Web to weave and corn to grind ;
Things are in the saddle,
And ride mankind.

                    "Ode," *Poems*.

As a contrast to this dwarfing of the man by specialized
labor Mr. Emerson took keen pleasure in every instance that
he saw of Yankee "faculty" among his neighbors in the
country. The war brought out much of this versatile talent.
He especially enjoyed the bright and interesting narrative by
Major Theodore Winthrop of the equality of the Massachusetts men to each new difficulty in the march to Washington
in 1861. See Theodore Winthrop's *New York Seventh
Regiment ; Our March to Washington*, in *The Atlantic
Monthly* for June, 1861.

Page 169, note 1. Carlyle, in a letter written to his friend
in April, 1839, had said of conditions in England : —

"Scarcity, discontent, fast ripening towards desperation,
extends far and wide among our working people. God help
them! In man is yet small help."

Page 170, note 1. Among Mr. Emerson's notes on England are the following on her rule in India : —

"The English repair the old, and dig new canals for the
irrigation of the country, cross the immense Empire with
macadam roads, educate the native population in good schools;
advance natives to public employment, and aim ' to elevate
more and more the social condition of the peoples of Hindo-
stan, and to put them in condition of administering their own
affairs one day, by aid of the principles and the laws whose
utility England will have made them comprehend, and carefully taught them the beneficent application.' Magnificent
this, — the gradual detachment of the colonies which she has

planted, which have grown to Empires, and then are with dignity, and with full consent of the mother country, released from allegiance. Go — I have given you English language, laws, manners; disanglicanize yourselves if you can. United States, Canada, Australia, Cape of Good Hope, West Indies — East Indies. . . . It has become necessary to govern India by carefully selected agents — young men of thorough education and high ability, tried in the service. India is practically a profession to be studied as methodically as law or medicine.''

Page 173, note 1. One is reminded here of the glamour which Scott by his *Waverley Novels* had thrown around the nobility of England, even for readers of democratic predilections; and yet with a fairness and humanity, Tory though he was, towards the humble vassal and down-trodden peasant.

" There 's Derby and Cavendish, dread of their foes;
   There 's Erin's high Ormond and Scotland's Montrose!
   Would you match the base Skippon and Massey and Brown
   With the Barons of England that fight for the Crown ? ''
                                    " The Cavalier," *Rokeby*.

Page 173, note 2. Mr. Emerson used to tell his children of an old miracle-play in which Jesus, before submitting to be crucified, stood on his rights of knighthood as a direct descendant of King David, and challenged Pontius Pilate to single combat.

Page 175, note 1. Fuller's *Worthies*, vol. ii. In Mr. Emerson's notebook he gives these two fine pictures of the earl, from Fuller: " At a joust in France, fighting with Sir Collard Fines, he so bore himself that the French thought he was tied to the saddle, and to confute their jealousies, he alighted and remounted." "Crossing into Normandy, the ship was tossed with such a tempest that Warwick caused himself and lady and infant son to be bound to the mainmast, with his armour and coat of arms upon him, that he might be known and buried aright. Yet he died in his bed."

Page 176, note 1. The Bear and Ragged Staff was the full cognizance of the Earls of Warwick.

Page 178, note 1. Reliquiæ Wottonianæ. This was George Villiers, the favorite of James I. and Charles I., the first duke after the revival of the title. There had been Dukes of Buckingham of the House of Stafford, but the title became extinct with the execution, by Richard III., of "the deep-revolving wily Buckingham."

Page 178, note 2. In Shakspeare's *Richard III.*, on the morning of the battle of Bosworth Field, fatal to him, this duke, a stanch adherent of the usurper, finds this scroll in his tent: —

"Jockey of Norfolk, be not too bold,
  For Dickon thy master is bought and sold."

Page 178, note 3. Compare the *Earth-Song* in "Hamatreya" in the *Poems*.

Page 179, note 1. Jamblichus of Chalcis, in the fourth century B. C., a Syrian Neo-Platonist. Of him Mr. Emerson said more than once in his journals, "I expect a revival in the churches to be caused by the reading of Jamblichus."

Page 180, note 1. Opportunity to test this statement seemed to be at hand during Mr. Emerson's visit. In a letter to his wife, April 20, 1848, he wrote, "I read the newspaper daily, and the revolution, fixed for the 10th instant, occupied all men's thought until the Chartist petition was actually carried to the Commons."

Page 181, note 1. The residence of the Duke of Suther-
-land. Of his visit there Mr. Emerson wrote to a friend: —

JUNE 21st, 1848.

The Duchess of Sutherland sent for me to come to lunch
with her at two o'clock, and she would show me Stafford
House. Now you must know this eminent lady lives in the
best house in the Kingdom, the Queen's not excepted. I
went, and was received with great courtesy by the Duchess,
who is a fair, large woman, of good figure, with much dignity
and sweetness, and the kindest manners. She was surrounded
by company, and she presented me to the Duke of Argyle,
her son-in-law, and to her sisters, the Ladies Howard. After
we left the table we went through this magnificent palace,
this young and friendly Duke of Argyle being my guide. He
told me he had never seen so fine a banquet hall as the one
we were entering; and galleries, saloons, and ante-rooms were
all in the same regal proportions and richness, full everywhere
with sculpture and painting. We found the Duchess in the
gallery, and she showed me her most valued pictures. I
asked her if she did not come on fine mornings to walk alone
amidst these beautiful forms; which she professed she liked
well to do. She took care to have every best thing pointed
out to me, and invited me to come and see the gallery alone
whenever I liked. I assure you in this little visit the two
parts of Duchess and of Palace were well and truly played.
. . . I had seen nothing so sumptuous as was all this. One
would so gladly forget that there was anything else in England than these golden chambers and the high and gentle
people who walk in them! May the grim Revolution with
his iron hand — if come he must — come slowly and late to
Stafford House, and deal softly with its inmates!

Concerning the meeting between this noble lady and Mr. Emerson, his friend wrote to him: —

I hope you penetrated the Armida Palace and did your devoir to the sublime Duchess and her Luncheon yesterday! I cannot without a certain internal amusement (foreign enough to my present humor) represent to myself such a conjunction of opposite stars! But you carry a new image off with you, and are a gainer, you. *Allons.* . . .

Yours ever truly,

T. CARLYLE.

Page 181, note 2. Of Northumberland House, which stood until 1874 in Trafalgar Square, Augustus Hare said: — "One only of the great Strand palaces survived entire till our own time, and our own generation has seen and mourned the loss of Northumberland House, one of the noblest Jacobean buildings in England and the most picturesque feature in London."

Page 184, note 1. Mr. Emerson, though sympathizing with the rising of the people to assert their proper rights, took a certain pleasure in the courage shown by both sides when the storm threatened. In a letter home he said: — "One thing is certain: that if the peace of England should be broken up, the aristocracy here — or, I should say, the rich — are stouthearted and as ready to fight for their own as the poor; are not very likely to run away." He gives this instance of "standing by one's order" from the previous century: —

"Earl Spencer when asked why he left Fox and voted for the War (in 1793), wrote: —

"'I will be very frank with you. My lot is cast among the nobility. It is not my fault that I was thus born, and that

I thus inherit. I wish to remain what I am, and to hand my father's titles and estates down to my heirs. I do not know that I thus seek my own gratification at the expense of my country, which has been very great, free and happy, under this order of things. I am satisfied that if we do not go to war with the French, this order of things will be destroyed. We *may* fall by the War, but we *must* fall without it. The thing is worth fighting for, and to fight for it we are resolved.' "

Page 184, note 2. The following notes on English politics were used in lectures on Mr. Emerson's return: —

"The English youth, highborn, has a narrow road to travel. Besides his horse and gun and his clubhouse, all he knows is the door of the House of Commons. So aristocratic is the frame of society, that the House of Commons is in the hands of the House of Lords. The Commons are the lords that shall be. Of the 658 members of the lower House, 455 have been lately shown to be representatives of the House of Lords. Before 1832 the House was violently patrician. In 1793, it was declared in a petition presented to the House by the (afterward) Earl Grey, that 307 members were put into the House by 154 persons, owners and patrons of boroughs. The Reform Bill in 1832 reduced the patronage, yet a majority of seats in the House may be filled by the nominees of the nobility. Of the Cabinet, one half is usually peers, and the other half relations of peers. Thus the aristocracy have the direction of public affairs. They naturally prize this as a career. 'Politics,' said the Duke of Norfolk to Shelley, ' is the proper career of a young man of ability in your station. That career is most advantageous, because it is a monopoly.' A little success in that line goes far, since the number of competitors is limited. In such a Parliament class-legislation is inevitable; and offices and pensions are given to those who have votes and patronage to buy them with. Mr. Peyronnet Thompson's theory of aristocracy is, 'To make one of a family strong enough to compel the public to support all the rest.' And it only needs to look into the files of newspapers opposed to the Government in the last century to find many ugly anecdotes, which, after all allowance for party exaggeration, expose the manner of saddling the public with pensions for their children, relatives, tutors, and even bastards. The Duke of Beaufort's will left annual sums to his younger sons, which, with great naïveté, he devised should be paid *until they should obtain places or pensions to certain amounts, under Government.*

"An Earl of Uxbridge, with an estate of £60,000 a year, obtained an annual pension for his daughter of £300, in her own name; and after her marriage, another pension of the like sum to her, in the list of Scotch pensions, under her new name of Erskine. She continued to draw both, and the journals had their joke on the double Lady Louisa.

"These abuses were much mended by the Reform Bill. In 1780, Mr. Pitt said in the House that, 'Without a reform in Parliament, it was impossible for any honest man to remain a minister of England.' "

Page 184, note 3. Commissions in the army could then be bought.

Page 185, note 1. Again from the stray sheets on English politics: —

"One wonders how a Parliament thus constituted remains in any manner representative of the bulk of the population. But many of the younger nobles espouse the popular cause and the classes of trade and manufactures force their voices into the House. Men of brilliant popular talents like Burke,

Pitt, Mackintosh, Macaulay, Canning, Sheridan, sit for the close boroughs, and, one thing with another, we have got in modern times a wonderful assembly, its moral reputation much mended, though bribery is still permitted, but its intellectual and social reputation supreme.

"It is petulant — the common saying is that no question can be mooted, no statement made there but, out of 654 members, will find some fit and ready to sift it. That, especially, it is the most severe anthropometer or test of men. Canning said, when alarm was expressed at the probable return of O'Connell and his friends to Parliament, 'It is in Parliament I wish to see them. I have never known a demagogue who, when elected to a seat in this house, did not in the course of six months shrink to his proper dimensions.' "

Page 186, note 1.

"That repose
Which stamps the caste of Vere de Vere."
Tennyson, "Lady Clara Vere de Vere."

Of his experiences in London society Mr. Emerson wrote: "I am to say what is strange, but it so happened, that the higher were the persons in the social scale whom I conversed with, the less marked was their national accent, and the more I found them like the most cultivated persons in America."

Page 189, note 1. Jean de la Quintinie wrote a book on gardening which was translated into English by John Evelyn.

Arthur Young was an agricultural experimenter and writer in the last part of the eighteenth century, and wrote several important works on the subject of agriculture in England and the use of waste lands. His *Travels in France* is quoted by Carlyle often in his *French Revolution.* George III. contributed to his *Annals of Agriculture* under the name of Ralph Robinson.

In these *Annals*, Young highly praises the improvements in cultivation and cattle-breeding made by Robert Bakewell in the middle of the eighteenth century.

John Joseph Mechi, a great authority on scientific farming, attained remarkable results in Essex by irrigating his farm with liquefied manure by steam-power.

Page 189, note 2. In Dibdin's *Literary Reminiscences,* vol. I., xii.

Page 189, note 3. Mr. Emerson took great pleasure in the *naïf* account of his life and adventures, given by the valiant and philosophic Edward, Lord Herbert of Cherbury. He was the elder brother of George Herbert, the poet.

Page 190, note 1. Penshurst in Kent was Sir Philip Sidney's birthplace, and Wilton House the residence of his sister the Countess of Pembroke.

Sir Fulke Greville, Lord Brooke, wrote *The Life of the Renowned Sir Philip Sidney.*

Page 191, note 1. In the lecture " Natural Aristocracy " which Mr. Emerson gave in London, after granting the claims of the really great to honor and place, he said, " But mankind do not extend the same indulgence to those who claim and enjoy the same prerogative, but render no returns. The day is darkened when the golden river runs down into mud; when genius grows idle and wanton and reckless of its fine duties of being Saint, Prophet, Inspirer to its humble fellows, baulks their respect and confounds their understanding by silly extravagances. . . . To live without duties is obscene." He made so much allowance for the outrages to which the misdeeds of idle aristocrats might incite the poor and ignorant that Lord Morpeth urged him to suppress the passage, should he give the lecture again. It still stands in the essay on " Aristocracy " in *Lectures and Biographical Sketches.*

Page 192, note 1. George Selwyn (1719–91), the friend of Horace Walpole.

Page 193, note 1. Causes Célèbres Étrangères, publiées en France pour la première fois, et traduites de l' Espagnol, l' Italien et l' Allemagne. Paris: 1827–28. *Par une Société de jurisconsultes et de gens de lettres.*

Another work of the same kind is the *Causes Célèbres, Répertoire générale des causes célèbres anciennes et modernes, rédigé par une Société d' hommes de lettres sous la direction de B. Saint-Edme.* Paris: Rosier, 1834–35.

An English work appeared in 1849, entitled: *Celebrated Trials connected with the Aristocracy in the Relations of Private Life.* London: W. Benning & Co., 1849.

Page 195, note 1. A clergyman who prepared students for the examinations of admission to Oxford and Cambridge told the editor that, even in the colleges in which the standard of scholarship was very high, rank was, to some extent, accepted as an equivalent.

Page 195, note 2. History of English Universities, "Die englischen Universitäten," by Victor Aimé Huber (2 vols. Cassel, 1839–40), was translated into English by Francis William Newman.

Page 195, note 3.

"Some great estates provide, but not
A mastering mind, so both are lost thereby."
          Herbert, *The Church Porch.*

Page 197, note 1.

The lord is the peasant that was,
The peasant the lord that shall be.

. . . . . .

Who liveth in the palace hall
Waneth fast and spendeth all.
          "Woodnotes," II., *Poems.*

Page 199, note 1. This friend was Arthur Hugh Clough, the poet, and translator of Plutarch. Mr. Emerson, on his return, reviewed with much praise his poem "The Bothie of Tober-na-Vuolich," in the Massachusetts *Quarterly Review* (March, 1849), then edited by Theodore Parker.

Mr. Clough visited Mr. Emerson later and spent a winter in Cambridge. From Oxford Mr. Emerson wrote of dining at Exeter College with Palgrave, Froude, and other Fellows, and at Oriel with Clough and Dr. Daubeny. "They showed me the kindest attentions, . . . but more, they showed me themselves; who are many of them very earnest, faithful, affectionate, some of them highly gifted men; some of them, too, prepared and decided to make great sacrifices for conscience' sake. Froude is a noble youth to whom my heart warms. . . . Truly I became fond of these monks of Oxford."

Soon after leaving Oxford Mr. Emerson received a letter from Mr. Froude of which the following is an extract: —

EXETER COLLEGE [OXFORD], JUNE 6, [1848].
MY DEAR MR. EMERSON, —

. . . Your own visit here, short as it was, was not without its service to us; you left luminous traces of your presence in the words you scattered from you, which as yet the birds of the air have not devoured. Horace's *Segnius irritant animos*[1] is only half true. One sentence spoken is worth a hundred written. In a few years, I hope, even here in Ox-

---

[1] Segnius irritant animos demissa per aurem.

Horace, *Ars Poetica*, 180.

In speaking of theatrical representations, and the comparative effect on the spectator of things seen, or merely narrated by an actor, Horace explains that things addressed to the ear rouse the feelings more slowly than those presented to the eye.

v

ford, you will see whole acres yellow with the corn of your sowing, and logic-mills grinding it and professors baking it in their lecture-rooms into bread for hungry students.

Believe me ever

Your very much obliged

J. A. FROUDE.

Page 200, note 1. "Let the blessed bless; he is blessed, let him be blessed."

Page 201, note 1. Erasmus thus expressed his surprise and delight in Oxford, regenerated by the influence of John Colet, whither he had gone to study Greek (newly introduced by Grocyn), because he was too poor to go to Italy: "I have found in Oxford so much polish and learning that now I hardly care to go to Italy at all, save for the sake of having been there. When I listen to my friend Colet it seems like listening to Plato himself. Who does not wonder at the wide range of Grocyn's knowledge? What can be more searching, deep and refined than the judgment of Linacre? When did Nature mould a temper more gentle, endearing and happy than the temper of Thomas More?" [1]

Page 201, note 2. Albericus Gentilis (1552–1608), a celebrated jurist and early authority on international law. Driven from Italy and Austria by the Inquisition, he was recommended to University of Oxford by the Earl of Leicester and received with much honor there.

Page 201, note 3. Casaubon, the Swiss theologian and critic, protected and made royal librarian at Paris by Henry IV., was so annoyed by Catholic jealousy that he passed his latter days in England, where he was made prebendary of Canterbury.

1 Green's *Short History of the English People.*

Page 201, note 4. The *Life of William Morris* by J. W. Mackail, and the story of *Tom Brown at Oxford* by the late Thomas Hughes, give extraordinary pictures of sleepy and perfunctory instruction at Oxford colleges and the idle life there until the very recent awakening.

Page 202, note 1. Leviathan, or the Matter, Form and Power of a Commonwealth, Ecclesiastical and Civil, containing the complete system of Hobbes's materialistic philosophy.

Page 204, note 1. Huber's *History of English Universities,* vol. ii. p. 304.

Page 205, note 1. Five Years in an English University, by Charles Astor Bristed (1852).

Page 207, note 1. Mr. Emerson, always regretting that, as Dr. John Collins Warren said of him in his boyhood, " he had no *stamina,*" wrote thus to his friend Sterling in 1844: " I do not know how it happens, but there are but seven hours, often but five, in an American scholar's day; the twelve, thirteen, fifteen, that we have heard of in German libraries, are fabulous to us. Probably in England you find a mean between Massachusetts and Germany. The performances of Goethe, the performances of Scott, appear superhuman to us in their quantity, let alone their quality."

Page 209, note 1. Huber's *History of English Universities.*

Page 209, note 2. Bristed's *Five Years in an English University.*

Page 211, note 1. Later Mr. Emerson wrote: " At home I am still struck with the superior animal vigor of the average Englishman; as if the English were pasture-oaks, and the Americans fine saplings."

It should be remembered, however, that this was written

before the reaction towards due physical culture in America set in, which culminates now in extreme athleticism.

Page 212, note 1. Both these Russian posts were captured by the Allies in the Crimean War, but I cannot find evidence of personal hostile action taken by their governors. Perhaps stories of such were in the newspapers of the day.

Page 213, note 1. The " poetic influence from the heart of Oxford " evidently refers to Arthur Hugh Clough, Mr. Emerson's friend and host there, and four years later his guest in America, whose charming hexameter poem, *The Bothie of Tober-na-Vuolich,* was just published. Mr. Clough's increasingly liberal views made him feel bound in honor to resign his Fellowship, the holder of which is required to belong to the Church of England.

Page 213, note 2. Wordsworth, and, probably, Byron.

Page 215, note 1. As he says elsewhere, he felt that the Briton was temperamentally a worshipper of Fate. As for " this mountain of stone," he hoped that among the generation then rising in England would appear men who would, as he had done, remember Jesus' word: " If ye have faith as a grain of mustard seed, ye shall say unto this mountain, Remove hence to yonder place; and it shall remove; and nothing shall be impossible unto you."

Page 215, note 2. To this thought before Dundee Church he adds in his notebook, " And at other times I say, If idealists will work as well as these men wrought, we shall see a new world apace."

Page 216, note 1. The contemporary monkish chronicler of the deeds of Richard Cœur de Lion in Palestine. It is included in Bohn's *Chronicles of the Crusades.*

Page 217, note 1. Wordsworth, note to " Ecclesiastical Sonnets," XVIII. He also speaks of the Established clergy

of England as being, in many parts, " the principal bulwark
against barbarism."

Page 219, note 1. John Sterling, in a letter written to Mr.
Emerson in 1841, speculates as to what kind of audiences he
finds in America — audiences that must be very different from
those in England. He says: " Here we have not only the
same aggressive, material element as in the United States, but
a second fact unknown there, namely, the social authority of
Church Orthodoxy derived from the close connection between
the Aristocracy (that is, the Rich) and the Clergy. And
odd it is to see that, so far as appears on the surface, the last
twenty-five years have produced more of this instead of less." [1]

Page 220, note 1. Fuller's *Worthies of England.*

Page 220, note 2. Mr. Emerson notes that " Certain
doctrines are offensive to their mind; for example, the meta-
morphosis or passage of souls. Englishmen hate it. It vexes
the common sense." The possibility that he might become a
Frenchman or Spaniard might account for this fear. Swedenborg, Mr. Emerson mentions, found the English in a heaven
apart.

Page 221, note 1. From the notebook on England:
" Four things they believe in, namely, Shakspeare's genius,
commerce, pit-coal, and the steam-engine.

" English Church gets to be an enormous doll with old
ladies of both sexes to dress and dandle it."

Page 222, note 1. Journal, 1848. " At the dinner of
the Geological Club, I sat between Sir Henry De la Bèche
and Lord Selkirk. When I remarked that I understood the
accepted view of the creation of races to be, that many individuals appeared simultaneously, and not one pair only, Lord

1 *Correspondence between John Sterling and Ralph Waldo Emerson.*
Boston: Houghton, Mifflin & Co., 1897.

S. replied, that there is no geological fact which is at variance
with the Mosaic history.''

Page 223, note 1. Augustus Pugin, an Englishman of
French descent, an admirable architectural draughtsman. He
published in 1821 *Specimens of Gothic Architecture selected
from various ancient Edifices in England,* and later, other
important illustrated works of the same sort.

Page 224, note 1. Thomas Taylor (1758–1835), a remarkable scholar and apostle of Plato and the Neoplatonists.
He translated Aristotle, Plato, Proclus, Plotinus, Pausanius,
Jamblichus, and Porphyry. Niebuhr in his *Letters* says of
him, "Through a singular philosophical mysticism, derived
from the Platonist, he became an orthodox polytheist and adherent of the mystical interpretation of the popular religion of
the Greeks.'' In his translation of the *Cratylus* Taylor calls
Christianity "a certain most irrational and gigantic impiety.''

Page 224, note 2. English notebook. "The English have
no national religion and have imported the Hebrew.''

Page 224, note 3. The Saracens are pressing the little
force of the English Crusaders hard, and the battle seems going
against them. Richard, having done his utmost, thus makes
his *argumentum ad Deum:* "O God! O God, my God,
why hast Thou forsaken me? For whom have we foolish
Christians, for whom have we English come hither from the
farthest part of the earth to bear our arms? Is it not for the
God of the Christians? O fie! How good art Thou to the
people who now are, for Thy name, given up to the sword:
we shall become a portion for foxes. Oh how unwilling
should I be to forsake Thee in so forlorn and dreadful a position, were I Thy Lord and Advocate as Thou art mine. In
sooth my standards will in future be despised not through
my fault, but through Thine; in sooth not through any cow-

ardice in my warfare art Thou Thyself, my King and my God,
conquered this day, and not Richard Thy vassal!''

Page 224, note 4. In his sketch of the Rev. Dr. Ripley,
in *Lectures and Biographical Sketches*, Mr. Emerson gives
some amusing extracts from the diary of his great-grandfather,
the Rev. Joseph Emerson of Malden, on his purchase of a
''shay.'' '''The Lord grant it may be a comfort and blessing to my family,'' says the good man, like Pepys. But accidents and misgivings of conscience, because he deemed these
to be chastisements of the Lord for his pride, followed, and
in six months he sold this vehicle of wrath, as Pepys would
not have done.

Page 225, note 1. Showing a survival of a trace of the
spirit of the English of the twelfth century. The monk
Richard of Devizes in his chronicle relates with delight that
on the Coronation-day of King Richard, which happened to be
on Good Friday, '' About the self-same hour that the Son was
immolated to the Father, a sacrifice of the Jews to their father
the Devil began in all parts of the Kingdom ; '' and that they
'' despatched their blood-suckers with blood to hell.''

Page 225, note 2. Mr. Emerson notes this list of the
triumphs of English conscience and good sense over national
conservatism, in the nineteenth century : —

    1826. Catholic Emancipation.

    1832. Reform Bill.

    1846. Repeal of Corn Laws;
           Repeal of Navigation Laws.

    1834. West Indian Emancipation;
           Dissenters Chapels bill;
           Unitarians and Quakers in Parliament;
           Sugar duties abolished;
           Republics acknowledged.

Mr. Pitt said in Parliament in 1780, that, "without a reform in Parliament, it was impossible for any honest man to remain a minister of England."

Page 228, note 1. John Sterling, a man of brilliant parts and noble character, who had been in his youth and while his health permitted a curate devoted to his people, soon found his growing spirit cramped by the creed of the Church of England. He went through an experience like Emerson's, and they became close friends, through letters. Sterling wrote to his friend in December, 1841: "How remarkable it is that the critical and historical difficulties of the Bible were pointed out by clear-sighted English writers more than a century ago, and thence passed through Voltaire into the whole mind of Continental Europe, and yet that in this country both the facts and the books about them remain utterly unknown, except to a few recluses! The overthrow of our dead Biblical Dogmatism must, however, be preparing, and may be nearer than appears. The great curse is the wretched and seemingly hopeless pedantry of our Monastic Colleges at Oxford and Cambridge." [1]

Six months later he writes more hopefully: "Thought is leaking into this country. Even Strauss sells."

About the time of Mr. Emerson's first visit to England, Newman and Pusey had begun the Anglo-Catholic movement; ten years later Newman had formally retracted his charges against the Church of Rome, and in 1845 had joined that church, returning to England, during the time of Mr. Emerson's second visit, to establish religious houses there.

Page 228, note 2. Here are some further items from the English notebook: —

"They punish dissent: — they punish education. So late as

[1] *Correspondence of Emerson and Sterling.*

1831, marriages performed by Dissenters were illegal, and the children of such marriages bastards. So late as 12 Geo. III., a Catholic priest who married a Catholic and Protestant was liable to the punishment of death; and later to a fine of £500. So late as 59 Geo. III., 23 June, 1819, trial by single combat was abolished.

" ' Decent debility,' said Sydney Smith of the clergy."

Page 229, note 1. George Borrow, the Englishman who lived and wandered with the Gypsies to study them, the author of *The Zincali, Lavengro* (partly autobiographical), and *The Romany Rye.* He was for a time in the employ of the British and Foreign Bible Society.

Page 230, note 1. In conversation at a dinner-party where Mr. Emerson met him, " Macaulay said, he had arrested on its progress to be printed a bill for civilising and Christianising the natives of —— in Africa, appropriating —— thousand pounds, first for an expense of—— pounds for adjusting pipes, etc., on the paddle wheels of steamboat for squirting hot water on the natives," etc.

" A Unitarian," he said, " will presently be shown as a Dodo, — an extinct race."

Page 230, note 2. In acknowledging *English Traits,* December 2, 1856, Carlyle wrote : " That Chapter on the Church is inimitable ; ' the Bishop asking a troublesome gentleman to take wine,' — you should see the kind of grin it awakens here on our best kind of faces. Excellent the manner of that, and the matter too dreadfully *true* in every part. I do not much seize your idea in regard to ' Literature,' though I do details of it, and will try again. Glad of that too even in its half state ; not ' sorry ' at any part of it, — you Sceptic ! ' "

Page 230, note 3. On his return home Mr. Emerson

writes in his journal of the question of his wife : "Lidian asks if I saw the spiritual class. Oh no, I saw the ox and the ass, but rarely the driver."

Page 231, note 1. This thought of the passing of the Spirit, its newness, its surprise, is found again in the *Poems* in the last lines of "Woodnotes," II., and in "Worship."

Page 232, note 1. As introductory to this chapter this entry may be copied from Mr. Emerson's notebook of 1878 : "40 *per cent.* of the English people cannot write their names. One half of one *per cent.* of the Massachusetts people cannot, and these are probably Britons born.

"It is certain that more people speak English correctly in the United States than in Britain."

Page 233, note 1. "The Englishman," Emerson says in a lecture after his return, "stands in awe of a fact as something final and irreversible, and confines his thoughts and his aspirations to the means of dealing with it to advantage ; he does not seek to comprehend it, but only to utilize it for enjoyment or display, at any rate to adapt himself to it ; and he values only the faculties that enable him to do this. He admires talent and is careless of ideas. ' The English have no higher heaven than Fate.' "

Page 235, note 1. Mr. Emerson, though valuing the classics, and most careful in choosing the word that from its composition and association would most accurately give his meaning, sought plain Saxon words to make his thought clear to his lyceum audiences, and in many of his earlier published poems sacrificed music to vigor, as in the line —

Boon Nature yields each day a brag.

Later his ear became finer. His style is remarkably Saxon. If his children brought home the word *commence* from school he bade them forget it and say *begin*.

Page 237, note 1. Again the speech of the English King, in *Chevy-Chase*, on the fall of Percy, is recalled : —

> " I trust I have within my realms
> Five hundred as good as he."

Page 238, note 1. William Camden (1551–1623), who wrote the *Annals of the Reign of Queen Elizabeth.* James Usher (1580–1656), the Irish prelate, author of the *Annales Veteris et Novi Testamenti.* John Selden (1584–1664), " the great Dictator of Learning of the English nation," best known by his *Table-Talk.* Joseph Mede (1586–1628), the theologian who attempted the explanation of the *Book of Revelation* in his *Clavis Apocalyptica.* Thomas Gataker (1574–1654), a divine who edited the writings of Marcus Aurelius and wrote on the Stoics. Richard Hooker (1553–1600), the author of the *Ecclesiastical Polity.* Jeremy Taylor (1613–67), the chaplain of Charles I., wrote the *Liberty of Prophesying,* the *Great Exemplar,* but especially the *Holy Living and Holy Dying.* Mr. Emerson in " The Problem " calls him

> The younger *Golden Lips* or mines,
> Taylor, the Shakspeare of divines.

Robert Burton (1576–1640), who wrote the *Anatomy of Melancholy,* which Dr. Johnson said was the only book that ever took him out of bed two hours sooner than he wished to rise, and Byron found the most exciting and instructive medley of quotations and classical anecdotes. Richard Bentley (1662–1742), the head of Cambridge University, remarkable for his critical study of the classics. Brian Walton (1600–61), the editor of the Polyglot Bible from nine languages, and Oriental scholar.

Page 238, note 2. By comparison with what Mr. Emer-

son says later in this chapter, and elsewhere through the book
and in letters, it is evident that this tint of Platonism refers to
English scholars of another age, not to those he met.

Page 238, note 3. In the journal of 1838–39 Mr. Emerson wrote : " Bacon's perfect law of inquiry after truth
was that nothing should be in the globe of matter which was
not also in the globe of crystal ; that is, nothing should take
place as event in life which did not also exist as truth in the
mind."

Page 240, note 1. Mr. Emerson, impatient of the modern
writers on metaphysics, waiting in vain for the man who
should deal with the worlds of spirit and matter worthily, wished
to make his contributions, however fragmentary, towards the
grand theme. As early as 1835 he made notes towards this
end, beginning thus : " By the First Philosophy is meant
the original laws of the mind. It is the science of what is,
in distinction from what appears. It is one mark of them that
their enunciation awakens the feeling of the moral sublime, and
great men are they who believe in them. They resemble
great circles in Astronomy, each of which, in what direction
soever it is drawn, contains the whole sphere." Mr. Emerson's strength failed him when at length the opportunity seemed
to come to give some form and completeness to this work,
for which through the years he had made notes, in the invitation to give a course on Philosophy at Harvard University.
Many of the notes were already embodied in other lectures ;
the fragments of the course were collected by Mr. Cabot in
the opening paper of the volume called *Natural History of
Intellect.*[1]

Page 241, note 1. Bacon quotes here from Plutarch's

[1] See Cabot's *Memoir of Emerson*, vol. ii. p. 133 ; also his Prefatory
Note to *Natural History of Intellect.*

Morals a corrupted form of a saying of Heracleitus. I am indebted to Professor Wright of Harvard University for the following curious account of the steps of the perversion. Heracleitus wrote, αὔη ψυχὴ σοφωτάτη καὶ ἀρίστη, "a dry soul is wisest and best," as what is dry is most near to fire and fire is at the top of Heracleitus's upward way. Αὔη being an unusual word, a commentator explained it by putting ξηρή, a more usual word, as explanatory, beside it, so that now the sentence read αὔη (ξηρὴ) ψυχή, etc., which might be rendered "a dry (i. e. not moist) soul," etc. Then the original αὔη was dropped and ξηρή substituted in some versions. But before this was done, while αὔη and ξηρή stood side by side, some transcriber took αὔη for αὐγή (light), so the sentence now stood αὐγὴ ξηρή· ψυχὴ σοφωτάτη καὶ ἀρίστη, "the light is dry; soul is wisest and best," or, differently punctuated, "as a dry light the soul is wisest and best." It is the last form that Plutarch quotes.

The "dry light" is also alluded to in "Manners," *Essays, Second Series*, page 140.

Page 241, note 2. From the *Phædrus.*

Page 241, note 3. Jan Baptista van Helmont (1577–1644), the eminent Flemish physician, experimenter, and writer, author of the *Ortus* and the *Progressus Medicinæ*, *The Magnetic Cure of Wounds, The Image of God in Man*, and other works.

Page 242, note 1. Mr. Emerson refers to the Chaldæan Oracles, quoted often by Thomas Taylor. In his note-book he says they are "from Zoroaster, or else utterances of the Theurgists under Marcus Antoninus."

Page 242, note 2. The quotation from Spenser is from "A Hymne in honour of Beautie," the whole stanza being quoted on page 14 of *Essays. Second Series.*

Page 242, note 3. In a letter to Miss Fuller in 1841, Mr. Emerson speaks of " the joy with which in my boyhood I caught the first hint of the Berkeleyan philosophy, and which I certainly never lost sight of afterwards. . . . I could see that there was a Cause behind every stump and clod, and by the help of some fine words could make every old wagon and wood-pile and stone wall oscillate a little and threaten to dance ; nay, give me a fair field, and the selectmen of Concord and the Rev. Pound-me-down himself began to look unstable and vaporous." [1]

Page 242, note 4. Dr. Samuel Clarke (1675–1729), a clergyman and remarkable scholar, author of *The Being and Attributes of God*, as well as other religious and scientific works, important in their day. He translated some of Sir Isaac Newton's works into English. Of him Mr. Emerson notes, " 'T is curious, that Newton's theory of gravitation was introduced into the teaching of the Universities, by stealth. Sam Clarke taught, in tne text, the old Ptolemaic theory ; and, in the notes only, explained the new philosophy, which, of course, needed only to be explained in order gradually to supersede the old." James Harrington (1611–77), author of many political treatises, especially the *Oceana, The Grounds and Reasons for Monarchy Considered,* and *The Prerogative of Popular Government.*

Page 243, note 1. As confirming this love of the English, even of their scholars, to feel the solid ground of the understanding beneath their feet, may be quoted the remark of Dr. Paul Weber in his *History of Philosophy :* " English philosophy is to this day almost as empirical and positivistic as in the times of Bacon and Locke."

Page 244, note 1. Sterling, writing to Emerson in 1841,

[1] Cabot's *Memoir of Emerson,* vol. ii. p. 478.

said that, twenty years earlier, to the English mind "Wordsworth and Coleridge were mystagogues lurking in caverns,
and German literature thought of with a good deal less favor
than we are now disposed to show towards that of China."
Emerson, writing in answer to this and another letter, said :
"Your picture of England I was very glad to have. It con-
firms my own impressions . . . I think the most intellectual
class of my countrymen look to Germany rather than to England for their recent culture, and Coleridge, I suppose, has
always had more readers here than in Britain."

Page 245, note 1. It appears in Mr. Cabot's memoir that
Mr. Emerson read Hume — "the Scotch Goliath" he calls
him — at the age of twenty, and made probably overmuch of
Hume's doubts and objections in spiritual matters, in a letter to
his Aunt Mary, with purpose to stir her up to writing a vigorous letter of refutation.

Page 245, note 2. Mr. Emerson met Hallam at the house
of Mr. Milman, the historian, and dined with him later at
Lord Ashburton's, "sitting between Mr. Hallam and Lord
Northampton." He wrote, "Hallam was very courteous and
communicative and has since called on me." In the notebook he records : "Mr. Hallam asked me ' whether Swedenborg were all mad, or partly so.' He knew nothing of Thomas
Taylor, nor did Milman, nor any Englishman."

Page 247, note 1. Mr. Emerson dined with Dickens and
Carlyle at Mr. John Forster's. The writings of Dickens did not
attract him. He had read in one or two of the earlier books.
In 1837 he wrote in his journal : —

"Two or three events, two or three objects, large or small,
suffice to genius. Let dulness work with multitudes and mag-
nitudes. The poor Pickwick stuff (into which I have only
looked and with no wish for more) teaches this, that prose

and parlors and shops and city widows, the tradesman's dinner, and such matters, are as good materials in a skilful hand for interest and art as palaces and revolutions.''

He made the following entry in his journal two years later : '' I have read *Oliver Twist*, in obedience to the opinions of so many intelligent people as have praised it. The author has an acute eye for costume ; he sees the expression of dress, of form, of gait, of personal deformities ; of furniture, of the outside and inside of houses ; but his eye rests always on surfaces, he has no insight into character. For want of key to the moral powers, the author is fain to strain all his stage trick of grievance, of bodily terror, of murder and the most approved performances of Remorse. It all avails nothing. There is nothing memorable in the book except the flash, which is got at a police-office, and the dancing of the madman, which strikes a momentary terror. Like Cooper and Hawthorne he .has no dramatic talent. The moment he attempts dialogue the improbability of life hardens to wood and stone. And the book begins and ends without a poetic ray, and so perishes in the reading.''

I find this mention of Bulwer in the journal for 1842 : '' *Zanoni*. We must not rail if we read the book. Of all the ministers to luxury these novel-writers are the best. It is a trick, a juggle. We are cheated into laughter or wonder by feats which only oddly combine acts that we do every day. There is no new element, no power, no furtherance. It is only confectionery, not the raising of new corn ; and being such, there is no limit to its extension and multiplication. . . . But *Zanoni* pains us, and the author gets no respect from us because he speedily shows us that his view is partial ; that this power which he gives to his hero is a toy, and not flowing from its legitimate fountains in the mind, is a power for London, a divine power converted into a highwayman's pistol to rob and kill with.''

Mr. Emerson met Thackeray in England, and probably later in Boston. He read only one of his books ; of the painful impression left upon him by this he writes in the journal for 1850 : "Thackeray's *Vanity Fair* is pathetic in its name, and in his use of the name ; an admission it is from a man of fashion in the London of 1850, that poor old puritan Bunyan was right in his perception of the London of 1650. And yet now in Thackeray is the added wisdom of skepticism, that, though this be really so, he must yet live in tolerance of, and practically in homage and obedience to these illusions. And there is in the book an admission, too, which seems somewhat new in literature, akin to Froude's Formula in the *Nemesis*, that ' Moral deterioration follows on a diminished exchequer ; ' and State Street thinks it is easy for a rich man to be honourable, but that in failing circumstances, no man can be relied on to keep his integrity.''

Page 247, note 2. Mr. Emerson met Macaulay, '' that Niagara of information,'' as Fanny Kemble used to call him, at least twice, at private houses. Of the table-talk on one of these occasions Mr. Alexander Ireland, in his biographical sketch of Emerson, says : "He witnessed one of Macaulay's brilliant feats in conversation at a dinner where Hallam was one of the guests. The talk was on the question whether the ' additional letters,' lately published by Carlyle, were spurious or genuine. Emerson afterwards, describing the conversation, said: . . . ' Macaulay overcame everybody at the table, including Hallam, by pouring out with victorious volubility instances of the use of words in a different meaning from that they bore in Cromwell's time, or by citing words which were not in use at all until half a century later. A

v

question, which might have been settled in a few minutes by
the consent of a few men of insight, opened a tiresome controversy which lasted during the whole dinner. Macaulay
seemed to have the best of it ; still, I did not like the arrogance with which he paraded his minute information ; but
then there was a fire, speed, fury, talent and effrontery in
the fellow which were very taking.' ''

Mr. Ireland adds, '' Carlyle, in speaking of Macaulay, used
sometimes to exclaim, ' Flow on, thou Shining River,' following up with his accustomed loud shout of laughter.''

Page 248, note 1. Sir David Brewster, the biographer of
Sir Isaac Newton. Brewster was himself a successful investi-
gator in the field of optics, and a writer of distinction.

Page 248, note 2. Robert Hooke (1635–1703), the
eminent mathematician and physicist who disputed with Newton the honor of the discovery of the law of gravitation.
Robert Boyle (1626–91), the physical experimenter and
learned writer sometimes called '' the Christian Philosopher.''
Edmund Halley (1656–1742), the distinguished astronomer
and mathematician, the friend of Newton, whose *Principia* he
published at his own expense.

Page 249, note 1. Coleridge had died the year after Mr.
Emerson's visit to him, described earlier in this volume. Car-
lyle, in announcing his death to his friend, had written,
'' How great a Possibility, how small a realized Result ! ''

Among Mr. Emerson's papers is a short printed notice of his
own life and works, designed for a handbook of contemporary
biography sent by the English editor in 1859 to him for re-
vision and correction. It says, '' In 1849 Emerson visited
England, receiving a cordial reception from the literary society
of London '' [Mr. Emerson here added '' and rather alarm-
ing the religious society of Glasgow '']. The editor alludes

to *English Traits* as a work " singularly fair and justly appre-
ciative," but says that " his influence upon the British mind
has been comparatively limited. This circumstance is perhaps
accounted for by the fact that he is more an interpreter of
Coleridge and Carlyle than an original thinker." Mr. Emerson's marginal comment was, " He must be a superficial
reader of Emerson who fancies him an interpreter of Coleridge
or Carlyle."

Page 250, note 1. All Emerson's love for Carlyle was
needed to allow for his friend's attitude of despair for his day
and hopelessness for his generation. In the early letters Carlyle, while praising each particular work that his friend sent
him, was constantly urging on him his doctrine of Silence, ·
sitting still, — doing, not teaching. Fortunately Emerson listened to his Genius rather than to his friend. He writes in
his English notebook : " It is droll to hear this talker talking
against talkers, and this writer writing against writing. He has
such vigor of constitution that he can dispose of poison very
well. He is a bacchanal in the strong waters of vituperation."

Shortly before the publication of *English Traits* Emerson
wrote to Carlyle : " I say to myself, the high-seeing, aus-
terely exigent friend whom I elected, and who elected me,
twenty years and more ago, finds me heavy and silent, when
all the world elects and loves him. Yet I have not changed.
I have the same pride in his genius, the same sympathy with
the Genius that governs his, the old love with the old limitations, though love and limitation be all untold. And I see well
what a piece of Providence he is, how material he is to the
times, which must always have a solo Soprano to balance the
roar of the orchestra. The solo sings the theme ; the orchestra
roars antagonistically, but follows. And have I not put him
into my Chapter of ' English Spiritual Tendencies,' with all

thankfulness to the Eternal Creator, — though the chapter lie unborn in a trunk ? ' '

Page 250, note 2. In his journal for 1851, Mr. Emerson recalls the high esteem in which he had at first held Wilkinson for ability, power of labor, acute vision, " and especially the power I so value, and so rarely meet, of *expansion*, expansion such as Alcott shines with, but all this spoiled by a certain levity." He then laments his " changing his sphere from Swedenborg's mysticism to French Fourierism." Wilkinson, on his part, in a later criticism of Emerson for his limited acceptance of Swedenborg, made the amusing charge of narrow and timid Unitarianism.

Page 251, note 1. In a fragment of a lecture called " Anglo-Saxon " is this passage on the lack of original æsthetic sense : —

" The English race must take rank with the Roman and the Turk as being born for power, but without art. They cannot make a pattern for a pitcher, they cannot build well, or paint, or carve, or dance. Then England has no music. It has never produced a first-rate composer, and accepts only such music as has already been decided to be good in Italy and Germany. They seem to have great delight in these things, but not original appreciation; and value them as showy commodities, which they buy at great prices for pride. But they firmly hold what they have once been taught, — as well the peculiarities of a picture, or style of building, as the rule for breaking a line of battle; and all England thinks as one man, on the merits of the Italian masters, as on the genuineness of the canonical Bible. . . . ' England never did or can look at art otherwise than as a commodity it can buy.' Hogarth and Wilkie and Landseer with their humour and homeliness and veracity are truly national artists. In sculpture, never a quite

original genius. The superb scholarship of Flaxman's sculpture
is far the best they have had, and, in general, their artists
show total want of all object, with great powers of execution.
Their drawing has the highest finish but no grandeur.''

Page 254, note 1. This was written at the time when
Science, newly freed from bonds of *a priori* considerations of
Theology and Philosophy, was on its guard against other than
material considerations, especially in unimaginative England.
Mr. Emerson, with his belief that the same laws ruled mind
and matter, was impatient of this attitude and was more interested in the wide views of the German and French *savans.*
In John Hunter's work he took great interest. Comparative
anatomy, ever since at the museum of the *Jardin des Plantes,*
in 1833, he had been startled by the view of the upward series
of creation from monad to man, had commanded his respect.
Richard Owen, celebrated for his studies in this branch, had
shown him the Hunterian Museum of which he was curator,
and doubtless explained the ideas of evolution as far as they
were then recognized. Mr. Emerson very probably also met
Robert Brown, the great botanist and explorer of vegetable
physiology.

Page 254, note 2. He wrote in the notebook: ''The
people have wide range, but no ascending range in their speculations. An American, like a German, has many platforms of
thought. But an Englishman requires to be treated with tenderness if he wishes to climb.'' John Sterling, his friend, said,
'' Think if we had a dozen such to stand up for ideas, as Cobden and his friends do for machinery.''

Page 255, note 1. This was before William Morris's day,
who not only awakened his people to the hideousness of their
expensive furniture and stuffs, but gave them things beautiful
and honest, and said, moreover, that if a family could do but

one thing to beautify their home, the best would be to make, in the street in front of it, a bonfire of two thirds of the contents.

Page 256, note 1.   Here, as elsewhere in the book, Mr. Emerson only presents one aspect of the case.   In his poem "The Harp" he speaks of

> Scott, the delight of generous boys,

but he never outgrew his love for the poet and the man.   See in *Miscellanies* his remarks at the Scott Centennial Anniversary.

Page 257, note 1.   Before this visit to England, Mr. Emerson wrote much in two papers in the *Dial* (now included in the volume *Natural History of Intellect*) of

> Wordsworth, Pan's recording voice,

as he calls him in "The Harp."   In a late notebook he said, "I may say of Wordsworth what Cartwright said of Fletcher, —

"'What he would write, he was before he writ.'"

In 1870 Mr. Emerson made this note: "I ought to write a paper on Wordsworth partly from my *Dial* paper, and partly from MSS."   Some of the latter may appear in the extracts from the journals.   The following comparison of the poets, written in 1868, should, however, appear here: —

"Wordsworth is manly, the manliest poet of his age.   His poems record the thoughts and emotions which have occupied his mind, and which he reports because of their reality.   He has great skill in rendering them into simple and sometimes happiest poetic speech.   Tennyson has incomparable felicity in all poetic forms, and is a brave thoughtful Englishman, exceeds Wordsworth a hundred fold in rhythmic power and variety, but far less manly compass; and Tennyson's main purpose is the rendering, whilst Wordsworth's is just value of the dignity of the thought."

Page 258, note 1. Of his first meeting with Tennyson he writes : —

"I saw Tennyson first at the house of Coventry Patmore, where we dined together. I was contented with him at once. He is tall and scholastic looking, no dandy, but a great deal of plain strength about him, and, though cultivated, quite unaffected. Quiet, sluggish sense and thought; refined as all English are, and good-humoured. There is in him an air of general superiority that is very satisfactory. He lives with his college set, . . . and has the air of one who is accustomed to be petted and indulged by those he lives with. Take away Hawthorne's bashfulness, and let him talk easily and fast, and you would have a pretty good Tennyson." Yet, in most other accounts of Tennyson heard by Mr. Emerson, his silence, his devotion to his pipe and a certain dreamy helplessness are dwelt upon.

In the paper "Europe and European Books," written in 1843, reprinted from the *Dial* in *Natural History of Intellect,* may be found Mr. Emerson's feeling about Tennyson's poetry at that time. In the essay on "The Poet" (page 9) Tennyson is criticised. But in the journal of 1871, after some complaint at the sacrifice of natural strength to finish in Tennyson's second volume of poems, he adds : "And yet, tried by one of my tests, it was not found wholly wanting. I mean that it was liberating ; it slipped, or caused to slide a little, 'this mortal coil.' The poems of 'Locksley Hall' and 'The Talking Oak,' I bear cheerful witness, both gave me to feel a momentary share of freedom and power."

When he read "Ulysses" he was inclined to "question whether there is taste in England to do justice to the poet."

In 1846 he notes: "Tennyson and Browning, though full of talent, remind one of the catbird's knowing music." And again : —

"The office of poetry, I supposed, was Tyrtæan, — consoling, indemnifying ; and, of the Uranian, deifying or imparadising. Homer did what he could, — and Callimachus, Pindar, and the Greek tragedians ; Horace and Persius ; Dante was faithful, and Milton, Shakspeare and Herbert. But now shall I find my heavenly bread in Tennyson ? or in Milnes ? in Lowell ? or in Longfellow ? Yet Wordsworth was mindful of the office."

Page 259, note 1. Preface to translation of the Bhagavad Gîtâ (1785) by Sir Charles Wilkins.

Page 260, note 1. John Sterling, the unseen friend and correspondent, who died three years before this visit of Emerson's to England, was eminently one of this first class. Brilliant and faithful, an advancing mind and a poet, he illuminated the lives of his friends, even the sad Carlyle, his biographer, who loved him strangely, though flouting his hopes and purposes.

Page 261, note 1. John Baron Somers of Evesham, the eminent lawyer and Whig statesman, Lord Chancellor of England under William and Mary.

Page 262, note 1. Winthrop Mackworth Praed, the Greek scholar and poet, who was also in Parliament. John Hookham Frere, the diplomat and scholar, one of the founders of the *Quarterly Review.* William Maginn, the versatile Irish contributor to *Blackwood*, the *Quarterly Review*, *Fraser's Magazine*, etc. Theodore Edward Hook, a brilliant writer and society wit, noted for his successful conduct of *John. Bull*, a newspaper established in the interest of the King as against that of Queen Caroline. Thomas Hood, the poet, was editor of the *Comic Annual*, the *New Monthly* and Hood's magazines. His "Song of the Shirt" appeared first in *Punch*.

Page 264, note 1. Fragment of lecture on English Civilization : —

"England never stands for the cause of freedom on the Continent, but only for English trade. She did not stand for the freedom of Schleswig-Holstein, but for the King of Denmark. She did not stand for the Hungarians, but for Austria. It was accordant that Lord Palmerston, reputed liberal, should favor Louis Napoleon's usurpation. England meantime is liberal, but the power of England is with the aristocracy who never go for liberty unless England itself is threatened."

Page 266, note 1. The Times was founded by John Walter, who had purchased the patent method of "logography," a great improvement in printing. Issued at first as the *London Daily Universal Register*, in 1785, three years later the title became *The Times, or Daily Universal Register.* Walter's son, bearing his father's name, succeeded to the management, under which the journal prospered. The second John Walter died in 1847, and his son John conducted the paper for many years. Of the staff mentioned in the text it may be said that Edward Sterling, the father of John Sterling, was an able man. Thomas Barnes was a vigorous writer on English politics in *The Times*, and was editor for a quarter of a century. Mr. Emerson notes that "Horace Twiss makes the 'parliamentary digest' for £700 a year." John Oxenford was the translator of Eckermann's *Conversations with Goethe*, and was a dramatic critic.

Journal, 1849. "The *Times* newspaper attracts the American in London more and more, until at last he wonders that it does not more pique the curiosity of the English themselves. . . .

"He never sees any person capable of writing these powerful paragraphs; and, though he hears up and down in society now and then some anecdote of a Mr. Bailey or Mr. Mosely who sent his paper to *The Times*, and received in return twenty guineas, with a request that he would write again, and so that he did, in due time, become one of the Staff of the Journal, — yet one never hears among well-informed men as Milnes, Carlyle, Helps, Gregg, Forster, any accounts of this potentate at all adequate to the fact.

"They may well affect not to know or care who wrote it, at the moment when I observe that all they know or say, they read in it."

Page 268, note 1. Hansard's *Journal of the House of Commons* from 1774.

Page 271, note 1. The recantation in *Punch* of its ridicule of Lincoln, after his assassination, in the fine poem by Taylor, was valued by Mr. Emerson. He included it in his *Parnassus*.

Page 271, note 2. *The Times* dared tell the British public in the war of 1812 the astounding news that within the year two of their frigates had been obliged to strike their flags in duels with vessels of the almost ignored American Navy. Captain Mahan quotes this leader in one of his magazine articles. It is one of the few recognitions, in English writings, of the actions at sea in that war.

Page 272, note 1. In 1863, while our country was struggling for life with foes at home, and the armed intervention of England on behalf of her trade was threatening, Mr. Emerson wrote, and probably spoke, thus: "We are coming (thanks to the war) to a nationality. Put down your foot and say to England, I know your merits and have paid them in the past the homage of ignoring your faults. I see them still. But it is time to say the whole truth, — that you have

failed in an Olympian hour, that when the occasion of magnanimity arrived, you had it not, — that you have lost character. Besides ; your insularity, your inches are conspicuous,
and they are to count against miles. When it comes to divide
an estate, the politest men quarrel. Justice is above your aim.
You are self-condemned."

Page 274, note 1. As a contrast of the tempers and teaching of the friends, the motto of Emerson's essay on Art, printed
in the *Poems,* might be read.

Page 276, note 1. He wrote in the notebook on England
and America, in 1856 : "We read without pain what the
English say to the advantage of England to the disparagement
of America; for are not we the heir ?

" ' Percy is but the factor, good my lord.' "

Page 279, note 1. Choir Gaur, or Côr Gawr, meaning
Giant's circle or temple, is only a British name for Stonehenge,
derived from the Saxon Stanhengest.

Page 280, note 1. Early in the seventeenth century the
Jesuits of Antwerp resolved to perpetuate the memory of the
saints and martyrs of the Church by collecting and transcribing
the records and traditions concerning them, and the work
known as the *Acta Sanctorum* was begun by John Bolland
and continued by various hands through two centuries.

Page 281, note 1. Algernon Herbert ("late of Merton
College and the Inner Temple") in his work on Stonehenge, *Cyclops Christianus,* calls attention to the important
fact that there is no accurate or approximate description of the
structure by Roman authors, as there certainly would have been,
had they existed during the Roman occupation. The British
Bards, however, in the Triads speak of the Cor Emmrys
(circle of Emmrys or Ambrosius) as one of the "three

mighty achievements of the Isle of Britain." He says that the native authors declare that "the great Coî was constructed in the latter days of Britain after the Roman Emperors had ceased to govern her," that is, in the fifth century after Christ.

Page 281, note 2. In the first edition Mr. Emerson quotes Stukeley as follows : " Connected with Stonehenge are an avenue and a *cursus.* The avenue is a narrow road of raised earth, extending 594 yards in a straight line from the grand entrance, then dividing into two branches, which lead, severally, to a row of barrows, and to the *cursus,* — an artificially formed flat tract of ground. This is half a mile northeast from Stonehenge, bounded by banks and ditches, 3036 yards long, by 110 broad."

Page 282, note 1. In this chapter four similar names are used to signify two places (both in Wiltshire), and Mr. Emerson in his notes fell into some confusion among them. Ambresbury, or Ambresberie, is the old name for Amesbury, which he visited. Abury is the old name for Avebury, and at this place is the largest circle of Druid stones which exists in England.

Page 285, note 1. Apparently the charm of the nameless stream made the visitor name it for the " sacred river " of *Kubla Khan.*

Page 286, note 1. The blood of the grir byte rians stirred in the admirer of John Knox, h share their dislike for the organ, —

" The kist fu' o' whistles that mak's

Page 286, note 2. Arthur Helps, after genial and talented man, who, though busy of the English government, found time for wri

the best known of which are *Friends in Council* and *The Spanish Conquest of America*. Of him Mr. Emerson wrote to his wife : " One meets now and then here with wonderfully witty men, all-knowing, who have tried everything and have everything, and are quite superior to letters and science. What could they not if they only would ? I saw such a one yesterday, with the odd name, too, of Arthur Helps."

Page 288, note 1. The friends were daily finding, now that they were together, the truth which Carlyle sadly wrote two years later : " I see what a great deep cleft divides us, in our way of practically looking at this world, — I see also (as probably you do yourself) where the rock-strata, miles deep, unite again ; and the two poor souls are at one." Fortunately apart, each for the rest of his life could remember " there is still a brother-soul left to me alive in this world, and a kind thought surviving far over the sea !" [1]

On the voyage home Mr. Emerson wrote in the cabin some " Sea-weeds " to send to a valued friend in Boston. In these the story of his quiet presentation to the two good Britons, Carlyle and Helps, of the thoughts that were moving the best people in New England in that day, is told with more vivacity thus : " Two very good men, with whom I spent a Sunday in the country near Winchester lately, asked me if there were any Americans, if there were any who had an American idea ? or what is it that thoughtful and superior men with us would have ? Certainly I did not retort, after our country f   , by defying them to show me one mortal Englishman   d not live from hand to mouth, but who w his w   assured them there were such monsters rd by th   n, who believed in a future such as was   a p   should show it to them, they would

           Correspondence, vol. ii. p. 187.

think French communism solid and practicable in comparison. So I sketched the Boston fanaticism of right and might without bayonets or bishops, every man his own king, and all coöperation necessary and extemporaneous. Of course my men went wild at the denying to society the beautiful right to kill and imprison. But we stood fast for milk and acorns, told them the musket-worship [1] was perfectly well known to us, that it was an old bankrupt, but that we had never seen a man of sufficient valor and substance quite to carry out the other, which was nevertheless as sure as Copernican astronomy, and all heroism and invention must of course lie on this side. 'T is wonderful how odiously thin and pale this republic dances before blue bloodshot English eyes, but I had some anecdotes to bring some of its traits within their vision, and at last obtained a kind of·allowance ; but I doubt my tender converts are backsliding before this. — But their question which began the conversation was so dangerous that I thought of no escape but to this extreme and sacred asylum, and having got off for once through the precinct of the temple, I shall not venture into such company again, without consulting those same thoughtful Americans, whom their inquiry concerned.''

Page 291, note 1. *Macbeth*, Act V., Scene iii.

Page 293, note 1. He wrote from London: —

. . . ''I attend Mr. Owen's lectures at the Royal College of Surgeons; Faraday, at the Royal Institution; Lyell, Sedgwick, Buckland, Forbes, I hear at the Geologic Society; and two nights ago I dined with the antiquaries, and discussed Shakspeare with Mr. Collier. Dr. Carpenter has shown me his microscopes, Sir Henry De la Bèche his geologic

---

[1] Mr. John Forster, at a recent dinner-party, had '' called Carlyle's passion ' musket-worship.' ''

NOTES 399

museum, and I have really owed many valuable hours to the scientific bodies. Now the Picture Galleries are open, and I have begun to see pictures and artists."

It is interesting to see the eagerness with which Mr. Emerson sought facts from the workers in science, to translate into higher terms. He quotes Owen's utterances on palæontology in "Poetry and Imagination," saying that every good reader will recall expressions or passages in works of pure science which have given him the same pleasure he seeks in the poets. In the same essay he finds delight in Faraday's "spherules of force," and in "Greatness" proudly claims for the brave scholar the right "to weigh Plato, judge Laplace, know Newton, Faraday, judge of Darwin, criticise Kant and Swedenborg, and on all these arouse the central courage or insight." [1]

On the opening page of *Natural History of Intellect*, Mr. Emerson says that his desire to enumerate the laws and powers of the intellect was incited by the masterly manner in which these same scientific men had presented those of matter.

Page 293, note 2. Joanna Baillie, the friend of Scott, authoress of ballads in Scottish dialect and of many dramatic pieces, was at the time of Mr. Emerson's visit in her ninetieth year. Lady Morgan, *née* Owenson in 1783, a bright young Irish lady, early won repute by her songs and tales, especially "The Wild Irish Girl." She married Sir Thomas Charles Morgan, and with him travelled and lived abroad many years, writing many books, and finished her days in London, where she was very popular in society. Mrs. Anna Jameson, the well-known writer on Art. Mrs. Mary Somerville, the active-minded and successful student of physics, physical geography, astronomy and microscopy. Herself

[1] *Letters and Social Aims.*

a remarkable example of what a woman could accomplish, she was one of the earliest champions of equal opportunities and rights for women.

Page 294, note 1. The inbred hostility of Wordsworth, as a Borderer, to the Scot, and his traditionary ally the Frenchman, is interesting, recalling the old ballad of the Marches, —

> "God send the land deliverance
> Frae every reaving, riding Scot!
> We 'll sune hae neither cow nor ewe,
> We 'll sune hae neither staig nor stot!''

The name starred in the text by Mr. Emerson was *Carlyle*, as appears in the notebook.

Page 295, note 1. After speaking of the insularity of the English and their unwilling reception of ideas in science from foreign sources, Mr. Emerson notes: —

"So in literature and philosophy, — Plato has no readers in England, except as a Greek book. The expansive, the ideal tendency has no favor, but only the exact, the defining, the experimental. Thomas Taylor, the Platonist, is totally unknown in England. His translation of Plato is found in every public, and often in private libraries, in this country; never in England. I asked repeatedly among literary men for some account of him. But in vain. Poor Taylor in his day had insulted over the materialism and superstition of the times, and the dreadful sterility of times in which he fell, and sadly said: 'There does not appear to be any living author besides myself, who has made the acquisition of the Platonic Philosophy the great business of his life without paying the smallest attention to the accumulation of wealth.' And the modern multitude, which he despised, avenged themselves by forgetting him. Coleridge and Wordsworth slowly and against all opposition made their genius felt. Goethe was received with mean cavilling criticism in the leading journals, like the *Edinburgh* and *Blackwood*, and with supercilious silence by the rest. The German Philosophy has made few steps. The English hate transcendental ideas, like the mysticism of the Eastern philosophy and religion, and one may see it amusingly in the anxiety a late critic shows to absolve Taliessin, the Welsh Bard, from the imputation of such odious doctrines as the transmigration of souls. Materialism is much less offensive."

Page 297, note 1. Wordsworth's " Happy Warrior "

" Through the heat of conflict keeps the law
In calmness made, and sees what he foresaw."

Page 298, note 1. With the best intentions on both sides, the meetings with the lights of England were a little disappointing. Mr. Emerson wrote in a letter: —

LONDON, MARCH 20, 1848.

. . . What shall I say to you of Babylon ? . . . There is nowhere so much wealth of talent and character and social accomplishment ; every star outshone by one more dazzling, and you cannot move without coming into the light and fame of new ones. I have seen, I suppose, some good specimens, chiefly of the literary-fashionable and not of the fashionable sort. They have all carried the art of agreeable sensations to a wonderful pitch, they know everything, have everything, they are rich, plain, polite, proud and admirable. But though good for them, it ends in the using. I shall or should soon have enough of this play for my occasion. The seed-corn is oftener found in quite other districts. . . . Tennyson, whom I wish to see more than any other, is in Ireland, and I fear

V

I shall miss him. I saw Wordsworth to very good purpose in Westmoreland, and all the Scottish gods at Edinburgh. Perhaps it is no fault of Britain, — no doubt it is because I grow old and cold, — but no persons here appeal in any manner to the imagination. I think even that there is no person in England from whom I expect more than talent and information. But I am wont to ask very much more of my benefactors, — expansions that amount to new horizons.[1]

Page 300, note 1. In some sheets on English Civilization, evidently from a lecture given on his return, he writes: —

"Very intellectual people and very silent people, inaccessible on every other topic, grew garrulous on politics. 'Festus' Bailey I found only entertained by politics. Every man gives the same attention to public affairs as the Prime Minister. The whole British public read the *Times* newspaper with the punctuality with which they eat."

And again: "'English principles' mean monopoly of all kinds, forcing the Colonies, forcing Ireland to buy of England only; suppressing manufactures in Ireland and the Colonies; allowing freedom of conscience, but you must take the oaths to the English Church and State, if you will enter Parliament, the University, the Army, the professions, or the government — freedom of conscience certainly, build what chapel you like, but you must pay your tithe to the Anglican. Lord Eldon resists abolition of Slavery; resists Catholic Emancipation; resists Reform of Parliament; resists Reform in Chancery; resists Jewish franchise; resists abolishing impressment of seamen, 'which is the life of our navy;' resists abolishing capital punishment for small offences; too speculative to be safe; resists strikes or any attempt on the part of operatives to obtain

[1] *Letters of Emerson to a Friend.* Houghton, Mifflin & Co., 1899.

increase of wages; resists West Indian Emancipation — ' English principles' mean with a primary view to the interests of property.''

Page 301, note 1. From the notebook: —

" English Politics. Sir James Graham opened the letters of Mazzini. In 1837 Lord John Russell usurped the Constitutional functions of the Colonial Assemblies in Canada. In 1831 Lord Palmerston pronounced the rights of the Czar over Poland incontestable; in 1849, refused to allow the Roman patriots to land in Malta.''

As an instance of the spirit of British trade in dealing with the outside world, he mentions the inscription on the statue of Lord Chatham in the Guildhall in London, which records that, "under his administration, Commerce had been united with and made to flourish by War.''

Remembering the brutal element in the Anglo-Saxon stock on both sides of the Atlantic, he writes: —

" In that country as in this, they want great men, and the cause of right can only succeed against this gravitation or materialism by means of immense personalities. But Webster, Calhoun, Clay, Benton, are not found to be philanthropists but attorneys of gross interests.''

But Mr. Emerson recognizes their hopeful advance among the other nations.

" They have exceeded the humanity of other governments. Cheap postage they have adopted. Free Trade they have adopted. Reform Bill passed. Emancipation of Negroes, Abolition of Slave Trade. Impeachment of Hastings — Dissenters Bill. Exploring Expeditions — Elgin Marbles; Nineveh excavations: British Museum; the government is gentlemanlike. If any national benefit has been rendered, if arts have been advanced, science served, the government may be relied on to be just and generous to the man who has served them, — Paxton, Fellowes, Stephenson, Franklin, Rowland Hill. The power of England goes to show that domesticity is the tap-root which enables a nation to branch wide and high. They are the most humane of nations. Their rules and usages in War are distinguished by humanity. They spare the conquered. They will not fire on an enemy when they might hit their own men: the French will. They respect towns and private property."

Page 304, note 1. Here is an instance of the immediate use on another plane of a scientific generalization of John Hunter, which Mr. Emerson had probably heard from Richard Owen, — the *electric word*, as he calls it in the essay on " Poetry and Imagination" in *Letters and Social Aims.*

Page 304, note 2. François Huber of Geneva, having become blind, devoted himself with his wife to the study of bees and wrote *Nouvelles Observations sur les Abeilles.*

Mr. Emerson felt that the Englishmen, even more than the Americans of his generation, were, for the time, in the bonds of materialism, but that, as he had written in his " Self-Reliance," it was true of them, as of all: —

" If they are honest and do well, presently their neat new pinfold will be too strait and low, will crack, will lean, will rot and vanish, and the immortal light, all young and joyful, million-orbed, million-colored, will beam over the universe as on the first morning."

Page 309, note 1. George Cruikshank, the caricaturist, who used his art not merely to amuse, for he was an eager liberal and reformer. Of his illustrations of Dickens's novels I find this mention in the journal: —

" Alcott told me that, when he saw Cruikshank's drawings, he thought him a fancy caricaturist, but when he went